Workers' control in America

Workers' control in America

Studies in the history of work, technology, and labor struggles

David Montgomery
Yale University

Cambridge University Press

Cambridge
London   New York   New Rochelle
Melbourne   Sydney

Published by the Syndics of the Cambridge University Press
The Pitt Building, Trumpington Street, Cambridge CB2 1RP
Bentley House, 200 Euston Road, London NW1 2DB
32 East 57th Street, New York, NY 10022, USA
296 Beaconsfield Parade, Middle Park, Melbourne 3206, Australia

First published 1979
First paperback edition 1980
Reprinted 1981 (twice)

Printed in the United States of America
Typeset by Graphic Composition, Inc., Athens, Georgia
Printed and bound by Vail-Ballou Press, Inc., Binghamton, N.Y.

Library of Congress Cataloging in Publication Data

Montgomery, David, 1927 –

Workers' control in America.

1. Labor and laboring classes – United States – History.
2. Trade-unions – United States – History.
3. Industrial relations – United States – History.
I. Title.

HD8072.M74   331.8'0973   78 –32001
ISBN 0 521 22580 9 hard covers
ISBN 0 521 28006 0 paperback

To Claude and Edward
from our past for your future

Contents

Preface

My thinking and research on questions of workers' control in America has been strongly influenced not only by the lessons in trade unionism imparted by my friends and foes in United Electrical Workers Local 475, Teamsters Local 1145, and Machinists Local 459, but also by many colleagues with whom I have been privileged to discuss them during my sojourn in the academic world. Noteworthy among the latter are James Hinton, E. P. Thompson, and Fred Reid, with whom I discussed the past and present of the working class at Warwick University in 1968 and 1969, and the participants in the international round tables in social history of 1975–7. The late James Matles of the UE and the delegates to the three UE conventions with whom I shared parts of this investigation helped keep my thoughts in touch with reality.

Above all, I am indebted to my companions in the study of working-class history at the University of Pittsburgh: Bruce Laurie, Fred Barkey, Horace Huntley, Ronald Schatz, Mark McColloch, Neville Kirk, John W. Bennett, Joseph White, Maurine Greenwald, Peter Gottlieb, Steve Sapolsky, Shelton Stromquist, Dodee Fennell, Cecelia Bucki, Peter Rachleff, Dale Newman, Clare Horner, James Barrett, Frank Serene, Rob Ruck, Bob Kaplan, Patricia Simpson, Donald McPherson, Paul LeBlanc, Gregory Mihalik, Linda Nyden, Geoffrey Bauman, and Patrick Lynch. Every idea in these essays was influenced by their research and by my conversations with them, though, to say the least, they are by no means in unanimous agreement with the form in which my arguments appear here.

Betti Benenati-Marconi, Steven Fraser, and Martel W. Montgomery deserve special thanks for their indispensible roles in shaping this collection. Last but hardly least, I am indebted to the John Simon Guggenheim Memorial Foundation for the fellowship which made much of this research possible.

Finally I would like to acknowledge the publishers' permission for the use of the following articles: "Workers' Control of Machine Production in the Nineteenth Century," which originally appeared in *Labor History*

(Fall 1976), forms Chapter 1 and is reprinted by the permission of the publisher. "Immigrant Workers and Managerial Reform," which originally appeared in Richard L. Ehrlich, ed., *Immigrants in Industrial America, 1850–1920* (University of Virginia Press: Charlottesville, Va., 1977), is used for Chapter 2 by the permission of the publisher. "The 'New Unionism' and the Transformation of Workers' Consciousness in America," which originally appeared in the *Journal of Social History* (Summer 1974), forms Chapter 4 and is reprinted by permission of the publisher. "Quels Standards? Les ouvriers et la réorganisation de la production aux Etats-Unis (1900–1920)" originally appeared in *Le Mouvement Social* (January–March 1978), and is used for Chapter 5 with the permission of the publisher. "Facing Layoffs" first appeared in *Radical America* (March–April 1976); It forms Chapter 6 and has been reprinted by the permission of the publisher and co-author.

D. M.

Introduction

Two notions, the complexity of modern society and its need for constantly rising levels of productivity, have become something more than common assumptions of contemporary American social thought. They are its basic reference points. From those assumptions we derive, among other things, the belief that an economy based on highly sophisticated technology *must* be characterized by a detailed division of labor and by a professionally trained management, which monopolizes its planning, directive, and supervisory functions. Employees under their command may make only the most trivial decisions, whether they repeat mindless operations on an assembly line or occupy positions which require high technical competence. Responsibility for the desired rising levels of output, we are assured, must rest with experts who alone can comprehend the whole complex process. For all the popularity that "job enrichment" and "participation" experiments have enjoyed from time to time during the last sixty years, American business has held fast to the principle enunciated by President John Calder of the Remington Typewriter Company in 1912: "The last thing a good manager would think of doing would be to make his policies of shop management the subject of a referendum."[1]

From this point of view, it is considered to the benefit of the whole of society that management becomes ever more "scientific," not only in the sense of attaining increasingly precise knowledge of technology and of the physical nature of work, but also in improving its comprehension of the human relationships involved by means of social scientific research.[2] Only incurable romantics could chafe at this march of progress. Whatever complaints might once have been uttered against time and motion study or the dilution of industrial skills, Daniel Nelson assures us in his recent study of turn-of-the-century managerial reform, "the new factory environment was a vast improvement over the old, whether viewed from an economic or a social perspective."[3]

Even if that improvement bore a heavy price in cultural or psychological impoverishment (which many enthusiasts of "modernization" strenuously deny), the bottom line in the social calculation remains per capita income.

As Douglass C. North put it, in his concise survey of the "new economic history":

The importance of increasing productive capacity cannot be overemphasized. Redistributing income or eliminating depressions would result in less gain for the poor or the whole society than they would derive from an even relatively short period of sustained economic growth. The consequences of a compounded real per capita growth rate of 1.6 per cent per year dwarf all other welfare effects in our history (assuming no change in income distribution).[4]

To be sure, this way of thinking is far from novel. Bernard Mandeville advised his compatriots more than 250 years ago:

Then leave Complaints . . .
T' enjoy the World's Conveniences,
Be Fam'd in War, yet live in Ease,
Without great Vices, is a vain
EUTOPIA seated in the Brain . . .
Bare Virtue can't make Nations live
In Splendor; they, that would revive
A Golden Age, must be as free,
For Acorns, as for Honesty.[5]

Since Mandeville's time not only did Adam Smith offer the world a positive science of producing National Splendor, but Benjamin Franklin, Calvin Colton, Samuel Smiles, Horatio Alger, and a host of lesser publicists taught us to devote our lives to its pursuit. Charles Babbage, Andrew Ure, and Francis A. Walker, among others, also clearly analyzed the role of minute division of labor and the disciplined subordination of those who execute tasks in production to others who direct that work in attaining such a national goal (not to mention personal wealth). Frederick Winslow Taylor and his fellow pioneers in scientific management both showed the way to reduce work itself to such systematic control that the disciplining of the individual worker would supposedly no longer be a problem and claimed that the "mental revolution" involved in their reorganization of work would lay the basis for future social harmony, as well as future wealth. Their influence was evident in the writings of the Chairman of the Board of the American Management Association in the 1920s, Sam A. Lewisohn, who believed, *"The problem of distribution, which has so often been regarded as a drama, with labor and capital as the conflicting characters, turns out to be largely the prosaic task of using wage policies to increase national productivity."*[6]

To be sure, dissenters from this single-minded cult of productivity and expertise have been both numerous and articulate. Carter Goodrich, analyzing changes in the management of American coal mines during the 1920s, disputed the idea that "modernity" or "technological complexity" by themselves made inevitable what Harry Braverman was later to call "the degradation of work" in the twentieth century. "It is often said that modern society has chosen efficiency in production rather than richness in working life," wrote Goodrich. To the contrary, he argued that

society makes no choices as such, and the countless individual decisions out of which have come mass production as efficient as that at Ford's and jobs as dull as those at Ford's have most of them been made without the slightest reference to the quality of the working life that would result. . . . They are made on the basis of figures of output and cost and profit for the immediate business in the immediate future.[7]

Just as Goodrich located the source of the specific way in which industrial work has been impoverished in the quest of corporate leaders for profits, rather than in the mysterious workings of some such imaginary agency as "modernization" or the "preferences of society," so R. H. Tawney heaped scorn on those who were conscious of such social maladies as poverty, but whose pinched imaginations could conjure up no remedy other than "increasing productive capacity." Wrote Tawney:

When they desire to place their economic life on a better foundation, they repeat, like parrots, the word "Productivity," because that is the word that rises first in their minds; regardless of the fact that productivity is the foundation on which it is based already, that increased productivity is the one characteristic achievement of the age before the war [of 1914–18], as religion was of the Middle Ages or art of classical Athens, and that it is precisely in the century which has seen the greatest increase in productivity since the fall of the Roman Empire that economic discontent has been most acute.[8]

It is no mere coincidence that both Goodrich and Tawney wrote from the vantage point of close and sympathetic personal acquaintance with the workers' control movement of the years immediately following World War I. As the essays in this collection argue, industrial workers in America, like their counterparts in Europe, were at that very time vigorously and explicitly challenging management's pretentions and the value system which supported them. Those workers were keenly aware that the "science of work," as Harry Braverman said, was in reality "*a science of the management of others' work* under capitalist conditions," that is, where "labor power . . . is bought and sold."[9]

The first quarter of the twentieth century, therefore, was not only the epoch in which scientific management and assembly line production came to characterize industrial work in all the most advanced capitalist countries, it was also one in which the alternative of placing the factory under the collective direction of its operatives, clerks, and technicians was vigorously and creatively supported by millions of workers in all those countries.[10]

The practice and theory of workers' control, as developed in America during those years, provide the principal subject of these essays. At times the story involved little more than silent and opaque resistance to the demands and innovations of employers. At other times, workers in skilled crafts adopted and fought to enforce collective work rules through which they regulated human relations on the job and wrestled with the chronic menace of unemployment. As the case study of the machinists' union will show, the shop-floor conflict between managements' prerogatives and workers' control both undermined the effort of the National Civic Federation to win corporate executives to its dream of harmonious contractual relations between labor and capital and spurred on the rapid rise of socialism among the workers. The machinists' answer to "scientific management" was to demand a "truly scientific" reorganization of the whole society on a collectivist basis. Furthermore, during the period of World War I and its immediate aftermath, miners, metal workers, garment workers, railroad employees, and others simultaneously forced their employers to rescind various aspects of the new managerial practice and demanded the immediate adoption of their own plans for the reorganization of work relations from below.

Nevertheless, the battle for control of the workplace neither began nor ended in the opening years of this century. Consequently, these essays will also trace various aspects of the conflict before and after that time, always emphasizing the initiatives of the workers themselves, rather than the ways in which they were manipulated by those in authority over them. In the first period treated here, skilled craftsmen of the late nineteenth century, who exercised substantial autonomy in the conduct of their industrial work and the direction of their helpers, upheld an egalitarian moral code in opposition to the acquisitive individualism of contemporary bourgeois society, and militantly supported each other's efforts to impose their own work rules on their employers.

The second period is that of the early twentieth century, in which management tried to systematically assert its mastery over the workplace, and workers responded with an unprecedented quest for social power. The third phase is that of the 1930s and 1940s, when the economy's collapse pulled down the defenses which companies had assiduously built up around their new managerial prerogatives, especially during the twenties so that the government was forced to intervene directly in the re-shaping of work relations. The final phase is the present day, when the New Deal formula itself has entered a fatal crisis, and workers' demands and struggles are once again breaching the confines into which managerial authority and the law seemed once to have restricted them. Through all four of these periods, it will be evident, the famous terms "collective bargaining" and "wage and job consciousness" have never been adequate to describe the aspirations of American workers.

Both workers' submerged resistance and their articulate programs have turned out to be causes, as much as effects, of the rapid evolution and diffusion of managerial practice. The forms of personnel management, which have been hallmarks of up-to-date plant administration since the 1920s, especially represent a cooptive and repressive response to workers' initiatives. They cannot be adequately explained simply as a logical ex-tension of Frederick Taylor's "scientific" thinking. Sam Lewisohn showed his awareness of this dialectical relationship, while he linked it inseparably to his own insistence on management's leadership: "The modern workman has, it is true, an awakened imagination. He should be given a larger voice in matters affecting his status and his particular work. *But it is the employer, as the one responsible for administration, that must initiate him into his new role.*"[11]

Lewisohn's language sounds quite familiar to anyone acquainted with discussions of "the blue collar blues" found in business periodicals of the 1970s.[12] The reason management's concern with wildcat strikes, absen-teeism, drugs, and an apparent disappearance of "the work ethic" appeared to be new and surprising at this time, however, is that in the two decades which followed the Second World War all opposition to the cult of productivity and expertise seemed to have disappeared. With wage in-creases routinely linked to productivity gains and "management pre-rogative" clauses standard fare in union contracts, Daniel Bell's famous declaration of "the end of ideology" seemed plausible.[13] Corporate execu-tives, government officials, and union leaders all seemed to be speaking the same language.

In this period social scientists began to lump strikes, manifestoes, unions, revolutionary parties, anarcho-syndicalist leagues and other dis-tinctly working class activity under the condescending rubric "protest." *Industrialism and Industrial Man*, Clark Kerr's handy and familiar com-pendium of the new vogue, argued that the moment had arrived to discard, not only Marxism, but also the John R. Commons' school of labor history, which had for too long fixed historians' attention on "protest." What should concern scholars was "a more universal phenomenon affecting workers – the inevitable structuring of the managers and the managed in the course of industrialization." Lest their point be obscure, the authors added: "Not the handling of protest, but the structuring of the labor force is *the* labor problem in economic development."[14]

So pervasive was this style of thinking in academic circles that, when the civil rights campaigns and the struggle against the war in Vietnam awakened a profoundly radical consciousness among American students, very few participants in The Movement initially thought of industrial workers other than as inert victims of an alienating system, at best, and "hard hat" champions of the status quo, at worst. Moreover, most student activists rebelled against organization, deliberation, and theory per se, sensing in them the thin edge of their professors' doctrines of "complexity" and "expertise," against which they were in revolt. It was as though they believed, to paraphrase Hamlet, that the only role of thought was to "sickly o'er" the "native hue of resolution."

In quick succession France's May Events of 1968, the Prague Spring, Italy's "Hot Autumn" of 1969 and China's Cultural Revolution, each in its own way, placed the practice and theory of workers' control back again prominently on history's agenda. The ensuing wave of strikes in America, from West Virginia's "Black Lung" stoppage and the national walkout at General Electric onward through Lordstown and the shutdown of the post office system, sharply challenged management's authority and rationality, and often that of established union practice and leadership as well. By the mid-1970s the discontent and alienation of American workers had become favorite subjects of the popular press, business periodicals, and academic conferences. Although that discussion was very informative, it seldom breached the guidelines of the need for abler management. Radical movements which had originated in the New Left, however, turned their attention toward serious analysis of American economic life, and in the process began to orient their activities in much greater measure than before toward the work place, work relations, and the struggles of workers trying to find their way out of capitalist "rationality" into a genuinely rational form and purpose in industrial production.[15]

These historical developments have revived interest in both the origins of contemporary scientific management and the alternative ideas and practices advanced by workers in the epoch of its origins. To be sure, workers' demands and organizational forms of 1890 or of 1920 cannot simply be resurrected in 1980. Too much has changed in the basic configurations of economic activity and social life to allow that. On the other hand, a clearer memory of earlier industrial practices which sprang from the autonomy, social formations, and militancy of workers would not allow us to accept the argument that the technology and work relations of industrial enterprises are simply too complex to be subjected to workers' collective direction. It would certainly remind us that the cult of productivity and expertise enjoyed no popular consensus in the America of the early twentieth century. No one knew better than the workers themselves that they needed a much better standard of living than they then enjoyed, that only hard work and sound productive organization could produce such improvement, and that inefficiency and waste were built into the very fiber of the economic system. Their ideas of how to remedy the situation, however, were very different from those of their employers.

Notes

1 *Iron Age*, 89 (April 11, 1912), 913.
2 See David F. Noble, *America by Design: Science, Technology, and the Rise of Corporate Capitalism* (New York, 1977).
3 Daniel Nelson, *Managers and Workers: Origins of the New Factory System in the United States, 1880–1920* (Madison, Wis., 1975), 164.
4 Douglass C. North, *Growth and Welfare in the American Past: A New Economic History* (Englewood Cliffs, N.J., 1966), 3n. For an excellent discussion of the concept of "modernization," see Dean C. Tipps, "Modernization Theory and the Comparative Study of Societies: A Critical Perspective," *Comparative Studies in Society and History*, 15 (1973), 199–226.
5 Bernard Mandeville, *The Fable of the Bees: or, Private Vices, Publick Benefits*, with a commentary by F. B. Kaye, 2 vols. (Oxford, 1924), I, 36–7.
6 Sam A. Lewisohn, *The New Leadership in Industry* (New York, 1926), 199. The italics are in the original.
7 Carter L. Goodrich, *The Miner's Freedom: A Study of the Working Life in a Changing Industry* (Boston, 1925), 5–6. Braverman's phrase is in the title of his book *Labor and Monopoly Capital: The Degradation of Work in the Twentieth Century* (New York and London, 1974).
8 R. H. Tawney, *The Acquisitive Society* (New York, 1920), 4–5.
9 Braverman, 90.
10 See Ernest Mandel, ed., *Contrôle ouvrier, conseils ouvriers, autogestion anthologie* (Paris, 1970); James Hinton, *The First Shop Stewards' Movement* (London, 1973); Carter L. Goodrich, *The Frontier of Control* (New York, 1921, reissued London, 1975); Goodrich, "Problems of Workers' Control," *Locomotive Engineers Journal*, 57 (May 1923), 365–6, 415; Gwyn A. Williams, *Proletarian Order: Antonio Gramsci, Factory Councils, and the Origins of Italian Communism, 1911–1921* (London, 1975); Peter von Oertzen, *Betriebsräte in der Novemberrevolution* (Düsseldorf, 1963); Patrick Fridenson, ed., *1914–1918, L'autre front* (Paris, 1977).
11 Lewisohn, 84.
12 For a review of much of this literature, see John Zernan, "Organized Labor versus 'The Revolt Against Work': The Critical Contest," *Telos*, 21 (Fall 1974), 194–206.

13 Daniel Bell, *The End of Ideology: On the Exhaustion of Political Ideas in the Fifties* (New York, 1961).
14 Clark Kerr, John T. Dunlop, Frederick H. Harbison, and Charles A. Myers, *Industrialism and Industrial Man* (New York, 1964), 8.
15 See Braverman; Noble; Sidney Lens, *The Labor Wars* (Garden City, N.Y., 1974); Barbara Garson, *All the Livelong Day: The Meaning and Demeaning of Routine Work* (Garden City, N.Y. 1975); Jeremy Brecher, *Strike!* (San Francisco, 1972); Stanley Aronowitz, *False Promises: The Shaping of American Working Class Consciousness* (New York, 1973); James J. Matles and James Higgins, *Them and Us: Struggles of a Rank-and-File Union* (Englewood Cliffs, N.J., 1974); Dan Georgakas and Marvin Surkin, *Detroit: I Do Mind Dying* (New York, 1975); Rosalyn Baxandall, Linda Gordon and Susan Reverby, *America's Working Women* (New York, 1976); James Weinstein, *Ambiguous Legacy: The Left in American Politics* (New York, 1975); Gabriel Kolko, *Main Currents in Modern American History* (New York, 1976).

1. Workers' control of machine production in the nineteenth century*

"In an industrial establishment which employs say from 500 to 1,000 workmen, there will be found in many cases at least twenty to thirty different trades," wrote Frederick Winslow Taylor in his famous critique of the practices of industrial management which were then in vogue:

The workmen in each of these trades have had their knowledge handed down to them by word of mouth . . . This mass of rule-of-thumb or traditional knowledge may be said to be the principle asset or possession of every tradesman . . . [The] foremen and superintendents [who comprise the management] know, better than anyone else, that their own knowledge and personal skill falls far short of the combined knowledge and dexterity of all the workmen under them . . . They recognize the task before them as that of inducing each workman to use his best endeavors, his hardest work, all his traditional knowledge, his skill, his ingenuity, and his goodwill – in a word, his "initiative," so as to yield the largest possible return to his employer.[1]

Big Bill Haywood put the same point somewhat more pungently, when he declared: "The manager's brains are under the workman's cap."[2]

Both Taylor and Haywood were describing the power which certain groups of workers exercised over the direction of production processes at the end of the nineteenth century, a power which the scientific management movement strove to abolish, and which the Industrial Workers of the World wished to enlarge and extend to all workers. It is important to note that both men found the basis of workers' power in the superiority of their knowledge over that of the factory owners. It is even more important to note that they were referring not to "preindustrial" work practices, but to the factory itself.

The richly impressive work of Herbert Gutman in this country, E. P. Thompson in England, and others[3] has already unveiled to us the profound changes forced by the advent of industrial capitalism upon people's values and expectation, work habits, and sense of time, as well as the persistence with which working people clung to their traditional,

9

spasmodic, task-oriented styles of work and to a social code which was less tightly disciplined, less individualistic, and less exploitative than that which industrialization was imposing upon them. These studies have directed our attention to the experiences of the first generation of industrial workers, or, in the case of Gutman's conception, to the persistence of that "first-generation" experience over more than a century of American life.

My concern here, however, is not with the encounter of industrial with "preindustrial" ways, but rather with the patterns of behavior which took shape in the second and third generations of industrial experience, largely among workers whose world had been fashioned from their youngest days by smoky mills, congested streets, recreation as a week-end affair and toil at the times and the pace dictated by the clock (except when a more or less lengthy layoff meant no work at all).[4] It was such workers, the veterans, if you will, of industrial life, with whom Taylor was preoccupied. They had internalized the industrial sense of time, they were highly disciplined in both individual and collective behavior, and they regarded both an extensive division of labor and machine production as their natural environments. However, they had often fashioned from these attributes neither the docile obedience of automatons, nor the individualism of the "upwardly mobile," but rather a form of control of productive processes which became increasingly collective, deliberate and aggressive, until American employers launched a partially successful counterattack under the banners of scientific management and the open-shop drive.

Workers' control of production, however, was not a condition or state of affairs which existed at any point in time, but a struggle, a chronic battle in industrial life which assumed a variety of forms. Those forms may be treated as successive stages in a pattern of historical evolution, though one must always remember that the stages overlapped each other chronologically in different industries, or even at different localities within the same industry, and that each successive stage incorporated the previous one, rather than replaced it. The three levels of development which appeared in the second half of the nineteenth century were those characterized by (1) the functional autonomy of the craftsman, (2) the union work rule, and (3) mutual support of diverse trades in rule enforcement and sympathetic strikes. Each of these levels will be examined here in turn, then in conclusion some observations will be made on the impact of scientific management and the open-shop drive on the patterns of behavior which they represented.

The autonomous craftsman

The functional autonomy of craftsmen rested on both their superior knowledge, which made them self-directing at their tasks, and the supervision which they gave to one or more helpers. Iron molders, glass blowers, coopers, paper machine tenders, locomotive engineers, mule spinners, boiler makers, pipe fitters, typographers, jiggermen in potteries, coal miners, iron rollers, puddlers and heaters, the operators of McKay or Goodyear stitching machines in shoe factories, and, in many instances, journeymen machinists and fitters in metal works exercised broad discretion in the direction of their own work and that of their helpers. They often hired and fired their own helpers and paid the latter some fixed portion of their own earnings.

James J. Davis, who was to end up as Warren Harding's Secretary of Labor, learned the trade of puddling iron by working as his father's helper in Sharon, Pennsylvania. "None of us ever went to school and learned the chemistry of it from books," he recalled. "We learned the trick by doing it, standing with our faces in the scorching heat while our hands puddled the metal in its glaring bath."[5] His first job, in fact, had come at the age of twelve, when an aged puddler devised a scheme to enable himself to continue the physically arduous exertion of the trade by taking on a boy (twelve-year-old Davis) to relieve the helper of mundane tasks like stoking the furnace, so that the helper in turn could assume a larger share of the taxing work of stirring the iron as it "came to nature." By the time Davis felt he had learned enough to master his own furnace, he had to leave Sharon, because furnaces passed from father to son, and Davis's father was not yet ready to step down. As late as 1900, when Davis was living at home while attending business college after having been elected to public office, he took over his father's furnace every afternoon, through an arrangement the two had worked out between themselves.[6]

The iron rollers of the Columbus Iron Works, in Ohio, have left us a clear record of how they managed their trade in the minute books of their local union from 1873 to 1876. The three twelve-man rolling teams, which constituted the union, negotiated a single tonnage rate with the company for each specific rolling job the company undertook. The workers then decided collectively, among themselves, what portion of that rate should go to each of them (and the shares were far from equal, ranging from 19 1/4 cents, out of the negotiated $1.13 a ton, for the roller, to 5 cents for the runout hooker); how work should be allocated among them; how many rounds on the rolls should be undertaken per day; what special arrangements should be made for the fiercely hot labors of the hookers during the summer; and how members should be hired and progress through the various ranks of the gang.[7] To put it another way, all the boss did was to buy the equipment and raw materials and sell the finished product.

One cannot help being impressed by the fact that the Columbus iron rollers were conducting the operations of the firm in precisely the way J. T. Murphy and the Sheffield Workers' Council demanded that shop stewards should operate British industries in 1918, the union contracting with the employer to do the whole job, then performing that job without interference from employers.[8] But to make that analogy is to run too fast. The iron rollers of Columbus were not raising revolutionary demands, but pursuing commonplace practices. On the other hand, the practices themselves were both historically quite new (a "preindustrial" iron roller is a contradiction in terms), subject to incessant attacks by employers, and defended by the craftsmen's own disciplined ethical code.

Three aspects of the moral code, in which the craftsmen's autonomy was protectively enmeshed, deserve close attention. First, on most jobs there was a stint, an output quota fixed by the workers themselves. As the laments of scientific management's apostles about workers "soldiering" and the remarkable 1904 survey by the commissioner of labor, *Regulation and Restriction of Output*, made clear, stints flourished as widely without unions as with them.[9] Abram Hewitt testified in 1867 that his puddlers in New Jersey, who were not unionized, worked eleven turns per week (five and a half days), made three heats per turn, and put 450 pounds of iron in each charge, all by arrangement among themselves. Thirty-five years later a stint still governed the trade, though a dramatic improvement in puddling furnaces was reflected in union rules which specified eleven turns with five heats per turn and 550 pounds per charge (a 104 percent improvement in productivity), while some nonunion mill workers followed the same routine but boiled bigger charges.[10]

Stints were always under pressure from the employers, and were often stretched over the course of time by the combined force of competition among employers and improving technology. In this instance, productivity under union rules expanded more than three percent annually over three and a half decades. But workers clung doggedly to the practice, and used their superior knowledge both to determine how much they should do and to outwit employers' efforts to wring more production out of them. In a farm equipment factory studied in 1902, for example, the machine shop, polishing department, fitting department and blacksmith shop all had fixed stints, which made each group of workers average very similar earnings despite the fact that all departments were on piecework. In the blacksmith shop, which unlike the others had no union rule fining those who earned too much, workers held down the pace by refusing to replace each part they removed from the heaters with a cold one. They emptied the heaters entirely, before refilling them and then waited for the new parts to heat up.[11] Similarly, Taylor's colleague Carl Barth discovered a planer operator who avoided exceeding the stint while always looking busy, by simply removing the cutting tool from his machine from time to time, while letting it run merrily on.[12]

"There is in every workroom a fashion, a habit of work," wrote efficiency consultant Henry Gantt, "and the new worker follows that fashion, for it isn't respectable not to."[13] A quiver full of epithets awaited the deviant: "hog," "hogger-in," "leader," "rooter," "chaser," "rusher," "runner," "swift," "boss's pet"[14] to mention some politer versions. And when a whole factory gained a reputation for feverish work, disdainful craftsmen would describe its occupants, as one did of the Gisholt turret lathe works, as comprised half "of farmers, and the other half, with few exceptions, of horse thieves."[15] On the other hand, those who held fast to the carefully measured stint, despite the curses of their employers and the lure of higher earnings, depicted themselves as sober and trustworthy masters of their trades. Unlimited output led to slashed piece rates, irregular employment, drink and debauchery, they argued. Rationally restricted output, however, reflected "unselfish brotherhood," personal dignity, and "cultivation of the mind."[16]

Second, as this language vividly suggests, the craftsmen's ethical code demanded a "manly" bearing toward the boss. Few words enjoyed more popularity in the nineteenth century than this honorific, with all its connotations of dignity, respectability, defiant egalitarianism, and patriarchal male supremacy. The worker who merited it refused to cower before the foreman's glares – in fact, often would not work at all when a boss was watching. When confronted with indignities, he was expected to respond like the machinist in Lowell, who found regulations posted in his shop in 1867 requiring all employees to be at their posts in their work clothes when the first bell rang, to remain there until the last bell, and to be prevented from leaving the works between those times by locked doors:

Not having been brought up under such a system of slavery, [he recalled,] I took my things and went out, followed in a few hours by the rest of the men. Thinking perhaps that it might be of some benefit to the rest, I remained with them on the strike. They went back to work with the understanding that the new rules should not apply except in regard to the doors being locked. A few days after I went for my pay and it was politely handed me without the trouble of asking for it.[17]

Finally, "manliness" toward one's fellow workers was as important as it was toward the owners. "Undermining or conniving" at a brother's job was a form of hoggish behavior as objectional as running more than one machine, or otherwise doing the work that belonged to two men. Union rules commanded the expulsion of members who performed such "dirty work" in order to secure employment or advancement for themselves. When the members of the Iron Heaters and Rollers Union at a Philadelphia mill learned in 1875 that one of their brothers had been fired "for dissatisfaction in regard to his management of the mill," and that another member had "undermined" the first with the superintendent and been promised his rolls, the delinquent was expelled from the lodge, along with a lodge member who defended him, and everyone went on strike to demand the immediate discharge of both excommunicates by the firm.[18]

In short, a simple technological explanation for the control exercised by nineteenth-century craftsmen will not suffice. Technical knowledge acquired on the job was embedded in a mutualistic ethical code, also acquired on the job, and together these attributes provided skilled workers with considerable autonomy at their work and powers of resistance to the wishes of their employers. On the other hand, it was technologically possible for the worker's autonomy to be used in individualistic ways, which might promote his own mobility and identify his interests with those of the owner. The ubiquitous practice of subcontracting encouraged this tendency. In the needle trades, the long established custom of a tailor's taking work home to his family was transformed by his employment of other pieceworkers into the iniquitous "sweat shop" system.[19] Among iron molders, the "berkshire" system expanded rapidly after 1850, as individual molders hired whole teams of helpers to assist them in producing a multitude of castings. Carpenters and bricklayers were lured into piecework systems of petty exploitation. Other forms of subcontracting flourished in stone quarrying, iron mining, anthracite mining, and even in railroad locomotive works, where entire units of an engine's construction were let out to the machinist who filed the lowest bid, and who then hired a crew to assist him in making and fitting the parts.[20]

Subcontracting practices readily undermined both stints and the mutualistic ethic (though contractors were known to fix stints for their own protection in both garment and locomotive works), and they tended to flood many trades with trained, or semi-trained, workers who undercut wages and work standards. Their spread encouraged many craftsmen to move beyond reliance on their functional autonomy to the next higher level of craft control, the enactment and enforcement of union work rules. In one respect, union rules simply codified the autonomy I have already described. In fact, because they were often written down and enforced by joint action, union rules have a visibility to historians, which has made me resort to them already for evidence in the discussion of autonomy per se. But this intimate historical relationship between customary workers' autonomy and the union rule should not blind us to the fact that the latter represents a significant new stage of development.[21]

Union work rules

The work rules of unions were referred to by their members as "legislation."[22] The phrase denotes a shift from spontaneous to deliberate collective action, from a group ethical code to formal rules and sanctions, and from resistance to employers' pretentions to control over them. In some unions the rules were rather simple. The International Association of Machinists, for example, like its predecessors the Machinists and Black-smiths' International Union and the many machinists' local assemblies of the Knights of Labor, simply specified a fixed term of apprenticeship for any prospective journeyman, established a standard wage for the trade, prohibited helpers or handymen from performing journeymen's work, and forbade any member from running more than one machine at a time or accepting any form of piecework payment.[23]

Other unions had much more detailed and complex rules. There were, for example, sixty-six "Rules for Working" in the bylaws of the window-glass workers' Local Assembly 300 of the Knights of Labor. They specified that full crews had to be present "at each pot setting"; that skimming could be done only at the beginning of blowing and at meal time; that blowers and gatherers should not "work faster than at the rate of nine rollers per hour"; and that the "standard size of single strength rollers" should "be 40 × 58 to cut 38 × 56." No work was to be performed on Thanksgiving Day, Christmas, Decoration Day or Washington's Birthday, and no blower, gatherer or cutter could work between June 15 and September 15. In other words, during the summer months the union ruled that the fires were to be out.[24] In 1884 the local assembly waged a long and successful strike to preserve its limit of forty-eight boxes of glass a week, a rule which its members considered the key to the dignity and welfare of the trade.[25]

Nineteenth-century work rules were not ordinarily negotiated with employers or embodied in a contract. From the 1860s onward it became increasingly common for standard *wages* to be negotiated with employers or their associations, rather than fixed unilaterally as unions had tried earlier, but working rules changed more slowly. They were usually adopted unilaterally by local unions, or by the delegates to a national convention, and enforced by the refusal of the individual member to obey any command from an employer which violated them. Hopefully, the worker's refusal would be supported by the joint action of his shop mates, but if it was not, he was honor bound to pack his tool box and walk out alone, rather than break the union's laws. As Fred Reid put the point well in his description of nineteenth-century Scottish miners' unionism: "The strength of organised labour was held to depend upon the manliness of the individual workman."[26]

On the other hand, the autonomy of craftsmen which was codified in union rules was clearly not individualistic. Craftsmen were unmistakably and consciously group-made men, who sought to pull themselves upward by their collective boot straps. As unions waxed stronger after 1886, the number of strikes to enforce union rules grew steadily. It was, however, in union legislation against subcontracting that both the practical and ideological aspects of the conflict between group solidarity and upwardly mobile individualism became most evident, for these rules sought to regulate in the first instance not the employers' behavior, but that of the workers themselves. Thus the Iron Molders Union attacked the "berkshire" system by rules forbidding any of its members to employ a helper for any other purpose than "to skim, shake out and to cut sand," or to pay a helper out of his own earnings. In 1867, when 8,615 out of some 10,400 known molders in the country were union members, the national union legislated further that no member was allowed to go to work earlier than seven o'clock in the morning.[27] During the 1880s the Brick Layers' Union checked subcontracting by banning its members from working for any contractor who could not raise enough capital to buy his own bricks. All building trades unions instructed their members not to permit contractors to work with tools alongside with them. The United Mine Workers limited the number of helpers a bituminous miner could engage, usually to one, though the employment of several laborers by one miner remained widespread in anthracite mines through the First World War.

The Carpenters and the Machinists outlawed piecework altogether, for the same purpose. The Amalgamated Iron and Steel Workers required the companies to pay helpers directly, rather than through the craftsmen, and fixed the share of tonnage rates to which helpers were entitled.[28] All such regulations secured the group welfare of the workers involved by sharply rejecting society's enticements to become petty entrepreneurs, clarifying and intensifying the division of labor at the work place, and sharpening the line between employer and employee.

Where the trade was well unionized, a committee in each shop supervised the enforcement in that plant of the rules and standard wage which the union had adopted for the trade as a whole. The craft union and the craft local assembly of the Knights of Labor were forms of organization well adapted to such regulatory activities. The members were legislating, on matters on which they were unchallenged experts, rules which only their courage and solidarity could enforce. On one hand, the craft form of organization linked their personal interests to those of the trade, rather than those of the company in which they worked, while, on the other hand, their efforts to enforce the same rules on all of their employers, where they were successful, created at least a few islands of order in the nineteenth-century's economic ocean of anarchic competition.

Labor organizations of the late nineteenth century struggled persistently to transform workers' struggles to manage their own work from spontaneous to deliberate actions, just as they tried to subject wage strikes and efforts to shorten the working day to their conscious regulation. "The trade union movement is one of reason, one of deliberation, depending entirely upon the voluntary and sovereign actions of its member," declared the Executive Council of the AFL.[29] Only through "thorough organization," to use a favorite phrase of the day, was it possible to enforce a trade's work rules throughout a factory, mine, or construction site. Despite the growing number of strikes over union rules and union recognition in the late 1880s, the enforcement of workers' standards of control spread more often through the daily self-assertion of craftsmen on the job than through large and dramatic strikes.

Conversely, strikes over wage reductions at times involved thinly disguised attacks by employers on craftsmen's job controls. Fall River's textile manufacturers in 1870 and the Hocking Valley coal operators in 1884, to cite only two examples, deliberately foisted severe wage reductions on their highly unionized workers in order to provoke strikes. The owners' hope was that in time hunger would force their employees to abandon union membership, and thus free the companies' hands to change production methods.[30] As the treasurer of one Fall River mill testified in 1870: "I think the question with the spinners was not wages, but whether they or the manufacturers should rule. For the last six or eight years they have ruled Fall River."[31] Defeat in a strike temporarily broke the union's control, which had grown through steady recruiting and rule enforcement during years which were largely free of work stoppages.

Mutual support

The third level of control struggles emerged when different trades lent each other support in their battles to enforce union rules and recognition. An examination of the strike statistics gathered by the U.S. Commissioner of Labor for the period 1881–1905 reveals the basic patterns of this development.[32] Although there had been a steady increase in both the number and size of strikes between 1881 and 1886, the following twelve years saw a reversal of that growth, as stoppages became both smaller and increasingly confined to skilled crafts (except in 1894). With that change came three important and interrelated trends. First, the proportion of strikes called by unions rose sharply in comparison to spontaneous strikes. Nearly half of all strikes between 1881 and 1886 had occurred without union sanction or aid. In the seven years beginning with 1887 more than two-thirds of each year's strikes were deliberately called by a union, and in 1891 almost 75 percent of the strikes were official.

Secondly, as strikes became more deliberate and unionized, the proportion of strikes which dealt mainly with wages fell abruptly. Strikes to enforce union rules, enforce recognition of the union, and protect its members grew from 10 percent of the total or less before 1885 to the level of 19 to 20 percent between 1891 and 1893. Spontaneous strikes and strikes of laborers and factory operatives had almost invariably been aimed at increasing wages or preventing wage reductions, with the partial exception of 1886 when 20 percent of all strikes had been over hours. The more highly craftsmen became organized, however, the more often they struck and were locked out over work rules.

Third, unionization of workers grew on the whole faster than strike participation. The ratio of strike participants to membership in labor organizations fell almost smoothly from 109 in 1881 to 24 in 1888, rose abruptly in 1890 and 1891 (to 71 and 86 respectively), then resumed its downward trend to 36 in 1898, interrupted, of course, by a leap to 182 in 1894.[33] In a word, calculation and organization were the dominant tendencies in strike activity, just as they were in the evolution of work rules during the nineteenth century. But the assertion of deliberate control through formal organization was sustained not only by high levels of militancy (a persistently high propensity to strike), but also by remarkably aggressive mutual support, which sometimes took the form of the unionization of all grades of workers within a single industry, but more often appeared in the form of sympathetic strikes involving members of different trade unions.

Joint organization of all grades of workers seemed most likely to flourish where no single craft clearly dominated the life of the workplace, in the way iron molders, bricklayers, or iron puddlers did where they worked. It was also most likely to appear at the crest of the waves of strike activity among unskilled workers and operatives, as is hardly surprising, and to offer evidence of the organizational impulse in their ranks. In Philadelphia's shoe industry between 1884 and 1887, for example, the Knights of Labor successfully organized eleven local assemblies, ranging in size from 55 to 1,000 members, each of which represented a different craft or cluster of related occupations, and formulated wage demands and work rules for its own members. Each assembly sent three delegates to District Assembly 70, the highest governing body of the Knights for the industry, which in turn selected seven representatives to meet in a city-wide arbitration committee with an equal number of employers' representatives. Within each factory a "shop union" elected by the workers in that plant handled grievances and enforced the rules of the local assemblies, aided by one male and one female "statistician," who kept track of the complex piecerates.[34]

There is no evidence that local assemblies of unskilled workers or of semiskilled operatives ever attempted to regulate production processes themselves in the way assemblies of glass blowers and other craftsmen did. They did try to restrict hiring to members of the Knights and sometimes regulated layoffs by seniority clauses. For the most part, however, assemblies of operatives and laborers confined their attention to wages and to protection of their members against arbitrary treatment by supervisors.[35] On the other hand, the mere fact that such workers had been organized made it difficult for employers to grant concessions to their craftsmen at the expense of helpers and laborers. Consequently, the owners were faced simultaneously with higher wage bills and a reduction of their control in a domain where they had been accustomed to exercise unlimited authority.

Table 1. *Strike trends, 1881–1905*

Year	No. of strikes (1)	Workers involved (000) (2)	% wage strikes (3)	% ordered by unions (4)	% sympathy strikes (5)	No. sympathy strikes (6)
1881	471	101	79.8	47.3	0.8	2
1882	454	121	75.4	48.5	0.9	3
1883	478	122	77.2	56.7	0.6	2
1884	443	117	74.1	54.2	2.0	6
1885	645	159	72.9	55.3	3.1	20
1886	1432	407	63.0	53.3	2.9	37
1887	1436	273	54.8	66.3	4.7	71
1888	906	103	55.2	68.1	3.8	34
1889	1075	205	59.0	67.3	6.1	67
1890	1833	286	50.9	71.3	9.9	188
1891	1717	245	48.9	74.8	11.5	204
1892	1298	164	50.4	70.7	8.9	117
1893	1305	195	58.8	69.4	4.5	62
1894	1349	505	63.7	62.8	8.8	120
1895	1215	286	69.6	54.2	0.6	7
1896	1026	184	57.6	64.6	0.6	7
1897	1078	333	66.2	55.3	0.7	9
1898	1056	182	63.0	60.4	0.8	9
1899	1797	308	59.4	62.0	1.5	29
1900	1779	400	59.0	65.4	1.5	29
1901	2924	396	46.6	75.9	2.4	71
1902	3162	553	51.2	78.2	2.6	87
1903	3494	532	51.5	78.8	2.4	88
1904	2307	376	42.2	82.1	3.7	93
1905	2077	176	44.5	74.7	2.7	61

Sources: The number of strikes and the number of workers involved (1 and 2) are taken from U.S. Commissioner of Labor, *Twenty-First Annual Report* (1906), 15. Wage strikes as a percent of all strikes (3) is from J. H. Griffin, *Strikes* (1939), 76. The percentage of strikes ordered by unions, the percent of all strikes represented by sympathetic strikes, and the number of sympathetic strikes (4, 5, and 6) are from Florence Peterson, *Strikes in the United States, 1880–1936* (1937), 32–3.

Moreover, workers who directed important production processes were themselves at times reluctant to see their own underlings organized, and frequently sought to dominate the larger organization to which their helpers belonged. A case in point was offered by the experience of the Knights of Labor in the garment industry, where contractors were organized into local assemblies of their own, supposedly to cooperate with those of cutters, pressers, tailors, and sewing-machine operators. Contractors were often charged with disrupting the unionization of their own employees, in order to promote their personal competitive advantages. Above all, they tried to discourage women from joining the operators' assemblies. As the secretary of a St. Louis tailors' local assembly revealed, contractors who were his fellow Knights were telling the parents of operators that "no dissent girl [sic] belong to an assembly."[36]

On the other hand, the experience of the Knights in both the shoe and garment industries suggests that effective unionization of women operatives was likely to have a remarkably radicalizing impact on the organization. It closed the door decisively both on employers who wished to compensate for higher wages paid to craftsmen by exacting more from the unskilled, and on craftsmen who were tempted to advance themselves by sweating others. In Philadelphia, Toronto, Cincinnati, Beverly, and Lynn both the resistance of the manufacturers to unionism and the level of mutuality exhibited by the workers leapt upward noticeably when the women shoe workers organized along with the men. Furthermore, the sense of total organization made all shoe workers more exacting in their demands and less patient with the protracted arbitration procedures employed by the Knights. "Quickie" strikes became increasingly frequent as more and more shoe workers enrolled in the order. Conversely, the shoe manufacturers banded tightly together to destroy the Knights of Labor.[37]

In short, the organization of all grades of workers in any industry propelled craftsmen's collective rule making into a more aggressive relationship with the employers, even where it left existing styles of work substantially unchanged. The other form of joint action, sympathetic strikes, most often involved the unionized skilled crafts themselves, and consequently was more directly related to questions of control of production processes. When Fred S. Hall wrote in 1898 that sympathetic strikes had "come so much in vogue during the last few years,"[38] he was looking back on a period during which organized workers had shown a greater tendency to walk out in support of the struggles of other groups of workers than was the case in any other period in the history of recorded strike data. Only the years between 1901 and 1904 and those between 1917 and 1921 were to see the absolute number of sympathetic strikes approach even *half* the levels of 1890 and 1891.

There were, in fact, two distinct crests in the groundswell of sympathetic strikes. The first came between 1886 and 1888, when a relatively small number of disputes, which spread by sympathetic action to include vast numbers of workers, caught public attention in a dramatic way. The Southwest railways strike of 1886, the New York freight handlers' dispute of 1887, and the Lehigh coal and railroad stoppages of 1888 exemplified this trend. None of them, however, primarily involved control questions, in the sense they have been described here.

The second crest, that of 1890–2, was quite different. It was dominated by relatively small stoppages of organized craftsmen. In New York state, where the Bureau of Labor Statistics collected detailed information on such stoppages until 1892 (and included in its count strikes which were omitted from the U.S. Commissioner of Labor's data because they lasted less than a single day or included fewer than six workers), the number of establishments shut by sympathetic strikes rose from an average of 166 yearly between 1886 and 1889 to 732 in 1890, 639 in 1891, and 738 in 1892. Most of them involved the employees of a single company, like the fifteen machinists who struck in support of the claims of molders in their factory or the four marble cutters who walked out to assist paper hangers on the same site. A few were very large. When New York's cabinet makers struck to preserve their union in 1892, for example, 107 carpenters, 14 gilders, 75 marble cutters and helpers, 17 painters, 23 plasterers, 28 porters, 12 blue stone cutters, 14 tile layers and helpers, 32 upholsterers, 14 varnishers, 149 wood carvers, and others walked out of more than 100 firms to lend their support.[39]

Eugene V. Debs was to extoll this extreme manifestation of mutuality as the "Christ-like virtue of sympathy," and to depict his own Pullman boycott, the epoch's most massive sympathetic action, as an open confrontation between that working-class virtue and a social order which sanctified selfishness.[40] It is true that the mutualistic ethic which supported craftsmen's control was displayed in its highest form by sympathetic strikes. It is equally true, however, that the element of calculation, which was increasingly dominating all strike activity, was particularly evident here. As Fred S. Hall pointed out, sympathetic strikes of this epoch differed sharply from "contagious" strikes, which spread spontaneously like those of 1877, in two respects. First, the sympathetic strikes were called by the workers involved, through formal union procedures. Although figures comparing official with unofficial strikes are not available, two contrasting statistics illustrate Hall's point. The construction industry was always the leading center of sympathetic strikes. In New York more than 70 percent of the establishments shut by sympathetic action between 1890 and 1892 were involved in building construction. On the other hand, over the entire period of federal data (1881–1904) no less than 98.03 percent of the strikes in that industry were called by unions.[41]

Second, as Hall observed, the tendency toward sympathetic strikes was "least in those cases where the dispute concerns conditions of employment such as wages and hours, and [was] greatest in regard to disputes which involve questions of unionism – the employment of only union men, the recognition of the union, etc."[42] The rise of sympathetic strikes, like the rise of strikes over rules and recognition, was part of the struggle for craftsmen's control – its most aggressive and far-reaching manifestation.

It is for this reason that the practice of sympathetic strikes was ardently defended by the AFL in the 1890s. Building trades contracts explicitly provided for sympathetic stoppages. Furthermore, at the federation's 1895 convention a resolution carried, directing the executive council to "convey to the unions, in such way as it thinks proper, not to tie themselves up with contracts so that they cannot help each other when able." The council itself denied in a report to the same convention that it opposed sympathetic strikes. "On the contrary," it declared, "we were banded together to help one another. The words union, federation, implied it. An organization which held aloof when assistance could be given to a sister organization, was deserving of censure." even though each union had the right to decide its own course of action.[43]

On the other hand, not all unions supported this policy by any means. Under the right conditions it was just as possible for work processes to be regulated by the rules of a craft union which stood aloof from all appeals to class solidarity, as it was for an individual craftsman to identify his functional autonomy with his employer's interests through subcontracting. Precisely such a solitary course was proudly pursued by the locomotive engineers and firemen. In general, where a union was strong enough to defy its employers alone and where no major technological innovations threatened its members' work practices, it tended to reach an accommodation with the employers on the basis of the latter's more or less willing recognition of the union's work rules.

Two examples will suffice. One appeared in stove molding, where eight years of protracted strikes and lockouts followed the National Stove Founders' Defense Association's 1882 denunciation of the "one-sided cast-iron rules" of the Molders' Union, from which it envisaged "no appeal except through a bitter struggle for supremacy." But the molders' indispensable mastery of the art of casting satiny smooth stove parts, their thorough organization, and their readiness to strike again and again enabled the Molders Union to prevail with little help from other unions. In 1890 the employers' Defense Association signed a national trade agreement, which provided for arbitration of all disputes and tacitly accepted the union's authority to establish work rules.[44] In sharp contrast to machinery molders, who often joined machinists, boilermakers, and other metal tradesmen in strikes, participation by stove molders in sympathetic strikes was practically unheard of.

Similarly, bricklayers and stonemasons proved eminently capable of defending themselves, seldom found their rules seriously challenged, and consequently felt little need for joint action with other trades, except during campaigns for shorter hours. The forceful but conservative form of craft control which they represented is evident not only in the refusal of the Bricklayers' and Masons' International Union to send representatives to New York City's Board of Walking Delegates or to affiliate with the AFL, but also in the reluctance of its members to engage in sympathetic strikes. Between 1890 and 1892 only four New York firms were shut by bricklayers and four by stonemasons in sympathetic actions. By way of contrast, during the same three years sympathetic strikes by carpenters in that state closed 171 firms and similar stoppages by cloakmakers another 152.[45]

Furthermore, employers in many industries banded together in the early 1890s to resist sympathetic strikes, union rules and union recognition with increasing vigor and effectiveness. Sympathetic lockouts were mounted by employers' organizations to deny striking workers alternative sources of employment or financial support. Legal prosecutions for conspiracy in restraint of trade, including use of the Sherman Anti-Trust Act against the Workingmen's Amalgamated Council of New Orleans for the city-wide sympathetic strike of 1892, and court-ordered injunctions provided supplementary weapons. In this setting, unionized craftsmen suffered a growing number of defeats. Whereas fewer than 40 percent of the strikes of 1889 and 1890 had been lost by the workers, 54.5 percent of the strikes of 1891 and 53.9 percent of those of 1892 were unsuccessful. This level of defeats was by far the highest for the late nineteenth century, and would not be approached again until 1904.[46] The losses are all the more remarkable when one recalls that these were record years for union-called strikes (as opposed to spontaneous strikes) and that throughout the 1881 to 1905 period strikes called by unions tended to succeed in better than 70 percent of the cases, while spontaneous strikes were lost in almost the same proportion. The explanation for the high level of defeats in calculated strikes of 1891 and 1892 lies in the audacity of the workers' demands. Official strikes over wages remained eminently successful. The fiercest battles and the bitterest losses pivoted around union rules and recognition and around sympathetic action itself.

Consequently trade unionists began to shy away from sympathetic strikes in practice, despite their verbal defenses, even before 1894. The statistical appearance of a crescendo of sympathetic strikes in 1894 followed by an abrupt collapse is misleading. Hall suggests that crafts other than the building trades were becoming hesitant to come out in sympathy with other groups, especially with workers from other plants, from 1892 onward. Although the New York data ends that year, it seems to bear him out in an interesting way. The total number of sympathetic strikes in New York was as great in 1892 as it had been in 1890. On the other hand, 67 percent of those strikes had been in the building trades in 1890, as compared to 69 percent in 1891 and 84 percent in 1892. One wishes the figures had continued, to reveal whether the small numbers of such strikes after 1895 were confined to construction. In any event, even in 1892 more than 100 of the 120 establishments outside of the building trades which were hit by sympathetic strikes were involved in a single conflict, that of the cabinet makers. And the workers ultimately abandoned that battle in total defeat. In this context the resurgence of such strikes in 1894 appears as an aberration. Indeed, the Pullman boycott and the bituminous coal strike together accounted for 94 percent of the establishments shut by sympathy actions in the first six months of that year.[47]

In short, historians have, on the whole, been seriously misled by Norman J. Ware's characterization of the period after the Haymarket Affair as one of "Sauve qui peut!"[48] As craftsmen unionized, they not only made their struggles for control increasingly collective and deliberate, but also manifested a *growing* consciousness of the dependence of their efforts on those of workers in other crafts. They drew strength in this struggle from their functional autonomy, which was derived from their superior knowledge, exercised through self-direction and their direction of others at work. This autonomy both nurtured and in turn was nurtured by a mutualistic ethic, which repudiated important elements of acquisitive individualism. As time passed functional autonomy was increasingly often codified in union rules, which were collectively "legislated" and upheld through the commitment of the individual craftsmen and through a swelling number of strikes to enforce them. Organized efforts reached the most aggressive and inclusive level of all in joint action among the various crafts for mutual support. When such actions enlisted all workers in an industry (as happened when women unionized in shoe manufacturing), and when they produced a strong propensity of unionized craftsmen to strike in support of each other's claims, they sharply separated the aggressive from the conservative consequences of craftsmen's autonomy and simultaneously provoked an intense, concerted response from the business community.

In an important sense, the last years of the depression represented only a lull in the battle. With the return of prosperity in 1898, both strikes and union organizing quickly resumed their upward spiral, work rules again seized the center of the stage, and sympathetic strikes became increasingly numerous and bitterly fought. Manufacturers' organizations leapt into the fray with the open-shop drive, while their spokesmen cited new government surveys to support their denunications of workers' "restriction of output."[49]

On the other hand, important new developments distinguished the first decade of the twentieth century from what had gone before. Trade union officials, who increasingly served long terms in full-time salaried positions, sought to negotiate the terms of work with employers, rather than letting their members "legislate" them. The anxiety of AFL leaders to secure trade agreements and to ally with "friendly employers," like those affiliated with the National Civic Federation, against the open-shop drive, prompted them to repudiate the use of sympathetic strikes. The many such strikes which took place were increasingly lacking in union sanction and in any event never reached the level of the early 1890s.[50]

Most important of all, new methods of industrial management undermined the very foundation of craftsmen's functional autonomy. Job analysis through time and motion study allowed management to learn, then to systematize the way the work itself was done. Coupled with systematic supervision and new forms of incentive payment it permitted what Frederick Winslow Taylor called "*enforced* standardization of methods, *enforced* adoption of the best implements and working conditions, and *enforced* cooperation of all the employees under management' detailed direction."[51] Scientific management, in fact, fundamentally disrupted the craftsmen's styles of work, their union rules and standard rates, and their mutualistic ethic, as it transformed American industrial practice between 1900 and 1930. Its basic effect, as Roethlisberger and Dickson discovered in their experiments at Western Electric's Hawthorne Works, was to place the worker "at the bottom level of a highly stratified organization," leaving his "established routines of work, his cultural traditions of craftsmanship, [and] his personal interrelations" all "at the mercy of technical specialists."[52]

Two important attributes of the scientific management movement become evident only against the background of the struggles of the nineteenth-century craftsmen to direct their own work in their own collective way. First, the appeal of the new managerial techniques to manufacturers involved more than simply a response to new technology and a new scale of business organization. It also implied a conscious endeavor to uproot those work practices which had been the taproot of whatever strength organized labor enjoyed in the late nineteenth century. A purely technological explanation of the spread of Taylorism is every bit as inadequate as a purely technological explanation of craftsmen's autonomy.[53] Second, the apostles of scientific management needed not only to abolish older industrial work practices, but also to discredit them in the public eye. Thus Taylor roundly denied that even "the high class mechanic" could "ever thoroughly understand the science of doing his work," and pasted the contemptuous label of "soldiering" over all craft rules, formal and informal alike.[54] Progressive intellectuals seconded his arguments. Louis Brandeis hailed scientific management for "reliev[ing] labor of responsibilities not its own."[55] And John R. Commons considered it "immoral to hold up to this miscellaneous labor, as a class, the hope that it can ever manage industry." If some workers do "shoulder responsibility," he explained, "it is because certain *individuals* succeed, and then those individuals immediately close the doors, and labor, as a class remains where it was."[56]

It was in this setting that the phrase "workers' control" first entered the vocabulary of the American labor movement. It appeared to express a radical, if often amorphous, set of demands which welled up around the end of World War I among workers in the metal trades, railroading, coal mining, and garment industries.[57] Although those demands represented very new styles of struggle in a unique industrial and political environment, many of the workers who expressed them could remember the recent day when in fact, the manager's brains had been under the workman's cap.

Notes

* The research for this study was assisted by a fellowship from the John Simon Guggenheim Memorial Foundation.

1 Frederick Winslow Taylor, *The Principles of Scientific Management* (New York, 1967), 31–2.

2 William D. Haywood and Frank Bohn, *Industrial Socialism* (Chicago, n.d.), 25.

3 Herbert G. Gutman, "Work, Culture, and Society in Industrializing America, 1815–1919," *American Historical Review*, 78 (June 1973), 531–88; E. P. Thompson, "Time, Work-Discipline, and Industrial Capitalism," *Past and Present*, 38 (Dec. 1967), 56–97; E. J. Hobsbawm, "Custom, Wages and Workload in Nineteenth-Century Industry," in Hobsbawm, *Labouring Men* (Lon-

don, 1964), 344–70; Gregory Kealey, "Artisans Respond to Industrialism: Shoemakers, Shoe Factories and the Knights of St. Crispin in Toronto," *Canadian Historical Association, Historical Papers* (June 1973), 137–57; Paul G. Faler, "Workingmen, Mechanics and Social Change: Lynn, Massachusetts, 1800–1860" (unpublished Ph.D. dissertation, University of Wisconsin, 1971); Bruce G. Laurie, "The Working People of Philadelphia, 1827–1853" (unpublished Ph.D. dissertation, University of Pittsburgh, 1971); David Montgomery, "The Shuttle and the Cross: Weavers and Artisans in the Kensington Riots of 1844," *Journal of Social History*, 5 (Spring 1972), 411–46.

4 The question of industrial generations has been treated in American history largely in terms of leaders. See David Montgomery, *Beyond Equality: Labor and the Radical Republicans, 1862–1872* (New York 1967), 197–229; Warren R. Van Tine, *The Making of the Labor Bureaucrat: Union Leadership in the United States, 1870–1920* (Amherst, 1973), 1–32. For more fundamental social analyses, see Leopold H. Haimson, "The Russian Workers' Movement on the Eve of the First World War," unpublished paper, presented at the American Historical Association convention, 1972; Michelle Perrot, *Les Ouvriers en grève: France 1871–1890*, 2 vols. (Paris, 1974), I, 312–95.

5 James J. Davis, *The Iron Puddler: My Life in the Rolling Mills and What Came of It* (Indianapolis, 1922), 91.

6 Ibid., 85, 92–3, 96, 114, 227. The issue of promotion of helpers to puddlers' furnaces provoked strikes by helpers against puddlers in the 1870s. See John H. Ashworth, *The Helper and American Trade Unions* (Baltimore, 1915), 83, 93–4.

7 Minute Books, Lodge No. 11, Rollers, Roughers, Catchers and Hookers Union (Columbus, Ohio), July 14, 1873– April 28, 1876 (William Martin Papers, University of Pittsburgh library).

8 Ernest Mandel, ed. *Contrôle ouvrier, conseils ouvriers, autogestion, anthologie* (Paris, 1970), 192–7. See also Carter Goodrich, *The Frontier of Control* (New York, 1921).

9 Frederick Winslow Taylor, "Shop Management," *Transactions of the American Society of Mechanical Engineers*, 24 (1903), 1337–456; U.S. Commissioner of Labor, *Eleventh Annual Report*, "Regulation and Restriction of Output" (Washington, D.C., 1904).

10 United Kingdom, Parliament, *Second Report of the Commissioners Appointed to Inquire into the Organization and Rules of Trades Unions and Other Associations* (Parliamentary Sessional Paper, 1867, xxxii c3893), 2; "Restriction of Output," 243.

11 "Restriction of Output," 198–9.

12 U.S. Commission on Industrial Relations, *Final Report and Testimony Submitted to Congress by the Commission on Industrial Relations* (64th Congress, 1st session, Washington, D.C., 1915), 893–4.

13 Henry L. Gantt, *Work, Wages, and Profits* (2nd, ed. rev., (New York, 1919), 186.

14 "Restriction of Output," 18.

15 P. A. Stein to *Machinists' Monthly Journal*, 15 (April 1903), 294.

16 See "What One Trade Has Done," *John Swinton's Paper*, March 23, 1884. Cf. Peter N. Stearns, "Adaptation to Industrialization: German Workers as a Test Case," *Central European History*, 3 (1970), 303–31.

17 Massachusetts Bureau of Statistics of Labor, *Report of the Bureau of Statistics of Labor for 1871*, 590–1.

18 Associated Brotherhood of Iron and Steel Heaters, Rollers and Roughers of

the United States, "Report on Communications. The Year's Term Having Closed July 10th, 1875," February 25, 1875. For more on "dirty work" and "one man-one machine" rules, see Amalgamated Association of Iron and Steel Workers, *Proceedings* (1877), 52, 75; "Restriction of Output," 101–5, 226–7.

19 On the origins of "sweating" in the needle trades, see Conrad Carl testimony, U.S. Congress, Senate Committee on Education and Labor, *Report of the Committee of the Senate upon the Relations between Labor and Capital*, 3 vols. (Washington, D.C., 1885), I, 413–21; Louis Lorwin, *The Women's Garment Workers* (New York, 1924), 12–23.

20 Ashworth, 67–72; Robert A. Christie, *Empire in Wood: A History of the Carpenters' Union* (Ithaca, N.Y., 1956), ch. 5; Paul Worthman, "Black Workers and Labor Unions in Birmingham, Alabama, 1897–1904," *Labor History*, 10 (Summer 1969), 374–407; Jacob H. Hollander and George E. Barnett, *Studies in American Trade Unionism* (New York, 1912), 147–8; *Iron Age*, 91 (January 30, 1913), 334; *Machinists' Monthly Journal*, 16 (April 1904), 321.

21 Cf. Benson Soffer, "A Theory of Trade Union Development: The Role of the 'Autonomous' Workman," *Labor History*, 1 (Spring 1960), 141–63.

22 The Typographers still call their rule book the Book of Laws. See Selig Perlman, *A Theory of the Labor Movement* (New York, 1928), 262–72; Seymour Martin Lipset, Martin A. Trow, and James S. Coleman, *Union Democracy* (Garden City, N.Y., 1972), 160–226.

23 "Restriction of Output," 101–8; Charles B. Going, "The Labour Question in England and America," *Engineering Magazine*, 19 (May 1900), 161–76; Hollander and Barnett, 109–52.

24 *By-Laws of the Window Glass Workers*, L.A. 300, Knights of Labor (Pittsburgh, 1899), 26–36.

25 "What One Trade Has Done," *John Swinton's Paper*, March 23, 1884.

26 Fred Reid, "Keir Hardie's Conversion to Socialism," in *Essays in Labour History, 1886–1923*, Asa Briggs and John Saville, eds. (London, 1971), 29. See also Montgomery, *Beyond Equality*, 142–53; David A. McCabe, *The Standard Rate in American Trade Unions* (Baltimore, 1912).

27 *Proceedings of the Eighth Annual Session of the Iron Molders' International Union* (Philadelphia, 1867) 10, 14, 40–1; Ashworth, 36, 38, 68.

28 See note 20.

29 Samuel Gompers, "The Strike and Its Lessons," in *A Momentous Question: The Respective Attitudes of Labor and Capital*, John Swinton, ed., (Philadelphia and Chicago, 1895), 311.

30 See Philip T. Silvia, Jr., "The Spindle City: Labor, Politics and Religion in Fall River, Massachusetts, 1870–1905" (unpublished Ph.D. dissertation, Fordham University, 1973), ch. 3; Jon Amsden and Stephen Brier, "Coal Miners on Strike: The Transformation of Strike Demands and the Formation of the National Union in the U.S. Coal Industry, 1881–1894," forthcoming in *The Journal of Interdisciplinary History*; Andrew Roy, *A History of the Coal Miners* (Columbus, Ohio, 1902), 220–42.

31 Massachusetts Bureau of Statistics of Labor, *Report*, 1871, 55.

32 See Table 1, Ch. 1.

33 John H. Griffin, *Strikes: A Study in Quantitative Economics* (New York, 1939), 107. A splendid discussion of the increasing role of calculation in nineteenth-century strikes may be found in Perrot, I, 101–80; II, 424–85, 574–606.

34 Augusta E. Galster, *The Labor Movement in the Shoe Industry, with Special Reference to Philadelphia* (New York, 1924), 49–57.

35 See, for example, the agreement between Carpet Weavers' National Assembly

No. 126, Knights of Labor and E. S. Higgins & Co., in New York Bureau of Statistics of Labor, *Fourth Annual Report, 1886* (Albany, 1887), 256. Much more research is needed on the demands of unskilled workers, but note the sharp contrast in the types of demands presented by craftsmen and laborers when each group met separately during the Bethlehem Steel strike. U.S. Congress, Senate, *Report on the Strike at the Bethlehem Steel Works* (Senate Document No. 521, Washington, D.C., 1910), 26–32.

36 Abraham Bisno, *Abraham Bisno, Union Pioneer* (Madison, Wis. 1967), 77–8, 135–7; John W. Hayes Papers, Catholic University of America, LA 7507, LA 2567, LA 10353. The quotation is from Gustive Cytron to John Hayes, Nov. 1, 1893. Hayes Papers, LA 10353. See Ashworth, passim, on the domination of helpers' unions by locals of craftsmen.

37 Galster, 55–7. See also Alan C. Dawley, "The Artisan Response to the Factory System: Lynn Massachusetts, in the Nineteenth Century" (unpublished Ph.D. dissertation, Harvard University, 1971); Kealey, 145–7; James M. Morris, "The Cincinnati Shoemakers Lockout of 1888," *Labor History*, 13 (Fall 1972), 505–19.

38 Fred S. Hall, *Sympathetic Strikes and Sympathetic Lockouts* (New York: Columbia University Studies in History, Economics and Public Law, No. 26, 1898), 29.

39 New York Bureau of Labor Statistics, *Report, 1890*, 936–49; *Report, 1891*, Part II, 732–45; *Report, 1892*, 124–39.

40 Eugene Debs, "Labor Strikes and Their Lessons," in Swinton, *Momentous Question*, 324–5.

41 U.S. Commissioner of Labor, *Twenty-First Annual Report* (Washington, D.C., 1906), 21–2, 33–4, 81–2. The calculation of the percentage of New York sympathetic strikes involving the building trades are my own, from the New York Bureau of Labor Statistics data.

42 Hall, 33.

43 E. Levasseur, *The American Workman* (Baltimore, 1900), 237–9; Hall, 102–3. The quotations from the AFL are in Hall, 102–3.

44 Hollander and Barnett, 226–31. The quotation is on p. 226. The trade agreement is reprinted on pp. 230–1.

45 John R. Commons, *Trade Unionism and Labor Problems* (First Series, Boston, 1905), 66–7; Philip Taft, *The A. F. of L. in the Time of Gompers* (New York, 1957), 25, 29, 251. On sympathetic strikes in New York, see note 39.

46 Hall, 36–51, 70–8; John T. Cumbler, "Labor, Capital, and Community: The Struggle for Power," *Labor History*, 15 (Summer 1974), 395–415; Almont Lindsay, *The Pullman Strike* (Chicago, 1942), 122–46, 203–73; Edwin E. Witte, *The Government in Labor Disputes* (New York and London, 1932), 26–31, 61–82; Gerald G. Eggert, *Railroad Labor Disputes: The Beginnings of Federal Strike Policy* (Ann Arbor, Mich. 1967), 81–191; United States v. Workingmen's Amalgamated Council of New Orleans, et al., 54 Fed. 994 (1893); Florence Peterson, *Strikes in the United States, 1880–1936* (Washington, D.C.: U.S. Dept. of Labor Bulletin No. 651, August 1937), 34.

47 Hall, 37–8.

48 Norman J. Ware, *The Labor Movement in the United States, 1860–1895* (New York and London, 1929), xii.

49 Clarence E. Bonnett, *Employers Associations in the United States: A Study of Typical Associations* (New York 1922); Commons, *Trade Unionism and Labor Problems*, passim; "Restriction of Output."

50 See Van Tine, 57–112; Mark Perlman, *The Machinists: A New Study in American Trade Unionism* (Washington, D.C., 1956), 20–36, 48–50.

51 Taylor, *Principles of Scientific Management*, 83.

52 F. J. Roethlisberger and W. J. Dickson, *Management and the Worker: Technical vs. Social Organization in an Industrial Plant* (Cambridge, Mass.: Harvard University Business Research Studies, No. 9, 1934), 16–7. Cf. Harry Braverman, *Labor and Monopoly Capital: The Degradation of Work in the Twentieth Century* (New York and London, 1974).

53 For basically technological interpretations of scientific management, see David Landes, *The Unbound Prometheus* (Cambridge, 1969), 290–326; Samuel Haber, *Efficiency and Uplift: Scientific Management in the Progressive Era, 1890–1920* (Chicago and London, 1964); Hugh G. J. Aitken, *Taylorism at Watertown Arsenal: Scientific Management in Action, 1908–1915* (Cambridge, Mass., 1960).

54 U.S. Congress, House of Representatives, *Hearings before the Special Committee of the House of Representatives to Investigate the Taylor and other Systems of Shop Management*, 3 vols. (Washington, D.C. 1912), 1397.

55 Louis Brandeis, "Brief before the I.C.C., January 3, 1911," in *Selected Articles on Employment Management*, Daniel Bloomfield ed. (New York, 1922), 127.

56 John R. Commons et al., *Industrial Government* (New York, 1921), 267.

57 See Arthur Gleason, "The Shop Stewards and Their Significance," *Survey*, 41 (January 4, 1919), 417–22; Carter Goodrich, "Problems of Workers' Control," *Locomotive Engineers Journal*, 62 (May 1923), 365–7, 415; Evans Clark, "The Industry is Ours," *Socialist Review*, 9 (July 1920), 59–62; David Montgomery, "The 'New Unionism' and the Transformation of Workers' Consciousness in America, 1909–1922," *Journal of Social History*, 7 (Summer 1974), 509–29.

2. Immigrant workers and managerial reform

"Our immigrant labor supply has been used by American industry in much the same way that American farmers have used our land supply," wrote William M. Leiserson in 1924.

But just as the disappearance of free land has led farmers to conserve their soil and to put a considerable investment into maintaining and improving it, so the restrictions on immigration brought about by the war and legislation have led employers to conserve the skill and strength of their labor and to put a considerable investment into training and improving it.[1]

Leiserson's description of the use of immigrant workers early in the twentieth century was accurate, even if his depiction of more recent practice was overly optimistic. A closer look at the interaction between immigrant behavior and the reform of managerial practice, however, suggests that important changes in that practice began even before America's entry into the war and that the immigrants themselves were active agents in bringing the changes about.

There were, in fact, three types of reform in managerial behavior during the first two decades of this century that need to be distinguished. The first, which may be called corporate welfare, involved paternalistic measures initiated by employers with the primary intention of changing their employees' social attitudes, work habits, and life styles. The endeavors of corporate "sociological departments," like those of later "Americanization" plans, can best be understood by reference to Herbert Gutman's discussion of the "recurrent tension over work habits" generated by the encounter of newcomers, steeped in preindustrial cultures, with demands of modern industry for orderly, regular habits. The basic thrust of welfare reform, seen in this context, was to hasten the cultural transformation of the immigrants by promoting the attitudes of "thrift, sobriety, adaptability, [and] initiative" that would allow employers to assign them easily to industrial tasks.[2]

The second type of reform was the professionalization of personnel management. Born of a sense that labor turnover had reached crisis proportions in the years after 1910 and propelled forward by the rapidly mounting tendency of immigrants and native workers alike to strike and to restrict output in organized fashions, the personnel management movement developed trained executives whose mission it was to cope with grievances arising at work and thus to stabilize and pacify the daily operations of the concern. Proponents of the new profession claimed credit for "a reduction in working time lost, a reduction in labor turnover, the elimination of serious labor disputes, the development of esprit de corps, greater production, betterment of physical and social conditions of employees, a reduction of sickness and accidents and the Americanization of aliens."[3] It was, furthermore, through their efforts that the three species of reform were ultimately blended into the American Plan of the 1920s.

The third type of reform was scientific management, or Taylorism, in the strict sense of the term. It was concerned with the systematic organization of production and with the instruction and enticement of the employee to perform his specific work assignment in "the one best way." Frederick Winslow Taylor himself considered welfare reforms "of secondary importance" and insisted that they "should never be allowed to engross the attention of the superintendent to the detriment of the more important and fundamental elements of management." The goal of scientific management, in Frank Gilbreth's words, was "the establishment of standards everywhere, including standard instructions cards for standard methods, motion studies, time study, time cards, [and] records of individual output."[4] Although personnel management was to develop in part as an effort to resolve some of the failures and internal contradictions of scientific management, Taylor and his colleagues clearly believed that careful selection and training for job assignments, a well-organized flow of work, job assignments, and incentive pay would suffice to keep labor contented and loyal.

Scientific management could "barely be said to have made any impression outside of machine shops," observed President John Calder of the Remington Typewriter Company in 1913.[5] Even if Calder had overstated the point, the direct impact of scientific management had been felt primarily by skilled workers, whose control over the way they performed their tasks it challenged. Before the economic crisis of 1907–9, therefore, corporate welfare was the only one of these three types of management reform that had affected immigrant workers, and even its influence was not particulary widespread.

Immigrants and industry

In the first decade of this century employers apparently felt little need
to conserve, train, or improve their immigrant workers. Those immigrants
who came with artisan or industrial skills tended to abandon their old
trades in America, largely because they found little demand here for the
ancient crafts they had learned abroad. Although almost 100 thousand
shoe makers came to America between 1900 and 1910, the number of
immigrants engaged in that occupation actually declined during those
years from 75 thousand to 55 thousand (about a fourth of the industry's
total force). Similarly, the number of curriers, blacksmiths, bookbinders,
and cabinetmakers who deserted their former occupations exceeded the
number of new arrivals in that decade. Some immigrant artisans, like
Italian marble cutters, did practically monopolize a shrinking trade here.
Others, like the 214 thousand foreign-born carpenters, were sufficiently
numerous (26 percent of all carpenters) to discourage metropolitan employers from training apprentices. Nevertheless, almost half of the newly
arrived carpenters left the trade.[6]

Most immigrants at that time, however, had no artisan skills to abandon.
By the estimates of the Immigration Commission, 54 percent of the men
and 44 percent of the women among the immigrants it studied had worked
in agriculture in Europe, and not more than 10 percent of them entered
farm work in the United States. To turn the point around, in only two
of the major industries it examined – clothing and silk manufacture –
had two-thirds or more of the immigrants worked at the same occupation
abroad.[7] Although silk manufacturing in the United States differed little
from that in Western Europe, the factories that employed about half of
the clothing workers by 1910 demanded very different work habits from
those of the shtetl tailor.

For the great mass of twentieth-century immigrants, therefore, the
skill and knowledge required by manufacturing occupations in which
they were engaged were embodied not in their training but in the technical
organization of the factory itself. The mental component of their labor
was not their property, but their employers'. They were, to use Karl
Marx's vivid phrase, "brought face to face with the intellectual potencies
of the material process of production, as the property of another, and
as a ruling power." Science, "a productive force distinct from labour,"
had been pressed "into the service of capital."[8]

Where laboratory science and production engineering determined the
tasks to be performed in minute detail, there was little evident need to

"train and improve" the immigrants. The 20 thousand workers at Good-year Rubber, who applied themselves furiously to minute but often heavy tasks at the molds and ovens, were checked by one inspector for every ten producers. Almost all production workers were on piecework, so that failure to produce at a rapid pace brought immediate deprivation of income. A "flying squadron" of 800 men, largely recruited from outside the firm after the strike of 1913, was trained by a three-year course to cover any job in the plant. Hence the 600 to 700 employees who quit each month and had to be replaced were of little concern to the company though it did find the daily average of 500 first-aid cases costly. Earlier Goodyear had tried to reduce turnover, but it concluded by 1919 that such efforts were futile and concentrated its attention on careful training of supervisory personnel.[9]

The general complex of oil, chemical, and rubber industries constituted the fastest-growing sector of nonfarm employment between 1870 and 1910, with a 1,900 percent increase in employment, and the Goodyear pattern prevailed throughout. Goodyear was remarkable only in that no more than a third of its workers were foreign born. For these industries in general, two-thirds of the employees were immigrants, and in the New Jersey centers three-fourths. Steel, meat packing, and textiles also coupled minute tasks with detailed supervision, so that the flow of operations needed to produce the final product confronted the immigrant as a self-motivating technological monster into which he might fit himself as best he could. Upton Sinclair's description of the awesome impact of a Chicago slaughterhouse on a Lithuanian peasant mirrored the sentiments of steelworkers, who sensed, quite consciously, that the mill had a life of its own.[10]

On the other hand, the experience of immigrants within these vast incarnations of science in the service of capital made a mockery of Taylor's appeals for scientific selection and training of workmen. In general, immigrants were assigned to their tasks, and even transferred from one work group to another, by the absolute authority of their foremen. They learned what to do and how to do it from their workmates. "I've had almost no instruction on any of my jobs from the bosses," noted Whiting Williams, the plant manager who lived for a year as a worker. "[They have] been too busy or else their bosses didn't think it was worth the time. But, Jiminy! I've had a lot of it from my buddies: Only most of that has been to help me get by with as little personal effort and discomfort as possible."[11]

In short, the immigrants' encounter with the factory impressed them not so much with system and rationality as with arbitrary, petty tyranny wielded by gang leaders, skilled workmen, and hiring bosses. "We went to the doors of one big slaughter house," recalled Antanas Kaztauskis:

There was a crowd of about 200 men waiting there for a job. They looked hungry and kept watching the door. At last a special policeman came out and began pointing to men, one by one. Each one jumped forward. Twenty-three were taken. Then they all went inside, and all the others turned their faces away and looked tired. I remember one boy sat down and cried, just next to me, on a pile of boards. Some policemen waved their clubs and we walked on.[12]

On the nine piers of Manhattan's Chelsea docks, there might have been twenty-five hundred jobs on a busy day. Invariably some five thousand men hung around the dockside saloons, and Longshoremen's Rest in hopes of shaping up. Word spread through the ethnic neighborhoods behind each pier by the "Longshore Gazette" (that is, word of mouth) when a new ship was to be loaded or unloaded. Regular gangs were hired with some consistency, but even their members dared not leave a job once they had been hired. The man who could not "stick it" for twenty-eight hours or more of continuous work might lose his place on a "good gang." When one man left a ship, another was taken on in his place, and the first would rejoin the waiting throng if he returned another day. Aside from the fruit crates kept on hand to lift casualties out of the holds, there were no facilities for the workers' needs. So abundant was manual labor on the New York docks that not a single pier had even installed a moving crane before 1914. Mechanical hoists were found in Liverpool and Hamburg, where dockers' unions were strong. The winch, block and tackle, and muscular back were the hoists of New York. Safety precautions were correspondingly simple. If a rope looked dangerously frayed to a docker, he cut it.[13]

In stark contrast to the tenets of scientific management, the wages of hundreds of thousands of immigrants were fixed by common labor rates. For longshoremen in New York the rate was $0.33 an hour for day work in 1914; for packinghouse workers $0.18; at Republic Steel in Youngstown, $0.195; and in the New York building trades, where possibly two-thirds of the laborers were Italians, $3.00 a day. Fully 40 percent of the workers in each of these industries were paid the common labor rate, and in each case the irregularity of employment for this grade left most of them averaging $10.00 to $11.00 a week. Common-labor earnings turned out to be not only homogeneous among occupations but remarkably stable over the years, until the numerous laborers' strikes of 1914 and 1916. "Class wages," charged the scientific management apostle Henry Gantt, led to inefficiency, inequity, and a "low tone" in the factory.[14] But few employers heeded his advice when they hired laborers.

Piecework wages

There was at the same time a widespread belief among employers that simple piecework, also at odds with scientific management principles, was the best pay system for immigrants, and, above all, for immigrant women. Wherever workers spent the day on tasks that allowed measurement of the results of individual exertion, employers tended to pay them by the piece. That form of payment tempted newcomers, who were eager to maximize their earnings in what they anticipated would be a short career on the job, to strain themselves to the limit. In the clothing industry, where experience sufficed to teach a worker the technical mysteries of the trade, the piecework system easily lent itself to the subcontracting of work, both outside, through sweatshops, and within the modern factory. One worker, paid by the piece, employed others to work for him. But inside contracting was not confined to clothing. It also appeared in some eastern machinery works, like United Shoe Machinery and Baldwin Locomotive, where journeymen machinists directed the exertions of less skilled workmen in the fabrication of complex components for which bids were let.[15]

Piecework was often applied to workers who were gang leaders or setup men, as a means of increasing the output of their subordinates. In cotton textiles, for example, loom fixers, second hands, and menders were often paid premiums based on the output of the weavers in their rooms. The weavers exerted themselves to the limit of their endurance, tending eight to twelve looms apiece. Women fell ill and "asked out" with such frequency that the companies of Fall River kept a large crew of standby women for "sick weaving." "But that don't make no matter," said one woman who struck there in 1904. "There's plenty waitin' at the gates for our jobs, I guess. The Polaks learn weavin' quick, and they just as soon live on nothin' and work like that."[16]

Piecework and hourly rates not only tended to yield very similar weekly earnings for immigrants, they also placed on the worker the full burden of any inefficiency on either his part or his employer's. In shoe factories, where the highly competitive market and frequent style changes made workers shift frequently from one job lot to another, employers were notoriously lax about planning and routing work through their plants. "Go through any shift at any time of day," charged the Federated American Engineering Societies' study of the 1920s, "and you will find some operators in every department waiting for shoes."[17] The waiting piece-workers were on the job but earning nothing.

Even worse was the evolution of New York's piano industry, where 90 percent of the workers were foreign born by 1919. Piecework had become universal as the primarily Italian immigrants moved in. At the same time the manufacturers discontinued the practice of stocking parts when orders were slack, as they had formerly in order to retain their craftsmen. They began working only to fill orders, so that seemingly interminable working hours alternated with closings of whole departments or plants. Overabundant labor had induced a retrogression to the most primitive managerial methods.[18]

The sophisticated incentive-pay schemes promoted by the advocates of scientific management made little progress outside of the metalworking industries. A survey of factory wage plans undertaken by the National Industrial Conference Board in 1924 found 56 percent of the workers on hourly wages, 37 percent on piecework, and only 7 percent on premium or bonus plans.[19] But employers seemed to be convinced that simple piecework was especially effective in inducing high output from immigrant women. The sausage and canning departments of the Chicago packing houses were the special domains of piecework and of Slavic women. The women stogie makers, cannery workers, candy dippers, clothing makers, laundry workers, core makers, coil winders, glass packers, hand-screw operators, and sheet-mill openers studied by Elizabeth Butler were all on piecework.[20]

There is, in fact, some evidence to suggest that young, single women were less likely than male pieceworkers to hold their output down to a stint set by the peer group. When the union gospel swept through the packing houses of Chicago between 1900 and 1904, women workers enrolled en masse, formed a local of their own to insure representation for themselves in the leadership, and waged an aggressive battle to raise their wage rates. Yet they alone of all the packing house workers made no effort to reduce their output. Similarly, in 1917, when women were introduced as metal polishers into the arms works of Bridgeport, the metal polishers' union quickly succeeded in equalizing the piece rates paid to women and to men (a demand unions often raised during the war in hopes of retarding the employment of women), only to find that employers ardently preferred women even without lower wage rates. The reason was that the women ignored the union's ceiling on a day's output, which was rigidly respected by all the men.[21]

The decisive variable in this response to piece rates, however, seems to have been age not sex. Most of the women involved in the cases cited were in or close to their teen-age years, and young males were equally notorious for their proclivity to "rate busting." Furthermore, there is clear evidence, albeit from later years, of women bacon packers (a relatively good job that tended to be dominated by women with considerable seniority in the firm) rigidly policing output quotas of their own making.[22]

On the other hand, the responses of different groups of women workers to incentive plans suggest that variables other than age and nativity could influence the behavior of women workers. When Henry Gantt set task quotas for the bobbin winders at the Brighton Mills in New Jersey, where almost all the women were immigrants, he found that the older women quickly made the rates, while many young girls failed and quit. It is possible that in textiles, where married women often made elaborate childcare arrangement in order to remain in the mills, they were especially anxious to hold their jobs. Similarly, when Joseph and Feis Company tried to make its Clothcraft Shops in Cleveland a model of modern management, it found that the young women in its employ failed to increase their output in order to earn a bonus. In this case, however, the company probed more deeply and learned that most of the women turned all of their earnings over to their parents. It tried the remedy of sending investigators to the homes of its employees to estimate their families' financial needs. Having determined for each woman a specific sum to be deducted from her pay and sent directly to her family, the firm had the rest of her earnings then paid separately to her. The scheme worked: output and incentive earnings shot up.[23] It may be that the traditional patterns of family relationships in a woman's nationality were as important as age and martial status in determining her reaction to piecework or incentive pay.

In any case Joseph and Feis was not the only employer to use so-phisticated welfare plans in an effort to change the culture patterns of his employees. "Improved machines demand improved men to run them," William H. Tolman observed in 1914, and he found two thousand firms that had already sought to promote such improvement through welfare plans for their million and a half workers. Thereafter interest in professional personnel management, scientific management, and welfare programs increased as employers sought to counter what, from their perspective, was a disheartening tendency, especially on the part of immigrant labor, to thwart their expectations of high productivity. None of these companies outdid the Ford Motor Company, which sent 100 sociologists to check on the family cohesiveness, home cleanliness, civic participation, and spending habits of its workers, in order to determine which of them were worthy to participate in the company's "prosperity sharing" wage scale. Ford's plan was based on the assumption that "efficiency was to be a by-product of the clean and wholesome life."[24]

Henry Ford's approach was unusual, but his assumption was shared by other large employers. More than a decade before the Ludlow Massacre prompted John D. Rockefeller, Jr. to pioneer in the development of personnel management, the Colorado Fuel and Iron Company had established a sociological department, which looked into every aspect of the workers' lives, from diet and drinking habits to public school curriculum. Its director, Dr. R. W. Corwin, explained that the company's employees were "drawn from the lowest classes of foreign immigrants . . . whose primitive ideas of living and ignorance of hygienic laws render the department's work along the line of improved housing facilities and instruction in domestic economy of the utmost importance."[25]

The welfare secretary of the American Iron and Steel Institute expressed special concern with changing the habits of workers in matters that were beyond the direct control of the employers. He urged careful tutelage of the immigrant in the

regulation of his meals, the amount, the character and the mastication of them, the amount and character of drink, the hours of rest and sleep, the ventilation of rooms . . . washing of hands before meals, daily washing of feet, proper fitting of shoes, amount and kind of clothing, care of the eye, ear and nose, brushing of the teeth, and regularity of the bowels. Cultivation of cheerful thoughts has much to do with the body. Another thing that the workman should be taught, [he concluded,] is that the first condition of health is fruitful toil. We are made to labor.[26]

Immigrant response to "scientific management"

As Herbert Gutman has pointed out, however, immigrant laborers were not passive clay to be molded by the requirements of American industry, but brought with them preindustrial work habits that shaped their responses to the environment they found here. On the other hand, the work pattern of "alternate bouts of intense labour and of idleness," which E. P. Thompson found to prevail "wherever men were in control of their own working lives," was but partially contested by the tasks to which immigrants were assigned. In steel, meat packing, chemicals, construction, longshore, and clothing, employment was extremely irregular, but the laborer himself had no control over the timing of the "alternate bouts" of toil and enforced idleness. The Chicago packing houses, for example, slaughtered three-fourths of their cattle on Monday, Tuesday, and Wednesday. A small force sufficed for the remaining days of the week. Only when the workers were organized and aggressive did the companies request their commission buyers to stabilize the flow of cattle to the stockyards, so that employment in the packing houses might be less sporadic.[27]

Even at work the immigrant's exertion was often spasmodic, especially where the 12-hour day prevailed. A study conducted by the steel industry in 1912 to counter agitation against the 7-day week revealed that the idle time of an open-hearth crew ranged from 54 percent of the turn of a second helper to 70 percent for a steel pourer. Similarly hot-blast men at blast furnaces were found to toil furiously during 38 percent of the turn, moderately for 3 percent, and lightly, if at all, for 47 percent, and to spend the remaining 12 percent watching the furnace. Testimony of the workers themselves confirms this impression. At one moment an open-hearth laborer might hoist a hundred pound sack of coal on his shoulder, race toward a ladle of white hot steel and hurl the sack into it. Ten minutes later he might be asleep, especially if it was the night turn.[28]

The immigrant laborer, furthermore, had one standard remedy for disgust with his job – he quit. Systematic studies of labor turnover were first undertaken during the economic boom of 1912–13 in the metal trades, where the cost to employers of breaking in new workers was especially burdensome. Annual turnover rates ranging from 100 percent to 250 percent of the original labor force were found to be commonplace. The Ford Motor Company hired 54 thousand men between October 1912, and October 1913, to maintain an average work force of thirteen thousand.[29] By far the greatest cause of separations was resignation, rather than discharge or layoff, and, understandably, the number of workers quitting spiraled upward in prosperous times.

Furthermore, though better-paid workers and those with several years' seniority or more were slow to quit, newcomers in laborers' or operatives' tasks moved through American factories as though they were revolving doors. Studies conducted in the meat packing and textile industries in the 1920s confirmed these patterns. Almost three-fourths of the separations found by Alma Herbst in Chicago packing houses involved workers with less than three months' service. At Cheney Brothers silk mill in Paterson, N.J., the general turnover rate for 1922 was 30 percent, but among those with a tenure of six months to a year the rate was 239 percent.[30]

Much as they distressed employers, however, individual and traditional responses of immigrants, such as the high propensity to quit, celebration of national holidays in defiance of foremen's threats, "blue mondays," and binges, which in fact might easily last a week or two, were not the only ways immigrants coped with the new industrial setting. The vastness and anonymity of the factory, mine, construction site, or pier should not blind us to the spontaneous formation of small informal groupings, which were the focal points of the immigrants' daily experience. In fact, the impersonal quality of the mill or dock itself made both sanity and survival depend on personal attachments to other workers. Older hands taught newcomers the techniques of survival and the covert forms of collective resistance—"lift it like this, lotsa' time, slow down, there's the boss, here's where we hide, what the hell!"

Two aspects of this phenomenon deserve close attention. First, foremen and gang leaders themselves frequently organized their subordinates' deception of higher management. Anxious to protect their own performance records and bonuses, foremen were wise to keep their crews large, production standards sufficiently lax to make the group's output look good to higher authorities, and a sense of good will among the workers should some emergency call for special bursts of exertion. Many of the spontaneous strikes by immigrants in the second decade of this century were in protest against the discharge of a popular foreman. Conversely, in the needle trades many strikes were led by inside contractors, that is, by the "sweaters" themselves.[31]

Second, immigrants entering industrial society encountered not only the expectations and culture patterns of their employers but also the culture and techniques of survival and struggle of the American-born workers. There is considerable evidence from coal mines and railroad-car shops, where native or British-born workmen and new immigrants worked together in small, mixed groups, that the former initiated the latter into those attitudes toward work and employers which they considered socially acceptable. For example, the impulse of peasant immigrants to work furiously when an authority figure was present and loaf in his absence (a tendency that persisted strongly in steel mills) was soon exchanged in coal mines or car shops for the craftsman's ethic of refusing to work while a boss was watching. Similarly, greenhorns soon learned from veteran workers how to safeguard their piecework scales against reductions by systematically limiting their individual outputs and ostracizing the spoilers, who maximized their output. The manager of the American Can Company's Brooklyn plant was convinced that, though piecework was "best for foreigners," there was an evident "tendency on the part of natives and Americanized immigrants to limit production" under the system.[32]

Neither the craftsman's bearing toward his boss nor the group-related stint of pieceworkers was preindustrial. Immigrants who adopted those behavior patterns had exchanged portions of their traditional culture, not for the values and habits welfare plans sought to inculcate, but for working-class mores.

Consequently, where immigrants encountered strong unions whose doors were open to them, as in the coal mines and the Chicago packing houses before 1904, they adroitly made use of those unions to frustrate their employers' demands for a frenzied pace of work. John R. Commons's insightful study of the Chicago packing houses before the 1904 strike revealed that each of the many amalgamated craft unions, except the women's local, succeeded in establishing a "scale of work." Output per man-hour fell between 16 percent and 25 percent for the city's packing houses as a whole.[33]

After 1910 each period of economic boom unleashed a rash of strikes by native craftsmen and immigrants alike, and the steady growth of unions in basic industries made them a part of the daily lives of millions of immigrants. Employers' complaints about the declining level of exertion among their employees then became almost universal. When the National Association of Credit Men surveyed 169 companies early in 1920, 70 percent of the respondents claimed that their workers were not as efficient as they had been in 1913–14. Full employment, high turnover, unrest, and unions were blamed for an alleged decline in individual output of roughly one-fourth, which was especially evident among immigrant workers.[34] On the New York docks, where no mechanical improvements offset the changing behavior of the unionized longshoremen, productivity per worker fell by one-half between 1914 and 1919, according to a Department of Labor study.[35]

As previously indicated, these developments spurred a new interest in time study, detailed supervision, systematization of work flow, and the other accoutrements of scientific management throughout American industry after the war.[36] These reforms were diffused within the context of personnel management, which by then was well established. In 1911 fifty company officials had met to form the Employment Managers' Association. They were the pioneers of the new profession. By 1918 the association could gather 900 members at its convention. Harvard, Dartmouth,

Rochester, and Columbia were all then offering university courses to train these executives, and Princeton was to be added to their number by means of a Rockefeller grant in 1922.[37]

Personnel managers by the war's end were asserting their importance by demanding salaries, deference, carpets, and office furnishings equal to those of the production superintendents. Their formulas for promoting higher productivity and reducing labor turnover, industrial strife, and the peril of unionization included systematic hiring procedures, a large staff to handle workers' grievances on and off the job, and employee representation plans to encourage a sense of participation by the workers in the execution of company policies. Scientific management and extensive welfare activity were easily grafted onto this core to create the American Plan.[38]

By 1923 the American Plan had succeeded in excluding unions from most industries and persuading union leaders to oppose their members' restrictive practices in others. Nevertheless, it had not realized the corporate executives' dream of enlisting the "support, loyalty and undivided effort" of immigrant workers.[39] Stanley B. Mathewson's study *Restriction of Output among Unorganized Workers* concluded in 1930 that American workers were frustrating their employers' efficiency schemes, even without the help of unions. His account of a Mexican immigrant in an automobile plant, who was assigned to the final tightening of nuts on cylinder heads, casts doubt on the efficacy of all management's efforts of the three previous decades to train and improve its new labor force:

The engines passed the Mexican rapidly on a conveyor. His instructions were to test all the nuts and if he found *one* or *two* loose to tighten them, but if three or more were loose he was not expected to have time to tighten that many. In such cases he marked the engine with chalk and it was later set aside from the conveyor and given special attention. The superintendent found that the number of engines so set aside reached an annoying total in the day's work. He made several unsuccessful attempts to locate the trouble. Finally, by carefully watching all the men on the conveyor line, he discovered that the Mexican was unscrewing a *third* tight nut whenever he found two already loose. It was easier to loosen *one* nut than to tighten two.[40]

Notes

1 William M. Leiserson, *Adjusting Immigrant and Industry* (New York, 1924), 105.
2 Herbert G. Gutman, "Work, Culture, and Society in Industrializing America, 1815–1919," *American Historical Review* 78 (1973), 531–88; Don D. Lescohier,

The Labor Market (New York, 1919), 251–75. The phrase quoted is from W. H. Beveridge, in Lescohier, 268.

3 E. C. Gould, "A Modern Industrial Relations Department," *Iron Age* 102 (1918), 832–3.

4 Frederick Winslow Taylor, "Shop Management," *Transactions of the American Society of Mechanical Engineers* 24 (1903), 1454; Frank B. Gilbreth, *Primer of Scientific Management*, 2d. ed. (New York, 1914), 36.

5 John Calder, "Overvaluation of Management Science," *Iron Age* 91 (1913), 605.

6 "Occupations of Immigrants Before and After Coming to the United States" (typescript), David J. Saposs Papers, box 21, State Historical Society of Wisconsin, Madison, hereinafter cited as "Occupations of Immigrants"; U.S. Bureau of Census, *Sixteenth Census of the United States: 1940, Populations, Comparative Occupational Statistics for the United States, 1870–1940* (Washington, D.C., 1943), 104–12.

7 "Occupations of Immigrants." It is noteworthy that these two industries are among the very few in America where socialism and communism ever enjoyed large numbers of followers.

8 Karl Marx, *Capital: A Critique of Political Economy*, 3 vols. (Chicago, 1906), I, 396–7.

9 Goodyear Tire and Rubber Company, Schedule B, Interviews, Saposs Papers, box 21.

10 See "Occupations of Immigrants"; New Jersey, Department of Labor, *Thirty-Eighth Annual Report of the Bureau of Industrial Statistics* (Camden, 1916), 210–46; Upton Sinclair, *The Jungle* (New York, 1906); John A. Fitch, *The Steel Workers* (New York, 1910), 8–21.

11 Whiting Williams, *What's on the Worker's Mind, by One Who Put On Overalls to Find Out* (New York, 1921), 182–83.

12 Leon Stein and Philip Taft, eds., *Workers Speak: Self-Portraits* (New York, 1971), 74.

13 U.S., Congress, Senate, Commission on Industrial Relations, *Final Report and Testimony*, 11 vols., 64th Congress, 1st session, 1916, Document no. 415, III, 2051, 2212. Hereinafter cited as CIR.

14 The wage figures are from CIR III, 2053, 2056; IV, 3465; III, 1757; *Iron Age* 98 (January 30, 1916), 128; see also Robert Ozanne, *Wages in Practice and Theory* (Madison, Wis., 1968), 83–107; Henry L. Gantt, *Work, Wages, and Profits*, 2d ed. rev. (New York, 1919), 58.

15 Louis Lorwin, *The Women's Garment Workers: A History of the International Ladies Garment Workers' Union* (New York, 1924), 12–23, 149–50; *Iron Age* 91 (January 30, 1913), 334; *Machinists' Monthly Journal* 16 (1904), 321, and 18 (1906), 829–31.

16 Stein and Taft, 28–80. The quotation is on p. 30.

17 Federated American Engineering Societies, Committee on the Elimination of Waste in Industry, *Waste in Industry* (New York, 1921), 143. On the comparability of hourly and piecework earnings, see David Brody, *Steelworkers in America: The Nonunion Era* (Cambridge, Mass., 1960), 45–8; New Jersey, *Thirty-eighth Annual Report of the Bureau of Industrial Statistics*, 227–8.

18 Interview with Charles Dodd, president, Piano and Organ Makers Union, December 18, 1918, Saposs Papers, box 21.

19 Sumner H. Slichter, *Union Policies and Industrial Management* (Washington, D.C., 1941), 282n.

20 John R. Commons, "Labor Conditions in Slaughtering and Meat Packing," in *Trade Unionism and Labor Problems*, John R. Commons, ed. (Boston, 1905), 238–41; Elizabeth Beardsley Butler, *Women and the Trades: Pittsburgh, 1907–1908* (New York, 1911).
21 Commons, "Labor Conditions," 240–1; Federal Mediation and Conciliation Service Reports, file 33/567, Records of the Department of Labor, Record Group 280, National Archives, Washington, D.C.
22 See Stella Nowicki, "Back of the Yards," in *Rank and File: Personal Histories of Working-Class Organizers*, Alice and Staughton Lynd, eds. (Boston, 1973), 79.
23 U.S., Congress, House, *Hearings before the Special Committee of the House of Representatives to Investigate the Taylor and Other Systems of Shop Management* (Washington, D.C., 1912), 583–5; Robert T. Kent, "Employing Methods That Make Good Workers," *Iron Age* 98 (1916), 244–7.
24 William H. Tolman, *Social Engineering: A Record of Things Done by American Industrialists Employing Upwards of One and One-Half Million People* (New York, 1909) 2; John R. Commons, *Industrial Government* (New York, 1921), 13–25. The quotation is on p. 14.
25 Tolman, 54–5. The quotation is on p. 55.
26 Quoted in Gerd Korman, *Industrialization, Immigrants, and Americanizers: The View from Milwaukee, 1886–1921* (Madison, Wis., 1967), 122.
27 Gutman, 553; Thompson, "Time, Work-Discipline, and Industrial Capitalism," *Past and Present* 38 (1967), 73; CIR IV, 3490–1.
28 "Hours and Intensity of Steel Works Labor," *Iron Age* 89 (February 1, 1912), 312–13; interview with Slavish worker (Pittsburgh), B. C. O'Connell (Gary), Saposs Papers, box 26; Williams, 15–27.
29 Magnus Alexander, "Waste in Hiring and Discharging Men," *Iron Age* 94 (1914), 1032–3; Paul H. Douglas, Curtice N. Hitchcock, and Willard E. Atkins, *The Worker in Modern Economic Society* (Chicago, 1923), 310–13.
30 Alma Herbst, *The Negro in the Slaughtering and Meat-Packing Industry in Chicago* (Boston, 1932), 134–45; Horace B. Cheney, "What 86 Years Have Taught Us about Selecting Labor," *Monthly Labor Review* 18 (1925), 9.
31 See Stanley B. Mathewson, *Restriction of Output among Unorganized Workers* (New York, 1931), 30–52; Lorwin, 149–51; New Jersey, Bureau of Industrial Statistics, reports, 1911–16.
32 Carter Goodrich, *The Miner's Freedom: A Study of the Working Life in a Changing Industry* (Boston, 1925), 56; Williams, 128–49; Mathewson, 137–9; American Can Company, Schedule B, interviews, Saposs Papers, box 21.
33 Commons, "Labor Conditions," 227–8.
34 Commons, *Industrial Government*, 367–8. It is unfortunately impossible to test these claims, because the effects of workers' exertion cannot be isolated from those of technological improvement and economies of scale. The trend of output per man-hour was upward for the economy as a whole from 1913 to 1919. But the rate of growth for that period was remarkably uneven and consistently lower than the average rate for the period 1910–29 as a whole. See U.S. Department of Commerce, Bureau of the Census, *Historical Statistics of the United States, Colonial Times to 1957* (Washington, D.C., 1960), 599.
35 *Monthly Labor Review* 18 (1924), 109–17.
36 See *Waste in Industry*; Ozanne, 175, 181–2; H. Dubreuil, *Robots or Men? A French Workman's Experience in American Industry* (New York, 1930); Sam A. Lewisohn, *The New Leadership in Industry* (New York, 1926); Solomon Blum, *Labor Economics* (New York, 1925), 413–14.

37 Meyer Bloomfield, "The New Profession of Handling Men," *Annals of the American Academy of Political and Social Science* 61 (September 1915), 121–6; M. Bloomfield, "A New Profession in American Industry," in *Selected Articles on Employment Management*, Daniel Bloomfield, ed. (New York, 1922), 113–18; Clarence J. Hicks, *My Life in Industrial Relations: Fifty Years in the Growth of a Profession* (New York, 1941), 145–50.

38 See Bloomfield, "New Profession"; Lewisohn; Hicks; Commons, *Industrial Government*; Leiserson, 80–168.

39 Special Conference Committee, *Report of the Special Conference Committee. Revising and Supplementing the Progress Report Published July 24, 1919, and Including Annual Reports Dated December 15, 1922, and December 6, 1923* (New York, 1924), 5–6. I am indebted to Professor Stephen Scheinberg for this information.

40 Mathewson, 125–6.

3. Machinists, the Civic Federation, and the Socialist Party*

The International Association of Machinists was an average sized union before World War I, but it was known as "the war dog" of the American Federation of Labor. Its members, who constituted in 1900 roughly 10 percent of the 280 thousand machinists in large and small metal fabricating plants and in the country's railroad repair shops, were among the very first workers to feel the full thrust of scientific management, rapidly changing machine technology, and the open-shop drive. On the other hand, the trade itself was a product of the most advanced industrial development, and its proud practitioners envisaged themselves as masters of the world of lathes, milling machines, radial drill presses, blue prints, mathematical calculation, and precision work. It is symbolic of their self-image that their union's monthly journal regularly carried detailed discussions of the American and world socialist movements and hints on the latest ways to fashion, fit, and assemble the parts of steam locomotives.

Within the ranks of the IAM discussion of the role of the worker and of the labor movement in modern industrial society was lively and down to earth. Both the vision of organized collaboration between labor and capital, which was espoused by the National Civic Federation, and that of the workers' "co-operative commonwealth," offered by socialists, enjoyed articulate supporters, who pressed their respective cases in terms of the immediate problems facing their trade. For proponents of both points of view, the most urgent of these problems was the contest between scientific management and the machinists' efforts to regulate their own jobs.

Consequently, the IAM provides a useful case study of the meaning of the National Civic Federation to both workers and their employers and of the rising popularity of socialism among American workers before World War I. The narrative and analysis of ideological controversies among machinists and among their employers during the pre-war years which follows, therefore, may serve to illuminate the significance of both the NCF and the Socialist Party. Because the role of these two organizations has been of central importance in recent historical discussions of "corporate liberalism" in the twentieth century, this analysis should improve our understanding of that phenomenon, as well as help us understand the ideological significance of the struggle for workers' control.[1]

The Murray Hill Agreement

A pervasive sense that the great depression of the nineties had ended infused the delegates to the IAM's 1897 convention with determination to eradicate the evils that afflicted their craft forthwith. May 1, 1898 was the date enthusiastically set to institute the 8-hour day and at last to abolish all piecework. As the day of battle approached, however, the union's officers and members alike watched with visibly mounting anxiety the course of the titanic lockout of the Amalgamated Society of Engineers in England. The world's largest machinists' organization, one powerful enough to have instituted the 9-hour day in 1871 and to have enforced its elaborate rules over most of England's metal working industries, was locked for ten months in a nation-wide struggle for its very life. In February, 1898, the ASE signed the terms of surrender, opening all plants to nonunion men, promotion of handymen, and piecework. The Americans' zeal wilted at the news. The ASE, after all, had 78,450 members in 1897, and the IAM scarcely 15,000. May 1 passed without a strike. Machinists were to get their day's excitement instead from Admiral Dewey's victory at Manilla Bay.[2]

Two years later the union's fighting spirit had revived. This time its attention was focused on its four thousand members in Chicago. The leaders were wise to commit themselves to battle in that city, because the workers of Chicago had accomplished a fusion of craft organization with class solidarity on a level unmatched anywhere else in the land. The lament of the manager of Fraser and Chalmers (a part of the Allis Chalmers chain) concerning his experience during a molders' strike in the fall of 1899 illustrates vividly the role of class consciousness in sustaining craft organization there. The unions, said he,

had so boycotted our place that we could not buy a pound of castings in any shop in the United States; they had watched the railroads so that we could not ship tools out of the city. They had so picketed us that when we brought a load of men – we brought 202 men to Chicago and we put up a building, we built a restaurant and fed them, and we could not buy bread or food; they would not sell any member of our company or office staff a newspaper in the vicinity; we could not hire a carriage; and they went around and said, "If you sell anything to this house, if you supply this firm with anything for their men, we will withdraw our patronage and you will have to go out of business."[3]

District Eight, on behalf of all the IAM lodges of the city, presented 150 machine shops with a proposed agreement in January 1900. A 9-hour day, a closed shop, seniority rule for layoffs, recognition of shop committees and a minimum wage of twenty-eight cents per hour were all terms on which the employers gagged, so on March 1, some five thousand workers went on strike. The fact that more than forty thousand building tradesmen were striking at the same time meant that more work was then closed down in Chicago than had been the case at the height of the Pullman Boycott. Encouraged by Chicago's example, the union's district officers in Cleveland, Detroit, Patterson and Philadelphia also called out their members.[4]

It soon became apparent to Chicago employers that they could not win a total victory, and seventeen of the struck firms affixed their names to the union's terms. But the officers of the Chicago branch of the newly established National Metal Trades Association, which grew quickly in membership and prestige by taking command of the employers' side of the battle, searched for a formula which would minimize the cost of a general capitulation. They had little fear of the twenty-eight cent standard rate, because most machinists already earned more than that, and they decided to offer concessions on the 9-hour day and on union recognition. On the other hand they disliked reducing their work week six hours below that of their competitors in other cities. And they dreaded the prospect of being bound to settle grievances with what one of them called, the "arrogant, dictorial" unions of Chicago. Because the "average intelligence" of machinists is "not high," explained one manufacturer, formal recognition of their union "becomes license, license. If the local association can once maintain its control there is no end to what it will have afterward." The President of Western Electric concurred: "Well, we should not have a committee or what they call a steward, an official of the union, in our place to represent the union among our employees. We should not have it."[5]

The remedy for both problems was the same formula – negotiate a *national* agreement between the National Metal Trades Association and the top officers of the IAM. The 9-hour day would then apply to competitors everywhere in the country, and, as the president of Turner Brass suggested, "A man fitted to represent a national organization, or representing a national organization, would be an easier man to do business with, I believe."[6] Recognizing the opportunity for the greatest coup in their union's career, President James O'Connell and organizer Stuart Reid hastened to parlay Chicago's power into national recognition of their union. They reached an agreement to transfer the wage question, apprenticeship rules, and any other unsettled grievances present and future to a national board of arbitration composed of six union and NMTA representatives. A 57-hour week was to go into effect in six months, and a 55-hour week in one year – quite a victory on the hours' question. But Chicago's local demands were largely sacrificed in the process. There was no mention in the pact of a closed shop, minimum wage, or seniority. Most important for the future, the IAM agreed "that there is to be no limit in any way placed upon the production of the shop."[7] Two weeks of argument within the union's leadership ensued before a mass ratification meeting was staged at the Salvation Army hall on March 31. With the help of a big bass drum borrowed from the hosts and "beaten with tremendous effect when speeches were being made favorable to the agreement," but "always silent when they were unfavorable," a vote to endorse the contract and return to work was carried 3,028 to 396.[8]

From May 10 to May 18 New York's Murray Hill Hotel was the scene of intense bargaining between President James O'Connell, Vice-president D. D. Wilson, and Chicago's venerable Hugh Doran (a veteran of the Machinists and Blacksmiths International Union) for the IAM, and President D. McLaren of the U.S. Cast Iron Pipe Company in Cincinnati, W. L. Pierce of Brooklyn's Lidgerwood Manufacturing Company, and Edward Reynolds of the E. P. Allis Company in Milwaukee, for the NMTA. They agreed to improve upon the Chicago pact, by reducing the work week nationally to fifty-seven hours in six months and fifty-four hours (rather than fifty-five) in one year. The union consented to call off the strikes outside of Chicago, once a small raise had been granted to the Patterson strikers. No union shop was conceded, the agreement calling only for no discrimination by employers against union members. A machinist was defined in accordance with the union's constitution, but wages for each locality were left to future arbitration. The board of six was to sit permanently to hear future grievances from all over the country, no strikes were to be called during the life of the agreement, and each association undertook to enforce the settlement on its own members. Finally, the union reiterated its pledge to put no restrictions on production, though the panel never dealt specifically with the questions of piecework, two machines, and handymen, which the union side had tried to place before it.[9]

Douglas Wilson, the union's Socialist editor and vice-president, hailed the Murray Hill Agreement as pointing "the way out [of industrial strife] by the simple and scientific process of gradual change, so gradual that the movement is almost imperceptible."[10] Samuel Gompers and President O'Connell toured New England to recruit for the IAM on the basis of its achievement of the 9-hour day and the employers' pledge of no discrimination, while the NMTA's officers barnstormed the land to beat recalcitrant employers into line on the shorter week. Only a few minor firms left the NMTA when the 57-hour week went into effect in November.[11]

The NMTA's leaders justified their behavior by giving currency to the views of William Phaler, the experienced president of the National Founders' Association which had reached a national arbitration agreement of its own with the Iron Molders in 1899. Union officers are more reliable than their members, argued Phaler. Furthermore, unions usually won strikes for wage increases and lost other strikes. Hence there was need for arbitration machinery to handle wage disputes. Finally, he stressed, labor had to be induced to abandon "the idea that recognition of the union implies more than the agreement to make collective bargains between employer and employee . . . or to insist that it conveys the right to enforce rules and methods in the conduct of the business without the consent or co-operation of the employer."[12]

These developments naturally led officers of the IAM and NMTA to be the featured guests at the December, 1900 conference on industrial arbitration and conciliation convened by the National Civic Federation. Although its National Conference on Combinations and Trusts in the fall of 1899 had established the NCF's claim to being an institution which could assemble men of prominence in every walk of life to discuss weighty current issues, its energetic secretary Ralph M. Easley was convinced that it could also provide a practical agency for the establishment of industrial peace. He had assembled in June of 1900 an advisory council of some 500 members to guide the federation's work and lend their names to its prestige. Wilson of the IAM, President Martin Fox of the Iron Molders, Secretary-Treasurer William Gilthrop of the Boiler Makers and Secretary George Buchanan of the Bicycle Workers represented the metal trades in a union contingent that also included Gompers, Mitchell, McGuire and two of the labor movement's ancient warriors, George Schilling and George McNeill. Among the fifty-two representatives of "manufacturing" on the council were no fewer than twenty-two prominent metal trades' employers, including Chicago's William Chalmers and Stanley McCormick, Clem Studebaker and David M. Parry, who was soon to become the nemesis of the NCF. Judge E. H. Gary was one of the eight participants from steel. Textiles was the only other industry heavily represented (five members). Both the NMTA and the National Association of Manufacturers were represented as organizations on the council. [13]

The main thrust of the federation's work in this field was to promote stable contractual relationships between unions and associated groups of employers by means of both propaganda and direct intervention in industrial disputes. It sought to convince employers that the established leaders of major unions were both sufficiently honorable to adhere scrupulously to the terms of any agreement they might negotiate, and, thanks to the position accorded them by contractual recognition, firmly enough entrenched to be able to compel their members to do so as well. Labor's vexing demand for shorter hours could be met by coupling reduction of working time with the abandonment of workers' restrictions on output. This formula was called by Easley the essence of the Murray Hill Agreement. [14]

It was indispensible to the success of such a policy that the union leaders involved vigorously suppress sympathy strikes and strikes by their members in violation of the "sacred contracts." The employer had to be reassured that, though union officials might drive a hard bargain on wages and hours from time to time, the terms of settlement, in the first place, would apply through the trade association to his competitors as well as himself, and, secondly, that his production would not subsequently be interrupted by the injection into his plant of "irrational" issues of class solidarity, possibly arising from disputes which had nothing directly to do with him. The role of John Mitchell, UMW President, on this question made him NCF Secretary Easley's hero in the labor movement. Mitchell consistently rejected private suggestions that he pare down the demands of the coal miners he represented, even when they came from Easley. But during the 1902 anthracite strike he made use of the entire staff of the NCF's conciliation committee to barnstorm locals of the United Mine Workers in bituminous coal areas to help him suppress the movement among them for a sympathy strike. [15] Similarly during the 1901 machinists' strike O'Connell of the IAM called on lodges which had settled with their employers and unions of other metal trades not to join the strike, in order that employers who had contractual arrangements with the union should not be hurt. [16]

The suppression of sympathy strikes, therefore, was a critically important feature of the federation's conciliation activity. Class solidarity had been the traditional mainspring of craft union strength. Easley and his colleagues now offered established unions an attractive alternative:

national agreements between organized labor and organized business, binding on both sides. Strong unions could improve the conditions of their own members under this formula, without being distracted by the plight of less fortunate workers. There was even room for joint action among such unions, as is illustrated by the gradual evolution of the Federated Metal Trades. Sympathetic action among machinists, molders, metal polishers, blacksmiths, pattern makers and boiler makers had long been commonplace, and a league of their national officers had existed since 1894. But the movement for a formal federation with local affiliated councils, which was initiated in 1901 and finalized by a convention in 1906, aimed to promote arbitration of disputes and joint negotiations, and to suppress sympathy strikes, as well as moves to amalgamate the unions.[17] Such efforts were indeed timely, because the tendency of workers to engage in sympathy strikes, which had lain dormant through the late 1890s, reasserted itself vigorously between 1901 and 1904.[18] The National Civic Federation could reach its goal only if such "uncivilized" behavior by workers were contained.

But the promise of organized harmony enshrined in the Murray Hill Agreement did not even survive a single year. The November, 1900 reduction of hours took place with little ado everywhere except St. Louis, where the union demanded an increase of hourly wages to compensate for the loss of hours. The question did not arise elsewhere because metal trades employers, faced still with a booming market and a shortage of machinists, tended to dispense raises liberally when hours fell. Nevertheless, the St. Louis case sounded an ominous note: the NMTA executives refused to arbitrate it or any other wage question at the national level. Wages, they now contended, were for local determination.

O'Connell and other national officers had anticipated strikes in plants which were not affiliated with the NMTA and had begun a campaign as early as February, 1901, to mobilize the members in such companies for a battle to force their weekly hours down to fifty-four on May 18, in line with those of the Association's shops. But as that date approached, the IAM's leaders found themselves deluged with petitions from lodges which *were* covered by the Murray Hill Agreement, all demanding that the union insist on an hourly raise of 12½ percent to take effect with the final reduction of hours. On May 11, O'Connell and Wilson met for hours with the NMTA's administrative council in a futile effort to reach a national wage settlement. Convinced that the employers had betrayed the spirit of Murray Hill (by demanding a national treaty to settle the local Chicago strike one year, then referring national wage claims back to localities the next), prodded by the insistence of his members that they would not accept a loss of income with the reduction of hours, and confident that his union, which had enrolled over 32 thousand members by this time and clearly would bring at least 150 thousand workers into action, could weather any storm, O'Connell called a nation-wide strike for May 20, 1901.

The Chicago District on its own initiative met with the national NMTA officers to propose a compromise local settlement, instead of joining the walkout. When their reply was an offer of a 5 percent increase, taken as deliberately insulting since Chicago employers had already offered 6¼ percent, the district officers left the room calling for a strike. The next morning, Decoration Day, the city's IAM headquarters thronged with machinists eager to show their martial skills once again.[19]

The NMTA was ready to meet the challenge. Throughout the previous year its officers too had been deluged with complaints from their constituents. Emboldened by national recognition of their union, machinists had not only enrolled in the union in great numbers, but employers protested, had also demanded that all their work mates do the same and had refused to work in violation of union rules. Having rejected the demand for a closed shop in negotiations, employers now found their workers establishing it in practice by work stoppages and ostracism of nonunion men. And having traded a reduction of hours for the agreement of the union not to place any limits on production, they encountered adamant refusal by their employees to run two machines, peform piece-work or instruct handymen. Of what value was the written contract, protested President Walter L. Pierce of the NMTA, when "we ran up against this curious proposition that the restriction of production and the freedom of employment was [sic] subject to the constitution of the union?"[20]

The Murray Hill Agreement, of which the Civic Federation had been so proud, had broken down in mutual betrayal. Federation officers Wilson and Chalmers were hurling angry press releases at each other from opposite sides of the picket lines. To make matters worse, Easley had little time to spare for an effort to resuscitate the pact, because at the very same time two other members of this advisory council had engaged each other in a similar conflict: Judge Gary of U.S. Steel and T. J. Shaffer of the Amalgamated Iron and Steel Workers. That embattled union had not only broken its contracts in the Hoop Division by calling a general stoppage throughout the new steel corporation, but was also openly seeking sympathy strikes by coal miners and railroad workers (whose leaders also sat on the advisory council). Working day and night with the aid of Gompers and Mitchell, to hold steel to the NCF's philosophy of labor relations, restrain the other unions, nullify Shaffer's influence in his own union and ultimately drive him from office, Ralph Easley had little of even his proverbial energy to devote to the metal trades. His dream of organized harmony between labor and capital was coming apart.[21]

Metal trades employers, however, had lost all interest in Mr. Easley's dream. On May 28 the NMTA's administrative council had met in Chicago's Great Northern Hotel to adopt a new Declaration of Principles. Point one declared: "Since we, as employers, are responsible for the work turned out by our workmen, we must, therefore, have full discretion to designate the men we consider competent to perform the work and to determine the conditions under which that work shall be prosecuted." It went on to proclaim that no employer would deal with men on strike, that each would employ handymen and apprentices as he saw fit and that hours and wages were to be governed by local conditions. Although it assured readers that the NMTA would not discriminate against workers because of union membership or nonmembership, and would not countenance such premium systems as did not allow an average workman a fair wage, it adamantly asserted the employer's prerogative to use any pay system or production method he chose.[22]

This ringing declaration attracted many manufacturers to an open meeting of the NMTA in New York City, where employers mobilized their side for the battle which was beginning. Former President Pierce (who had signed the Murray Hill Agreement for the association) and President Phaler of the Founders' Association attended, and, Easley later reported, "did everything they could to stem the tide, but every manufacturer was so hot at O'Connell, for his alleged 'treachery,' that they were overwhelmed by the opposition." The "general declaration of war" Easley and his colleagues labored so hard to prevent, was enthusiastically carried.[23]

In Chicago itself, ironically, the employers' bark proved much worse than their bite. Only some two thousand machinists were on strike there by the second week in June, because ninety companies had already acceded to the union's demands. Fraser and Chalmers, however, held out for fifty-four weeks, its president (a member of the NCF council) swearing he would never again deal with the IAM. Its molders soon joined the strike, with wage demands of their own, and the company responded by hiring strikebreakers (more than twenty-five hundred of them by the end) and announcing that it was returning to the 10-hour day for all employees. That declaration brought the pattern makers and boiler makers on strike. The profusion of tents in which scabs were housed earned the plant the name Fort Chalmers.

In June 1902, however, the defeated company signed contracts with all of its unions again,, granting its machinists an increase of 11 percent, a minimum craft rate of thirty cents per hour, a 55-hour week, and a pledge to reinstate all strikers but three leaders. For the next four to five weeks the plant was in turmoil, as workers demonstrated constantly to speed up the rehiring of strikers and the dismissal of scabs. On August 5, the union men chased the remaining eight scab machinists down the street from the plant with dire threats. The company fired four men who were involved in the fracas, and quickly the plant emptied out once more. About a week later, company officials met with union officers and the shop committee, reinstated the discharged men and agreed to a straight 54-hour week. Work then resumed at Fraser and Chalmers, under union conditions, but hardly those envisaged by the NCF.[24]

All across the country the strikes dragged on into the fall of 1901. In mid-October, President O'Connell could still report 3,470 members walking picket lines from Atlanta to San Francisco.[25] In one respect, however, the defiant stance of the NMTA restored the situation which had existed before Murray Hill. Union power prevailed in Chicago, and the employers had crushed it elsewhere. On the other hand, the Murray Hill – Civic Federation interlude had left both sides more formidably organized for combat than they had been previously, and, though it left some prominent union leaders devoted to the NCF, it convinced metal trades employers and soon practically the entire business world of the folly of the Civic Federation's philosophy of industrial relations.

The Open Shop Drive

By September 1903 there were 243 thousand trade union members in Chicago. The city could challenge London for the title, trade union capital of the world. Possibly one-third of those members worked in the packing houses, where militant shop committees united the activists of dozens of craft unions (among them IAM lodge 208) in effective exercise of job controls.[26] The Chicago Federation of Labor defiantly used sympathy strikes as the touchstone of its success. With its help a coalition of ten unions even brought International Harvester under contract, and converted it to the 9-hour day.[27] The policy of sympathy strikes placed the teamsters' union in the forefront of the city's class conflict. The drivers' participation carried almost any strike into the streets of working-class neighborhoods, where assaults on scabs became community actions.[28]

Even the business depression of 1903–4 did not destroy the power of Chicago's organized workers, though it undermined it at several points. By turning a labor shortage into a labor surplus, however, the depression triggered a general assault on union power throughout the land. The IAM alone faced 134 strikes in 1904, in contrast to 56 the previous year, and 55 of those strikes were in Chicago. The expiration of the Chicago Metal Trades' Association's contract covering eighty-two plants in May 1904, allowed the association to demand wage cuts, two-machine operation and the introduction of "roughers" to perform machinists tasks of lesser skill at lower than the minimum pay. The union, in turn, demanded Saturday afternoon off, and when the employers responded by instituting a work week of five 10-hour days, the machinists went home en masse at the end of nine hours starting a general stoppage.

The city's Metal Trades Council brought out all its affiliates in sympathy with the machinists, and union teamsters blacklisted the products of struck plants. But soon the massive unemployment took its toll. Strikebreakers were mustered in large numbers, and the desperate efforts of pickets to keep them out of the plants brought countless arrests and prosecutions on their heads. In July the packing houses forced all their unions into a long strike, in which the workers were ultimately crushed. In September International Harvester and Pullman closed completely for two weeks, then reopened on a nonunion basis. With the teamsters' strike in the spring of 1905 the city erupted in class and racial violence, bringing President Roosevelt himself to town to inveigh against apostles of "class hatred" and to threaten the strikers with military occupation of their city. When metal trades employers began once more to sign contracts with the IAM in April, International Harvester, Link Belt, Pullman and others were missing from the roll. But the union still had pacts with more than 400 firms.[29]

Outside Chicago the militant metal trades' employers generally carried the day. In Dayton, Ohio, Sedalia, Missouri, Birmingham, Alabama, Cincinnati, Ohio, and Beloit, Wisconsin, employers' associations mobilized the local business communities to support companies battling the IAM. Their actions initiated a campaign on several fronts which quickly gained momentum throughout the land. The NMTA itself, guided by "commissioner" E. F. DuBrul (sarcastically called its "business agent" in the union press), provided struck employers with strategic advice, financial assistance, private detectives, legal assistance and a card file on every one of the 35 thousand workers employed by the Association's 325 firms.

It organized the Independent Labor League of America, which enrolled machinists and would-be machinists, who were ready to go anywhere in the land to replace strikers. By 1911 it had registered 6,600 machinists in Chicago alone.[30] With the aid of agencies like the Corporations Auxiliary Company, it honeycombed the unions with spies. A sensational expose of 1904 identified such detectives on the AFL Executive Council, among the national officers of several unions, federation field organizers, city trades assemblies and union convention delegates.[31] Such weapons allowed the NMTA in Portland, Oregon, to summon every machinist to a central office where he was confronted with a dossier on his past and forced to tear up his union book.[32]

These undertakings led employers' associations into judicial and political activity on a broad front. Primarily through the agency of the American Anti-Boycott Association, they pressed court cases against boycotts and sympathy strikes, successfully establishing judicial precedents for the issuance of injunctions and the collection of damages against unions in such cases. Not until the early 1920s did a series of United States Supreme Court decisions, among them the Hitchman Coal, Red Jacket Coal, and American Steel Foundries cases, create a uniform federal law controlling boycotting, picketing and sympathy actions by labor, but state courts and federal rulings in the Danbury Hatters case and Bucks Stove and Range case opened the way to widespread issuance of injunctions by local courts. Of the 1,845 injunctions Edwin Witte catalogued that had been issued against union activities between 1880 and 1930, 28 were issued in the 1880s, 122 in the 1890s, 328 in the first decade of the twentieth century, 446 in the second, and 921 in the 1920s.[33]

Much more important than injunctions and the famous court precedents in determing the outcome of strikes, however, was the behavior of local police and magistrates at the scene of disputes. The law of trespass, traffic obstruction, disorderly conduct and riot was so ambiguous in its definitions of crimes that the attitudes of law enforcement officials on the spot in fact determined the atmosphere surrounding picket lines. Awareness of this fact made militant metal trades' associations become very active in local politics and in movements for governmental and police reform. In the midst of the 1900 strike in Chicago employer spokesmen had denounced the protection their plants received from police as "a farce," and blamed their troubles on the fact that no fewer than twenty-two "laboring men" occupied important offices in city hall. One employer complained that the police solicited payments from companies wanting protection, then "never laid a hand on those men," while strikers shouted insults and threats at scabs.[34]

The employers' crusade for the "open shop," therefore, everywhere enlisted the participation of concerned citizens from all walks of life. Starting with the Modern Order of the Bees in Dayton and Citizens' Alliances in numerous towns, local merchants, academics, professional men, supervisory personnel, fraternity boys from universities and anti-union workers were enrolled in local associations to combat "union tyranny." In Minneapolis, salesmen for the Citizens Alliance toured the town selling twenty-five cent anti-union buttons bearing the caption, "Minneapolis Makes Good," while metal trades employers posted placards in their factories recounting their victories over the unions.[35]

President David M. Parry of the National Association of Manufacturers and head of the Overland Automobile Company soon emerged as national leader of the crusade. Under his guidance a national Citizens' Industrial Association was formed in 1903 to rally all "those who believe in the maintenance of law and order and the perpetuation of our free institutions," first to defend the country's workingmen against "the present programme of violence, boycotting, and tyranny now being carried out by the majority of labor unions," and second to resist "legislation of a socialistic nature."[36] Its leader C. W. Post of Battle Creek, Michigan, explained the CIA's mission in its first bulletin:

Do you hear the murmur and the mutterings and see the lightning flashes of the storm of public indignation rolling up in mighty grandeur? It is coming and coming fast. The 14,980,000 decent, upright, peaceful voters who love work and demand liberty are now arising in their might, and the text on the wall, writ by the hand of Almighty God, writ in letters of glistening steel, proclaims that the slimy red fingers of anarchy shall be crushed by the mailed hand of the common people and their law.[37]

It has become fashionable for historians to identify the various organizations involved in the Open Shop Drive with relatively small business concerns concentrated in the Middle West, in contrast to the NCF, which is seen as the agency of the sophisticated leaders of big business. There is much in the rhetoric of the two groups to make this view attractive. Parry and Post often inveighed against the sentimental Eastern clergymen and intellectuals, who had been duped by Gompers and Mitchell into believing that business could deal honorably with unions. Easley for his part loved to boast that his organization represented "more capital and men than the whole of the Parry outfit."[38]

On examination of the dispute in the metal trades, however, it appears that the difference between the NCF and the Open Shop Drive was not sociological but tactical. Both appealed to the same business groups. Around the time of Murray Hill, Easley's approach won a broad and powerful following. By 1903, however, few manufacturers of any size endorsed his view any longer. The two business groups confronted each other directly with conventions held almost simultaneously in Chicago in the fall of 1903, and the outcome was diasterous for the NCF. The NMTA openly aligned itself with the NAM and the Citizens' Alliances, as 600 manufacturers from all over the land gathered to demand freedom from union controls. Commissioner DuBrul of the NMTA, who precipitated the anti-union tirades at the Mechanical Engineers' convention after the presentation of Taylor's paper a few months earlier, now scoffed at the NCF. "What do they represent anyway?" he asked. "I have found them a lot of meddlers."[39]

Though Easley still assured Mitchell that, "the same employers, and they outnumber the others at the rate of twenty-five to one, are with us,"[40] there was little evidence to support his claim. The employer representatives on the NCF's advisory committee now numbered only sixteen, and half of them were from transportation. At the 1904 Trade Agreements Conference, convened by Easley to answer the Open Shop Drive, only small employers from printing, foundries and construction participated, and they spent their time furiously berating the AFL representatives present for their sins.[41] By this time, the Citizens Industrial Association had adopted as its own official platform eight demands against union regulations advanced by the NCF leader, President Charles Eliot of Harvard, himself.[42] In 1906, Easley cautiously put union labels only on those invitations to the annual NFC conference which were intended for labor's representatives.[43]

More important, from 1903 onward the manufacturers of importance who were active in the National Civic Federation participated in the organization's welfare and safety work, and not in its promotion of conciliation and trade agreements. But the NAM and NMTA also approved of welfare and safety work and engaged in it as heartily as did the NCF. In 1914 only three manufacturers took part in the NCF's committee on collective bargaining – representatives of Otis Elevator, International Paper, and Weinstock and Nichols. Early stalwarts like U.S. Steel, International Harvester and National Cash Register had gone over to the Open Shop crusade. There were fifty major employers in the Civic Federation's welfare department, but fewer than ten of them dealt with unions.[44]

When a frenzied burst of economic activity in the last quarter of 1906 and the first half of 1907 lent strength once more to the bargaining power of workers, almost as many workers went on strike across the land as had gone out in 1900 and 1901. The NMTA, Anti-Boycott Association, and Citizens Alliances were tested to the limit, but the NCF had no significant role to play. District six of the IAM won a raise, a minimum rate and a 50-hour week from twenty-two shops in the Pittsburgh area, and engaged twenty-five others in long strikes. Parry and Post visited the city, reorganized the Pittsburgh Manufacturers' Association and boasted of the support they received from U.S. Steel. Large firms, like the Mesta Machine Company of Homestead and the Pressed Steel Car Company of McKees Rocks (soon to be given national fame by the IWW) became the bastions of resistance, as the region was flooded with private eyes and state constabulary. The three district leaders of the IAM were all imprisoned, as was only appropriate in a year when Gompers and Mitchell themselves were sentenced to jail for violating an injunction against the Bucks Stove and Range boycott. By December 1907, however, plant closings everywhere had left a tenth of the union's total membership unemployed and another third "on miserably short time." Victory once again belonged to the militant employers.[45]

In a word, Easley and "the Parryites," as he called the Open Shop leaders, had battled for the minds of the same business constituency, and the Parryites had won. The reason for their victory, quite simply, is that the leaders of the AFL could not control their members sufficiently to end sympathy strikes, stoppages in violation of contracts, and traditional work rules. Both the NCF and the Parryites promised improved working conditions and fair treatment of union members to the workers and industrial peace and a free hand for the introduction of scientific management to the employers. Both business groups feared the collective power of workers at the plant level, but the effort to control that power through union agreements had proven less effective than the unilateral exercise of management control, backed by the concerted action of all employers in a given locality. The NCF's approach failed abysmally in the metal trades, while in most of the land the Open Shop approach was a smashing success. Hand-blown glass-works, potteries, paper factories and bituminous coal mines of the Central Competitive Field, in all of which traditional work patterns remained unchallenged in this decade, might provide models of collective bargaining as espoused by the Civic Federation. In the building trades its formula often worked well. But where management fought for control, the open-shop approach provided it with the most effective strategy.

Union leadership and the Civic Federation

The Open Shop Drive effectively checked the growth of unionism in the metal trades. The IAM had enrolled roughly 11 percent of the country's machinists in its ranks by 1901, and that proportion was to remain constant through 1913. Its rules and standards were upheld for the most part in small workshops, whose employers were dependent upon the skills of their journeymen to turn out short runs of diverse products, railroad carshops, where machinists still rebuilt whole sections of locomotives and where the speed of repair work was more important to the companies than the men's hourly wages, and in firms which manufactured tools and instruments for purchase by craftsmen, who looked for union labels. Aside from temporary increases during the furious strikes of 1904 and 1907, the union enlarged its membership during these twelve years, when it did so at all, primarily by admitting semiskilled operatives into its ranks. The average American machinist (especially if he worked for a large enterprise) encountered at least some elements of scientific management each working day in a nonunion setting.

Two important consequences flowed from this development for the nature of metal trades unions and the consciousness of metal workers. First, the differentiation between the salaried leaders of the union and the rank and file became more and more pronounced. Second, the leaders themselves divided into rival factions, one supporting the National Civic Federation and the other the Socialist Party.

The officialdom of the Machinists became quite professionalized, as the union's membership expanded from 18 thousand to 56 thousand, its treasury swelled and contractual relationships with many companies became routinized after 1900. The union paid annual salaries ranging from $1,000 to $1,500 to President O'Connell, editor Wilson of the *Machinists' Monthly Journal*, Secretary-Treasurer George Preston, the tight-fisted guardian of its funds, and two general organizers. There were seventeen business agents by 1900, elected by districts or by large locals. They were paid half their salaries by their home bodies and half by the Grand Lodge. Additionally an average of twenty organizers were assigned to specific missions at any one time. In 1901 the constitution was amended to provide for the election at large of five paid vice-presidents (increased to seven in 1903), each of whom worked in the field as a trouble-shooter, under the general direction of the president. Rank-and-file supervision of this salaried leadership was provided in the British fashion, by a general executive board of five machinists from the shops, who were elected by the membership to meet periodically (with lost time at four dollars a day and expenses paid from the union's treasury) and review the actions of the salaried officials.[46]

The national officers were a homogeneous group in important respects. Of the twelve leaders elected to national posts in 1903, eight had been born in the United States, three in Britain and one in Canada. All but the venerable Hugh Doran, who had been active since the 1870s, were between thirty-five and forty-five years old. Seven came from railroad shops. Two had been master mechanics in such shops, and another three had at one time or another operated businesses of their own. Seven had been members of the Knights of Labor in their younger days, and one had been prominent in the American Railway Union. Although only two of the twelve were Socialist Party members (George Preston and P. J. Conlon), the most ardent anti-Socialist on the executive board, Robert Ashe, a Massachusetts single-taxer, had been driven from his post in 1897. President O'Connell consistently opposed the Socialists in the running battle of resolutions at the AFL conventions, but within his own union during the first years of the century, he was more circumspect, and even inclined to declare: "I am as good a Socialist as any man in this hall."[47]

This homogeneity facilitated a general concurrence among the officers on a program of all-grades unionization of the machine shop, increased discretionary authority to the leaders in dealing with management, political action and broad education of the membership on social and economic questions. All of them were hostile toward DeLeon's Socialist Labor Party and venemous toward the IWW.[48] Although resolutions to endorse the Socialist Party or the "cooperative commonwealth" were consistently defeated at IAM conventions, the delegates of 1903 did agree to insert into their constitution the provision that their union encouraged "the wisest use of our citizenship based upon the class struggle upon both economic and political lines, with a view to restoring the common weal of our Government to the people and using the natural resources, means of production and distribution for the benefit of all the people."[49]

In a word, the IAM's officers easily came to view themselves as full-time specialists in labor–management relations. In this respect they were much like the salaried officers of other American unions of the epoch: born to workingclass families, veterans of union struggles since their late teens, and successful in their pursuit of careers in union leadership. "Up-to-date unionism," wrote the American Fabian Herbert N. Casson in the Machinists' paper, "will choose as its leaders men who can hold their own with the lawyers and capitalists – large minded, masterful men, who will everywhere command respect."[50] All of them agreed on the need to drill a profound sense of discipline and calculation into their members, who still so often walked off their jobs one fine spring day without previous discussion with either the boss or the union officers, then wired the headquarters: "Demands refused. Men walked out. Send man at once."[51] More and more leaders came to agree with Adolph Strasser that their task was to "represent the interests of the International Union, regardless of the local instructions of the strike committee." Specifically that meant "to bring about an amicable and honorable adjustment of the trouble as speedily as possible, thus saving the funds of the International Union, which would otherwise be wasted; and to maintain the honor and reputation of the International Union for fair dealing with union manu-facturers."[52]

It became increasingly evident as the twentieth century progressed that most strikes did begin on the initiative of the workers involved, and that the basic role of union leaders was to negotiate terms of settlement. From the vantage point of the Grand Lodge of the IAM, which spent $3,626,890.58 to support strikers and their families between 1899 and 1914, the quest for some more "progressive" and "civilized" form of industrial relations was inescapable.[53] The mediation work of the National Civic Federation and its promotion of trade agreements between em-ployers and unions seemed to provide the most viable and attractive alternative to picket lines, injunctions, arrests and interminable industrial warfare, on the one side, and the growing threat of compulsory arbitration legislation, on the other.[54] The few state conciliation services which existed had staffs which were not only far too small for the work facing them, but also composed primarily of former union officers, appointed for their services to the Democratic or Republican Party, and received by the employers with frosty suspicion. No federal mediation service existed before 1914.

The Civic Federation, therefore, provided trade union executives with an agency which did enjoy enough standing in the business community to escort employers and unionists to the bargaining table in 118 disputes

during 1902 and 1903 and 156 in 1905, after which its effectiveness in
all sectors of the economy fell off rapidly.[55] In its heyday the NCF offered
a means of settling disputes, which was not only less hazardous than
reliance on sympathetic strikes and boycotts, but also imported into
industrial controversies the businessmen's style of dealing with each other.
For example, Ralph Easley sent a note to John Mitchell of the United
Mine Workers during the 1902 anthracite strike asking, "Cant [sic] you
come on & take dinner with me," and adding that George Perkins of the
House of Morgan would join them afterwards to "compare notes." Lest
the evening appear all work, Easley continued: "If you & your private
secy [Miss Morris] want to go to something nice tonight let me know
& I will get tickets. 'When Knighthood was in Flower' with Julia Marlow
is a lovely thing."[56]

In addition to its conciliation work, the NCF was an instrument for
improving sanitary and safety conditions at work, and one which was
especially important to union leaders who tried to adhere to the Civic
Federation's doctrine of the sanctity of contracts. This role was illustrated
by a request from President Fox of the Iron Molders to the Civic Federation's Welfare Secretary, Gertrude Beeks, that she prevail upon foundry
owners to repair broken windows, reducing wintry drafts, install showers
and give the men lockers for their street clothes. Fox "had his hands
full in getting the wage-scale signed up year after year with a provision
for reasonable hours," a Federation spokesman explained, and "if he
undertook to get any physical betterment for the men the employers
would contend that he was only trying to stir up trouble and break con-
tacts."[57]

Understandably, then, the popularity of the NCF was more intense
and much longer lasting with conservative union leaders than it was in
the business world. No substitute for it was available until Congress
established the Federal Mediation and Conciliation Service in 1914. It
is more remarkable that in the fresh glow of the Murray Hill Agreement
the activities of the NCF were commended by all officers of the IAM,
including the Socialists.[58] The latter looked upon *both* the rising level of
Socialist votes and arbitration agreements like that reached at the Murray
Hill Hotel as signs of the "marvelous times." Despite the criticisms levelled
against the Civic Federation by the Socialist press from 1901 onward,
editor D. D. Wilson of the *Machinists Monthly Journal*, a party member,
saw no anomaly in placing two items, in immediate succession one directly
after the other in the same column of his paper, the first urging his readers
to study socialism and the second praising Marc Hanna of the NCF for

remarks "that would do credit to an advanced trade unionist."[59] Wilson denounced open-shop advocates for their devotion to an individualistic order which had already been undermined by "big modern capitalistic combinations," and suggested that if businessmen would only "work in harmony with the times, cooperate for the elimination of waste – economic waste – put away their competitive knives and tomahawks, adopt modern methods, they would assist in the industrial and social revolution that is in progress."[60]

The mounting fury and success of the open-shop drive shattered the ideological harmony of the IAM's leadership. The union's growth was brought to a halt in 1904, while strike expenditures continued to soar upward, and injunctions, spies and organized strike-breakers dogged its tracks. To President O'Connell and Special Counsel Frank Mulholland, the former president of the Allied Metal Mechanics, who became O'Connell's closest aide after the merger of the two unions, an alliance with the Civic Federation was vitally necessary – more necessary than ever – to combat the "Parryites" of the business world. At the 1907 convention they pleaded at length with the delegates not to pass a motion denouncing the NCF and got their way in a confusing voice vote. But by the time of the next convention (1911) a referendum had prohibited any officers of the IAM from belonging to the NCF by a vote of 11,469 to 8,008.[61]

Toward the cooperative commonwealth

The leaders and beneficiaries of the assault on the Civic Federation were the Socialists. Editor Wilson had hailed Eugene V. Debs' *Unionism and Socialism* in 1904 for its lucid presentation of the need to abolish capitalism and of the separate yet complementary roles of trade unions and socialist political action, without ever mentioning the pamphlet's castigation of union collaboration with the NCF.[62] Within another year, however, Wilson's faith in the work of the Civic Federation had turned to anxiety. The Federation's retreat before the rising tide of anti-union sentiment in the business world had culminated in the election of August Belmont as its president. Belmont, Wilson charged, had "hired and retained the most notorious strike breaker in the country" to defeat the unions on his New York subway lines.[63] The editor's warning to the machinists to be "alert" was underscored by the memory that the national bituminous trade agreement, widely touted by the Civic Federation as the outstanding model of its philosophy of industrial relations in practice, had survived the previous year only at the expense of a 5½ percent wage cut, imposed on miners over the angry protests of the union's convention.[64]

During the ensuing years Wilson simply stopped writing about the NCF, while his paper gave extensive coverage to the socialist movements of Europe and the Socialist electoral activites of IAM members in the United States. There was plenty of such activity for him to describe, and its nature is well illustrated by the cluster of manufacturing towns, then known as the Tri-Cities: Rock Island and Moline, Illinois, and Davenport, Iowa. Three Machinists' lodges were to be found there, one in the federal arsenal at Rock Island (81), one in Moline (548), where the John Deere Company had its farm machinery works, and one in Davenport (388).[65] By 1911, when the IAM held its national convention in Davenport, a new railroad lodge had also been formed in the area (695).

For almost a year, during 1905 and 1906, the Socialist Party locals of the area issued their own ten-cent newspaper, *The Tri-City Workers' Magazine*, which addressed itself directly to the concerns of these workers. Three questions were emphasized in its columns: the insecurity and anxiety of working-class life, the degradation of the craftsman in the modern factory, and the neglect of workers' needs by the Democratic and Republican politicians in the local governments.

Debts – debts everywhere – provided the rhetorical theme for the first of these issues. Work was so irregular, especially with seasonal layoffs every summer and fall in the farm equipment industry, and earnings under constantly shifting piece-rate standards so unreliable that every family was depicted as carrying a heavy tally of credit on the grocer's books, not to speak of the butcher's, the coal dealer's, the clothing store's and the furniture market's. But most agonizing of all was the effort to buy a home of one's own. Convinced that an able and industrious American workman should have had the security and comfort of his own frame house, the worker described in issue after issue put his neck determinedly into the yoke of staggering mortgage payments, only to be foiled cruelly by the next bout of unemployment.[66]

But on the job itself, matters were even worse, according to *The Tri-City Workers' Magazine*. A layoff of several hundred men at the arsenal early in 1906 reminded its employees once more of the tyranny of its administration, which had battled the IAM through strike after strike over handymen, time study, and incentive pay since 1897, until the 1906 convention of the AFL officially proclaimed it a "sweatshop." The efficiency rating system seemed the worst tyranny of all. Twice yearly each employee was rated for regularity in attendance, skill, accuracy, deportment and rapidity, and his pay was adjusted according to his performance on each of these counts during the previous six months. Looking out the window cost A. A. Gustafson twenty-five cents a day for the next semester, just as breaking a tool holder took four points off the score of Nels Alifas, in addition to a fine of $6.12.[67] And even though Alifas consistently scored 100 on deportment and attendance, when he left the arsenal to assume a union post, the major in charge noted on his record: "This man is a disturber; has been disrespectful to me, and under no circumstances would I employ him in a shop of my own."[68]

At John Deere's vast "corn planter works," according to the Socialist paper, the workers' lot was even harsher than at the arsenal. Piecework predominated, and in parts of the plant workers subcontracted the construction of machines, rushing and cheating each other. The atmosphere of the plant resembled that of the state penitentiary, but because "the piece work system sets every man at his fellow worker's throat, the corporation has them all in its grasp." There was but one remedy: to deal with the boss "politically as a class . . . Electing their class to power workers elect themselves."[69]

The indictment of capitalism presented in these local accounts, and the political remedy proposed, echoed the themes of Debs' famous pamphlet of 1904:

> In the capitalist system the soul has no business. It cannot
> produce profit by any process of capitalist calculation.
> The working hand is what is needed for the capitalist's tool
> and so the human must be reduced to a hand . . .
> A thousand hands to one brain – the hands of workingman,
> the brain of a capitalist.
> A thousand dumb animals, in human form – a thousand
> slaves in fetters of ignorance, their heads having run to
> hands – all these owned and worked and fleeced by one
> stock-dealing, profit-mongering capitalist. This is
> capitalism![70]

The only meaningful remedy for both the "penitentiary" in which the worker toiled and the want he suffered when the penintentiary did not want him, then, was for workers to use their political power to collectivize the factories and introduce a "truly scientific" management by the workers themselves.[71] But the Socialist Party members of the Tri-Cities were as much concerned with their family and community lives as they were with the inside of the factory. Their paper agitated incessantly against the bleak living conditions and barren community life of towns whose sole reason for existence seemed to be to provide hands when needed for the corn planter works: "Diptheria in Davenport," "Why People Go to Brick Munro's."[72]

Above all the Party campaigned for the establishment of free kindergartens at every public school. They argued that capitalist development had already transferred one traditional function of the family after another to the "mill and factory, bakeshop, school, dispensary and hospital." But the young child was left to be socialized "in the street," to a sense of subordination and humility, or to its sublimation in gang loyalties, unchallenged by either the former nexus of family activities or any consciously designed alternative. Despite the evident failure of the cities' schools to equip young workers with a firm sense of how to contend with the world into which they were soon to be sent, the argument concluded, free kindergartens offered the best hope for instilling "community ideals" into the child, developing a sense of solidarity through relationships with the other children, and encouraging through "close personal touch" with the teacher, "the high instincts latent" in the child's mind, "which under any other method of ordeal and routine lapse into disuse and oblivion." To win this goal, however, an intense political struggle was needed against "the school board, the conservative German element and the Catholic Clergy."[73]

The crusade for kindergartens reflected the anxiety of skilled workers over the fate of their children in the city's streets as clearly as the paper's treatment of consumer debt and home ownership manifested their problems of economic survival and its castigation of the factory "penitentiaries" mirrored their loss of control on the job. In the Tri-Cities, as in Brockton and Haverhill, Massachusetts, Schenectady, New York, Wheeling, Huntington and the Kanawha mining towns of West Virginia, Pitcairn and Wilmerding, Pennsylvania, and other communities where it has been studied closely, the Socialist Party appealed above all to unionized workmen during the first decade of the twentieth century. In all these towns its program was the "constructive socialism," which linked union struggles over job conditions to community reforms of desperate importance to workers. Nothing could be more misleading than to identify "sewer socialism" with bourgeois influence upon the party. The bourgeoisie, and only they, already had good sewers.[74]

Socialism of this sort had no insurrectionary bite and recoiled in fear before "the great slum population," which the Tri-Cities' most famous

IAM member, Kate Richards O'Hare called "the greatest danger to our state – the greatest menace to humanity – and civilization."[75] Its strong commitment to both parliamentary activity and trade unionism made its local organizations resemble a labor party as much as a revolutionary organization – if not more so.[76] The party's moderate leader Robert Hunter could argue with considerate merit in 1914 that the Socialist Party "is a labor party, more or less dominated even today by Trade Unionists, and all it needs to make it rank with its capitalist rivals in this country and to make it as powerful as the great labor parties of Europe . . . is the united support of all American labor organizations."[77]

In fact, Socialist votes did invariably grow together with union strength, including IWW strength after 1910, and they shrank rapidly where that union base was destroyed.[78] In the Tri-Cities themselves, it was only after the brief triumph of unionization during the war years and the party's very effective local anti-war activity, that the Socialists carried Davenport's elections.[79] Moreover, by that time the members of the national executive board of the party bore a striking resemblance to those of most unions' executive boards: They were predominantly self-educated and self-confident careerists up from the ranks of the working class.[80]

The fact remains, however, that the ranks of the Socialist Party were infused with a profound class consciousness and an ardent commitment to total change of the social system. Much as they liked to argue that the type of political action pursued by the AFL's executive council was ineffective by its own criteria,[81] they ultimately insisted that no measures which did not bring the workers to political power, collectivize industry and abolish the ethic of competition and greed would suffice to meet workers' needs. Consequently, the party instructed its locals to emphasize street speaking, pamphleteering, book selling and other educational work on behalf of socialism. Locals were to avoid meeting in saloons, where the atmosphere would repel women members and impede serious discussion, to rotate the chair regularly, "so that no one gets too much power and becomes the 'boss' of the local," and to make themselves all expert in deliberation about their own needs. "If we are to rule the world," the instructions advised, "we must train ourselves to think clearly, talk calmly, debate kindly but forcibly, and the training can be obtained in the Socialist Local as nowhere else."[82]

The Tri-Cities' Socialists projected the image of a socialist future in which no individual would gather in rent, interest or profits. At the very least, the 8-hour day would instantly become the practice throughout society, and union scale would be the lowest possible pay. The government would end its interference in people's personal lives, they predicted, and control of all social functions would revert to the smallest social groups that could manage their affairs efficiently. Furthermore, in contrast to the leaders of the IAM, they looked upon the new IWW with considerable sympathy, and, when Haywood, Moyer and Pettibone went on trial, all discussion of piecework and kindergartens was sidetracked in favor of a tireless campaign for their release.[83] In short, the intellectual dichotomy of reformism versus revolutionary activity obscures, rather than clarifies, the ideology of these workers.

The Socialist Party had no formula for coping with scientific management on the job. It was the trade union's task to deal with that problem as best it could, while the party charted the path out of capitalism in all its forms. To be sure, many socialist leaders of IAM lodges in Toledo, Detroit, Chicago, Schenectady and elsewhere, ardently favored amalgamation of the metal trades unions and more militant action to cope effectively with the Open Shop Drive, but the emphasis of the party was on political action. Its most prominent spokesman in the AFL, Max Hayes, asserted in 1907: "it is absurd for Socialists to waste a lot of valuable time in splitting hairs, over the question of industrial organization."[84]

The fact remains that the Open Shop Drive and managerial reform together were not only undermining the traditional bases of craft control, but they were also solidifying the local middle class as a whole against the labor movement in town after town (making the opposite sides of the tracks, so vividly depicted in John Steinbeck's novel *East of Eden*, political, as well as social antagonists), and through injunctions and police ordinances making the daily functioning of trade unions a political issue. These developments brought the Socialists into control of the IAM.

The economic boom of early 1907 brought more workers out on strike than had been the case in any other year between 1904 and 1910, among them the largest number of IAM members that had ever been out in any year of the union's history. New recruits swelled the union's membership by almost 40 percent in a single year. In New Orleans a general strike, led by Black and White dockers acting in remarkable harmony under Marxist leadership, prevented the executive council of the AFL from destroying the Socialist-led Brewery Workers Union. Then in the fall of the year the economy collapsed, leading to draconic layoffs and even more widespread short time for workers in most industries. The open-shop drive was dramatically joined by U.S. Steel, which expelled all remaining unions not only from its own plants, but from whatever mines, docks, shops, haulers and construction operations it could influence. As the crisis gave way to renewed prosperity in the summer of 1909, however, aggressive strikes in McKees Rocks, and Newcastle, Pennsylvania, the West Virginia coal fields and New York's garment markets, all ably conducted under Socialist or IWW leadership, contributed immensely to the prestige of the Left, while the general strike of 146 thousand workers in Philadelphia in 1910 and the briefly effective fusion of AFL and Socialist Party efforts in Job Harriman's campaign for the mayor's office in open-shop Los Angeles the next year bore eloquent testimony to the class solidarity, of which the Socialists preached.[85]

The results were evident at the polls and in the trade unions. Socialists won major municipal offices in seventy-four cities in 1911. Among them was Schenectady, where nine of the eighteen party members elected to the city government were members of the IAM.[86] Although Thomas Van Lear had not been successful in his 1910 bid to become mayor of Minneapolis, he emerged from the effort as the most prestigious Socialist in the union and leading strategist of the emerging "Progressive" bloc. Two national organizers for the party had toured locals of the IAM and United Mine Workers in 1909, and the party's national executive committee established a trade union department to systematize the propaganda and recruiting work they began. At the 1908 convention of the Miners, John Mitchell was retired from office, and Socialist delegates, who numbered 400 out of the 1,000 miners present, led an assault on the Civic Federation and successfully urged a resolution barring from union membership anyone who joined the army or militia. During 1911 and 1912 conservative leaders of long standing in several unions were driven from their offices by rebel movements under Socialist direction. Among them were James Moffit of the Hatters, Albert Berres of the Pattern Makers, John Lennon of the Journeymen Tailors, Hugh Frayne of the Sheet Metal Workers, William Huber of the Carpenters and James O'Connell of the Machinists.[87]

The forty-odd Socialist Party members among the delegates to the 1911 convention of the AFL introduced a series of resolutions calling for financial aid to the indicted McNamara brothers and endorsement of Socialist Job Harriman's campaign for mayor of Los Angeles, both of which carried unanimously, and for greater attention to unionization of unskilled workers, which was referred to the executive council. Their other proposals, that Federation officers be elected by referendum vote and that the Civic Federation be denounced, lost by the heavy margin of five thousand to twelve thousand.[88] Nevertheless the delegates' vote to "sustain the conception of the labor problem in the United States for

which The National Civic Federation stands,"[89] offered conservative unionists a frail reed with which to defend themselves now that that conception
had been repudiated by all decisive sectors of the business community.

Socialist – Conservative factionalism

The growing Socialist strength injected an intense spirit of factionalism
into all the work of the AFL, and especially into the Machinists' union
itself. The conservatives drew on three sources of strength for the battle:
their control of the administrative machinery of the Federation and of
most unions, an alliance with the Democratic Party, which grew constantly more intimate and more effective between 1906 and 1918, and
the pervasive influence of religion and of clergymen in many working-
class communities.

Control of the top offices of most unions provided conservatives with
effective instruments for dominating union conventions (or avoiding them
altogether), rewarding loyal activists with desirable jobs, undermining
the relations of dissidents with employers or other unions, and keeping
the image of themselves as constructive and indispensable leaders before
the eyes of the members.[90] Despite the Federation's much vaunted respect
for the autonomy of member unions, its officers consistently strengthened
the positions of conservatives in those unions and attacked Socialists. The
demise of the United Metal Workers at the hands of the executive council,
the harassment of the Brewery Workers by jurisdictional disputes and
their ultimate expulsion for a year (until the New Orleans general strike
forced the Federation to take the Brewery Workers back), and the council's
decisive support of John Tobin's leadership of the Boot and Shoe Workers,
after he had clearly lost the elections, provide only three of the most
dramatic instances of the council's important role.[91] By 1907 Secretary
Morrison instructed all AFL organizers in the fields to keep Socialist
leaders of affiliated unions under constant surveillance.[92] On the other
hand, when conservative officers of affiliated unions were voted out of
office, the council found places for them in the hierarchy of the federation
itself. O'Connell of the Machinists became president of the metal
trades department, Moffitt of the Hatters was made a legislative agent,
and Berres, Lennon and Frayne all found sinecures within the federation.[93]

Consequently the factional warfare was fought with intense bitterness.
At the 1911 convention of the IAM, for example, the two opposing blocs
were so tightly disciplined that in balloting for convention committees
and for resolutions, fewer than a dozen delegates ever deviated from the

side with which they had voted on the previous issue. James O'Connell directed his faction and Thomas Van Lear conducted the Socialist group with precision that was almost military. When the delegate of Rock Island's Arsenal Lodge No. 81 was discovered to be voting with the conservatives, his home lodge convened an emergency meeting and recalled him, because he was under instructions "to vote with the progressives on all questions." On the other hand, Lodge 147 of Providence, Rhode Island, which had not been able to send a delegate, wired its protest against the "radical proceedings now being carried on by the delegates." Out-going President O'Connell was openly bitter in his valedictory speech, and boasted to the delegates that he had job offers from the metal trades department and two agencies in Washington, where he could get ten thousand dollars a year for only two to three hours work a day. No one moved to offer him a vote of thanks for his twenty-one years of leadership.[94]

The relationship of Gompers and his associates with the Democratic Party were skillfully dissected by Robert Hunter at the time and have been analyzed well by several historians subsequently.[95] It is important here simply to note that, although such an alliance on the national level was clearly in the making from 1906 onward, with the formation of the federation's labor representation committee, it reached its fulfillment only during the administration of Woodrow Wilson, when the Democrats could and did deliver patronage, legislation and helpful investigations to the AFL in abundance. Before that time, the long-standing Republican connections of many trade union officers and the genuine conviction of others that involvement with either party should be studiously avoided, retarded the consummation of the alliance as effectively, at least, as did the protests of the Socialists. Of course, the generous and effective activities of Martin M. Mulhall in trade union circles on behalf of the Republicans encouraged this resistance, until they were sensationally exposed by a congressional investigation in 1913.[96] After 1912, however, the federal government under Wilson's administration succeeded where the NCF had failed: It promised the unions legislated standards for working conditions and mediation services bolstered by the government's authority.

The historic basis for the role assumed by the Democratic Party was the long-standing loyalty it had enjoyed from German and Irish Catholics. This fealty had been based on the party's persistent defense of their religious institutions and their traditional cultures against the homogenizing efforts of native Protestants, especially in connection with liquor licensing, parochial schools, Catholic charities, and sabbatarian legislation.[97] To this historic defense of "popular liberties" against oppressive government, the Democrats in many localities had added protests against police and judicial repression of strikes and boycotts, and during the Open Shop Drive this theme assumed increasing importance in the party's propaganda. The important point, however, is that the emerging alliance of the Democratic Party with the leadership of the AFL only supplemented a very old partisan loyalty of two ethnic groups of great importance among union members. That old attachment, furthermore, was based on cultural values to which clerical leaders could effectively appeal against the rising tide of socialism.

In fact, while the cause of corporate liberalism within the AFL had been linked to the Civic Federation (and before the Democratic Party and the state became its main instruments), the most significant clerical influences in the labor movement had come from the seminary and episcopal or presbytery level of leadership of Protestant denominations. Twenty-three Protestant clergymen and editors sat on the 1901 advisory council of the NCF, along with only Archbishop John Ireland and two editors from the Catholic Church. In 1906, Reverend Charles Stelzle, who had once done some machinist's work and belonged to the IAM, was seated in the AFL convention as a fraternal delegate from the year-old department of church and labor of the Presbyterian Church – a status equal to that of delegates from the Women's Trade Union League, the Farmer's Educational and Cooperative Union or the British Trades Union Congress. Three years later he was seated as a fraternal delegate from the Federated Council of the Churches of Christ in America, which was then engaged in a strenuous public campaign to persuade steel manufacturers to let their men off work on Sundays. Stelzle himself frequently lectured both the AFL and the Machinists on the dangers of Socialists and of foreigners generally ("a pretty rocky lot, anyway").[98]

Effective Catholic intervention, on the other hand, appeared first at the parish level, with resounding denunciations of socialism from the pulpit and from lay organizations in Brockton, Haverhill, Lynn and other Massachusetts towns, in Schenectady and in Buffalo, New York, in Butte, Montana, and in St. Louis. By 1906 the German Catholic Central Verein had undertaken to coordinate this struggle, drawing especially on the experience of worker-priests who had battled the Socialist leadership of the Brewery Workers Union in St. Louis. Its activity propelled Reverend Peter E. Dietz of Elyria, Ohio into the national limelight, when he came to the 1909 convention of the federation in Toronto, determined to enroll the "class-conscious children of our Holy Mother Church" within the union movement, which he envisaged as "the classic battle-ground of socialism in this country."[99]

Although it is clearly foolish to depict the Catholic Church as single-handedly halting the rise of socialism, the Catholic effort was important in two ways. First it helped organize a conscious and coordinated anti-socialist bloc in the leadership of the unions. Although the Militia of Christ for Social Service, launched with great fanfare at the 1910 convention of the AFL, was strictly an organization of high union officers and was itself dissolved by Reverend Dietz after only a year's existence, the Catholic caucus at executive council meetings, the Labor Mass at each convention of the federation and the effective presence of Father Dietz in the lobbies became regular and important features in the lives and activities of many top leaders of the AFL. Between 1910 and 1916, at least, those efforts strongly supported Gompers' leadership.[100]

Secondly, the Catholic Action movement provided an ideological antidote for socialism, which appealed to the sentiments of many American workers. In contrast to the NCF's celebration of big business as organized labor's potential ally, the sermons of Dietz, Archbishop John Glennon of St. Louis, and other priests who involved themselves in the labor movement, stressed the church's defense of "her children," the workers, against the rapacity of the rich. They drew upon the church's traditional hostility toward materialism when they challenged the Taylorite doctrine that the best society is that which maximizes productivity.[101] Although Dietz needed some careful instruction from John Mitchell to convince him that a union could not open its doors to all social classes or abhor strikes and boycotts, he learned to denounce "the sham competition of individual bargaining between master and working man," and to uphold unions as a check against "the parasitic industries that take and use up the life-blood of the successive relays of working men, casting the worn-out toiler upon the scrap heap." He pledged his church's aid to the struggle for "the living wage, reasonable hours and fair conditions."[102]

Above all the clergy who were engaged in this battle rested their case on a defense of the patriarchal family and on warnings against the growing power of the state in modern life. The doctrine of "the living wage," as developed by American Catholic thinkers had two important features: First, the wage, to which every workingman was entitled by "natural right," was based not on his productivity, but on his need as a person for "reasonable and frugal comfort." Second, it should be a wage sufficient for the father to support a family without any contribution by his wife or young children. "The welfare of the whole family, and that of society likewise," wrote John A. Ryan, "renders it imperative that the wife and mother should not engage in any labor except that of the household."[103] He cited with approval the declaration of a French congress of Christian workingmen, that the "wife become a wage worker is no longer a wife."[104]

Thus the aspiration so widely shared among workers for a home of their own, where the wife remained caring for the needs of the family, was elevated to the level of a doctrinal imperative, which ruled out such Socialist proposals as kindergartens. "We have . . . to preserve, without state control, our homes," preached Archbishop Glennon to the AFL delegates assembled in his city of St. Louis. "We utterly abhor the idea that the children are the wards of the state: – common property."[105]

The admonitions against the growing domain of governmental activity, suggested in these remarks, was often spelled out explicitly. Archbishop Glennon warned his listeners:

There is a strong tendency to obliterate individuality in the state. The state is the cure, the panacea for all our ills. Capital wants the state to affirm its banking systems, to guard their interests through an interstate law. There are some of our laboring people preaching a gospel that wants us to throw our lives, our homes and our children into the state, making the state our mother and father.[106]

To workers already anxious about business's increasing use of the government to control more and more aspects of social life, the Archbishop was saying that the socialist remedy was only more of the same. To those in fear of scientific management of the factory, he warned that the revolutionaries would bring a scientifically managed society. In this respect he echoed John Mitchell's famous denunciation of governmental paternalism:

The American-bred wage worker does not wish to be the ward of any man or system – classified, numbered, tagged, and obliged to carry a card of identification, or be subject to police control or employing class supervision. In fact, the American wage worker who is the product of our general system of education is about the equal of his fellow-citizens and needs only the fair opportunities promised in the principles of our republic to work out his own economic salvation.[107]

It is true that Catholic social doctrine did not always bear this antistatist bias. In fact, the first articulate Catholic social thought in America turned impulsively to welfare legislation as the cure for social ills, and by the 1920s that theme would once again be dominant.[108] Moreover, the ideas outlined here were by no means articulated by all of the clergy even at this time. Most of them either ignored the labor question altogether, or contented themselves with admonitions to the faithful like those of Cardinal Gibbons, to "foster habits of economy and self-denial," and shun "the slightest invasion of the rights and autonomy of employers."[109] Nor can anyone argue that the Socialists had no success among Catholic workers. In Milwaukee their candidates carried the city's Polish wards in 1910, and the secretary of the Connecticut state branch claimed that 70 percent of the party members there were Catholics.[110] Moreover, the largest bloc of right wing votes in the IAM came from the predominantly Protestant railroad lodges of the South, while many heavily Catholic lodges in the Northeast went for the Socialists.

The point is that at this critical moment in the development of the labor movement, there were Catholic thinkers in close touch with trade unionists who attacked the Socialists with arguments bound to be convincing to large numbers of workers. The clearest statement of their position appeared in Hillaire Belloc's provocative book, *The Servile State*, published in 1912. This work, which clearly influenced both Father John Ryan and the Guild Socialists of England, argued that the inherent tendency of modern capitalism was toward a society in which the whole working class more or less willingly submitted to state direction in all its affairs, in return for relief from the brutal insecurity it had suffered under nineteenth-century capitalism.[111] Corporate reformers and socialists stood together in the vanguard of this trend, said Belloc. Clear reflections of his arguments were to be heard in the 1916 convention of the IAM, when Catholic conservatives, now in opposition, defended syndicalist rebels against the union's Socialist leadership.[112]

The solidification of the Socialist and conservative blocks resulted in sharply drawn ideological battle lines among the delegates who assembled in Davenport, Iowa, for the 1911 convention of the IAM. Referendum votes earlier that year had already resulted in the repudiation of the National Civic Federation and in the defeat of President O'Connell by a Socialist militant from Providence, Rhode Island, William H. Johnston, by a vote of 13,321 to 15,300, with 42 percent of the membership participating.[113]

Eight sections of the union cast among them 70 percent of the votes in the presidential contest. The one offering by far the greatest number of votes to Johnston was that made up of the railroad lodges in Division 1, the lines from the Illinois Central (Chicago to New Orleans) westward to the Pacific Ocean. Johnston gleaned one-fourth of his votes from these 162 lodges, which cast 69 percent of their ballots for him and sent delegates loyal to the Progressive bloc from 107 lodges (82 percent of the total). His second, and much smaller, base of support lay in the industrial lodges of New England, which contributed 9 percent of his votes and sent left convention delegates from thirty-three lodges, as compared to twenty-five lodges for the right. In all 57 percent of the New Englanders' votes had gone to the Rhode Island Socialist.

An important cluster of lodges, which may be designated as those from open-shop cities, would include those of Minneapolis – St. Paul, Dayton, Portland, Cincinnati, Los Angeles, Detroit, Pittsburgh and vicinity, Toledo, Sedalia and Indianapolis. This group behaved in much the same pattern as the New England lodges, confirming the impression that Socialist voting strength came not only from its traditional base (the railroad lodges of Division 1), but also from the beleagured industrial centers where scientific management had made the greatest headway. Their votes were not numerous, because the lodges were mostly small, but 59 percent of their 1,779 ballots went to Johnston.

Johnston also won in Chicago, where ten lodges went with the left and eight with the right, and he obtained 65 percent of the total votes cast. As we have noted the Chicago lodges seemed to be somewhat less tightly factionalized than others throughout the country. In fact, 41 percent of the referendum votes from right-wing lodges went to Johnston, though only 18 percent of those from left-wing lodges went to O'Connell.

Division One, the open-shop cities, New England and Chicago, then, were the main contributors to the Socialist victory. The strength of the conservatives, on the other hand, was found in Division Three, New York and New Jersey, Philadelphia, and Canada. Division Three was comprised of railroad lines East of the Illinois Central and south of the Chesapeake and Ohio. Clearly this was no center of Catholic votes, but its fifty-nine lodges sent right delegates from thirty-eight of their number and gave O'Connell 62.5 percent of their votes. The southern railroad shop lodges supported the right almost as strongly as their western brothers did the left, and both cast very large votes.

Great conservative strength also lay in New York City. In the metropolitan region of New York and northern New Jersey a majority of the lodges (fifteen out of twenty-four) actually supported the left, but ten of them were in New Jersey. The lodges of New York were bigger and more solidly conservative, so that the region as a whole cast 64 percent of its votes for O'Connell, mostly through tightly disciplined right-led lodges. In fact, this area gave O'Connell his biggest single bloc of votes – 1,870, as against 1,672 from his second biggest source, his minority in Division One. The New York–New Jersey area may illustrate a significant exercise of power by the Catholic anti-Socialist movement.

The biggest surprise, however, came in Philadelphia, home city of

Taylorism. Although five of the city's nine lodges backed the Socialists at the convention, 86 percent of its votes went for O'Connell. One special circumstance makes this result all the more intriguing: The IAM's lodges in Philadelphia had been moribund, under the impact of scientific management and the open-shop drive, until the city's general strike of 1910. Great numbers of machinists had walked out at that time, especially in the Kensington district of the city, and there a new lodge had been formed (No. 466), which cast 1,510 votes for O'Connell (more than he got in all of New England or even all of Division Three) and 40 for Johnston. The city's other eight lodges cast 69 percent of their meager votes for Johnston, following the pattern of the open-shop cities and New England. But this one new lodge, born of a general strike, stood by the man who had been president at the moment of its birth.

The other conservative stronghold was Canada, where twenty-seven of the forty-two lodges supported the right, and 61 percent of their votes went to O'Connell. In conformity with familiar patterns of Canadian labor politics, 60 percent of the left lodges were in the West while three-fourths of the right-wing lodges were located in Ontario, Quebec and the Maritime Provinces. Although the sole surviving Toronto lodge voted for Johnston by a narrow margin, it had been battered into quiescence by management's systematization of production in the city's larger firms, the militant unity of the city's employers' association, which enjoyed injunctions on demand, and total defeat in a major strike of 1907. Elsewhere the union consisted mainly of railroad lodges, among whom fear that a Socialist administration might reduce their autonomy supplemented the admonitions of the Catholic movement. Moreover, a rival Christian labor movement was already in the field, not only in Quebec, but in Hull and other English-speaking parts of Ontario as well. Consequently the threat of a secession of Catholic members from an international union controlled by Socialists in the United States was serious.[114]

At the close of the 1911 convention, therefore, members of the Socialist Party were the leaders of a deeply divided machinists union of 54,300 members. Both they and their factional foes expressed bitter hostility to the employers' efforts to dislodge the skilled machinist from his position of power within the workplace, but they also opposed each other's notions of the proper political course for their union with equal bitterness. Moreover, two weeks before the convention opened, sixteen thousand workers on the Illinois Central and Harriman railroad lines had struck in defiance of the Grand Lodge, thus opening a running battle between the incoming Socialist leadership and a syndicalist opposition, which was to plague the union until its next convention in 1916. The strikers sought to unite all railroad repair shop workers, from clerks to laborers, in "system federations," which functioned independently from the various craft unions to which their members belonged (and on which they relied for strike benefits). Their leadership was strongly influenced by the North American Syndicalist League, which repudiated political action altogether and sought to impose workers' control directly through the collective strength of employees at the workplace.[115]

Conclusion

Historians who have analyzed the Progressive Era in terms of the triumph of "corporate liberalism" have tended to overestimate the significance and the success of the National Civic Federation.[116] Neither the effort of the NCF to establish voluntary cooperation between organized business and organized labor, nor any subsequent effort of the sort, ever enjoyed the decisive support of the country's business leaders. In the decade before World War I, as in the postwar era, the daily confrontation between management and workers over control within the workplace made it impossible for unions to play a mediating role in a way which was satisfactory to corporate executives. In fact, that conflict generated movements within major unions to depose leaders, who were friendly to the NCF, and to replace them with others, who were pledged to uproot the capitalist system, on which scientific management grew. Neither Easley's banquets for labor statesmen and captains of industry nor Taylor's exhortations to workers and managers to commit themselves to increasing output, rather than fighting over its division, could put an end to class conflict. Under the circumstances, even those corporate executives who experimented with the most liberal welfare schemes chose to be absolute masters of the work relations in their own factories.

On the other hand, two corollaries of the "corporate liberalism" thesis are substantiated by this case study. First, the conciliation efforts of the National Civic Federation proved to be extremely attractive to union executives. Although the Socialist Party quickly and accurately perceived a deadly peril to the integrity of the workers' movement and its independence of bourgeois domination in the work of the NCF, even Socialist leaders of the IAM were enamored of the Murray Hill formula. The decisive moment arrived, however, after the electoral triumphs of the Democratic Party in 1910–1912. Then the federal government offered its own coercive authority to perform the tasks at which the voluntary means of the NCF had failed. Its promise of mediation services bolstered by the government's authority, plus legislated standards for working conditions, proved irresistible to most union leaders. Moreover, the party which extended that promise held the historic loyalty of German and Irish Catholic workers, whose own cultural and religious leaders opposed socialism on grounds which were far more consistent with traditional working-class values than was the ideology of the NCF. Consequently, by the elections of 1916 Woodrow Wilson's Democrats, boasting among many union endorsements that of the IAM, walked off with the labor vote. In short, it was through the agency of the country's political machinery, rather than through voluntary associations of businessmen, that "corporate liberalism" most effectively wooed union leaders, in the epoch of World War I as in the 1930s.

Second, just as corporate executives sought to systematize their control of production after the 1890s, so they also devoted major efforts to restructuring the country's political machinery at the local, state, and federal levels, and to put it to their own use in rationalizing the market, financial, and educational environments in which they functioned. Through legislation, regulatory commissions, municipal reform, and the exercise of national power to promote the "open door" abroad for American enterprise, the state became an agency of social and economic change, whose activities were apparent to all Americans. Its police role in the open-shop drive was especially evident to trade unionists. The growing prominence and pervasiveness of government's activities persuaded millions of workers that they could not challenge management in the workplace, while ignoring its links to the state. By 1911 a majority of the members of the IAM voted for a new leadership, whose party wished to use the state to abolish capitalist relationships. Many more workers voted for a party which promised to use governmental authority to curb management. A revolutionary minority repudiated voting altogether, and advised workers to use their collective industrial power to "smash the state." All three groups affirmed this corollary of the argument advanced by historians of the "corporate liberalism" school: In the twentieth century the questions of workers' control and the role of the state had become inseparably intertwined.

Notes

* This essay consists of excerpts from two chapters of my forthcoming book *The Fall of the House of Labor*, to be published by the Cambridge University Press.
1 For recent discussions of corporate liberalism and socialism, see James Wein-

stein, *The Corporate Ideal in the Liberal State, 1900–1918* (Boston, 1968); Weinstein, *Ambiguous Legacy: The Left in American Politics* (New York, 1975); Gabriel Kolko, *Main Currents in Modern American History* (New York, 1976); John H. M. Laslett, *Labor and the Left: A Study of Socialist and Radical Influences in the American Labor Movement, 1881–1924* (New York and London, 1970); Ira Kipnis, *The American Socialist Movement, 1897–1912* (New York and London, 1952); John H. M. Laslett and Seymour Martin Lipset, eds., *Failure of a Dream? Essays in the History of American Socialism* (Garden City, N.Y., 1974). For an interpretation of the Civic Federation closer to that presented in this essay, see Philip S. Foner, *History of the Labor Movement in the United States*, 4 vols. (New York, 1947–65), III, 61–110.

2 *Machinists Monthly Journal* (hereinafter cited as *MMJ*), 9 (June 1897), 214, 247–8, 276–7; 10 (January 1898), 25; 10 (February 1898), 65, 75; 10 (April 1898), 230–1, 237–8; 10 (August 1898), 463–6; 10 (December 1898), 722–5. Only the Pittsburgh lodges struck, and they won the 9-hour day in sixty-six shops. Jacob H. Hollander and George E. Barnett, *Studies in American Trade Unionism* (New York, 1912), 129. See also Charles Boxton Going, "Labour Questions in England and America," *Engineering Magazine*, 29 (May 1900), 161–76. On the membership of the ASE and the IAM, see Sidney and Beatrice Webb, *Industrial Democracy* (London, 1897), 287; Mark Perlman, *The Machinists: A New Study in American Trade Unionism* (Cambridge, Mass., 1961), 33.

3 U.S. Industrial Commission, *Report of the Industrial Commission*, 19 vols. (Washington, D.C., 1901), 8, 8.

4 *MMJ*, 12 (March 1900), 196–8, 210–12, 235; *Industrial Commission*, 8, 6–7, 490–2.

5 *Industrial Commission*, 8, cxxiv, 6–7, 24–6, 180–2, 299, 500–3. The quotations are on pp. 6, 24, 299. See also *MMJ*, 12 (May 1900), 249–52.

6 *Industrial Commission*, 8,35, 490–2.

7 *MMJ*, 11 (May 1900), 254–5.

8 Ibid., 11 (May 1900), 255; 14 (July 1902), 424.

9 Ibid., 12 (June 1900), 311–49, 386–90; 12 (July 1900), 483–90; 12 (August 1900), 496–9. For the membership of the NMTA, see ibid., 12 (May 1900), 252–4. On the issues which the IAM tried unsuccessfully to raise, see ibid., 12 (May 1900), 290.

10 Ibid., 13 (January 1901), 32.

11 Ibid., 13 (January 1901), 29–33; 13 (April 1901), 198–202; 13 (May 1901), 261–3.

12 Robert M. LaFollette, ed., *The Making of America*, vol. VIII, *Labor* (Chicago, 1905), 88–99. The quotation is on p. 97.

13 The membership of the advisory council is from Franklin H. Head and Ralph M. Easley to John Mitchell, February 4, 1901, John Mitchell Papers, Box A3-9. Catholic University of America, Washington, D.C. See also Marguerite Green, *The National Civic Federation and the American Labor Movement, 1900–1925* (Washington, D.C., 1956), 11–12.

14 Ralph Easley to John Mitchell, April 27, 1903, and the enclosed clipping from the *New York Independent* (Mitchell Papers, Box A3-10).

15 Green, 43–51. For Mitchell's rejection of Easley's request, see Easley to Mitchell, August 4, 1902; Mitchell to Easley, August 6, 1902 (Mitchell Papers, Box A3-10).

16 *Chicago Record-Herald*, June 9, 1901.

17 On sympathy strikes, see section on "mutual support," ch. 1. On the Fed-

erated Metal Trades, see *MMJ*, 9 (1897), 141; 14 (May 1902), 254–5; 18 (April 1906), 354; 18 (May 1906), 452–3.

18 See section on "mutual support," ch. 1.

19 *MMJ*, 12 (February 1901), 63–4; 12 (May 1901), 257–8, 261–3; 14 (July 1902), 30–1, 424–6.

20 *Industrial Commission*, 8,509, 512–13; *Chicago Record-Herald*, June 9, 1901; Harry F. Dawes to Ralph M. Easley, July 8, 1901, copy included in Ralph Easley to John Mitchell, July 13, 1901 (Mitchell Papers A3-10); National Civic Federation, "Joint Trades Agreement Conference of the National Civic Federation, Held at the Fifth Avenue Hotel, New York City, Saturday, May 7th, 1905 at 10 A.M.," (typescript, Mitchell Papers, Box A3-10), 37–45. The quotation is on p. 37.

21 Green, 25–33; David Brody, *Steelworkers in America: The Nonunion Era* (Cambridge, Mass., 1960), 60–8; William Z. Foster, *The Great Steel Strike and Its Lessons* (New York, 1920), 12, 18–20. For Easley's moves against Shaffer, see Easley to Mitchell, November 26, 1901, November 29, 1901 (Mitchell Papers, Box A3-10). Selig Perlman and Philip Taft correctly spoke of this strike as "labor's defeat at the Marne." *History of Labor in the United States, 1896–1932* (New York, 1935), 97–109.

22 *MMJ*, 14 (June 1902), 329–30; *Chicago Record-Herald*, June 9, 1901

23 Easley to Mitchell, June 11, 1901. See also Easley to Mitchell, June 12, 1901, June 19, 1901, June 25, 1901 (Mitchell Papers, Box A3-10).

24 *Chicago Record-Herald*, June 9, 1901; *MMJ*, 14 (January 1902), 28–30; 14 (October 1902), 677–82. A bitter rivalry between the IAM and the Chicago branches of the Amalgamated Society of Engineers strengthened the hand of Fraser and Chalmers during the strike. ASE members spoke against the first strike on the picket lines and then during the second walkout offered to replace IAM strikers with its own members. The British union was consequently ostracized by the Chicago labor movement, and, in search of a home, helped found the IWW in 1905. See Lee S. Fisher and J. J. Keppler to *MMJ*, 15 (March 1903), 209–11.

25 James O'Connell to executive council of the AFL, October 15, 1901 (Mitchell Papers, Box A3-46).

26 John R. Commons, ed., *Trade Unionism and Labor Problems, First Series* (Boston, 1905), 36–64, 87–136; Green, 97. I am indebted to Steven Sapolsky for his insights into the Chicago labor movement of this epoch.

27 *MMJ*, 15 (September 1903), 831–3.

28 Commons, *Trade Unionism and Labor Problems*, 36–64; Jacob H. Hollander and George E. Barnett, *Studies in American Trade Unionism* (New York, 1912), 192–3.

29 *MMJ*, 16 (July 1904), 621–2, 637; 16 (September 1904), 821–2; 16 (November 1904), 970; 17 (February 1905), 138–9; 17 (April 1905), 323–5; 17 (October 1905), 916–18. Foner, *History*, III, 310–11; Perlman and Taft, 61–70; William M. Tuttle, Jr., "Labor Conflict and Racial Violence: The Black Worker in Chicago, 1894–1919," *Labor History*, 10 (Summer 1969), 411–16.

30 On the NMTA's open-shop drive, see Perlman and Taft, 129–35; Clarence E. Bonnett, *Employers' Associations in the United States: A Study of Typical Associations* (New York, 1922); *MMJ*, 16 (June 1903), 448; 17 (June 1905), 501; *Iron Age*, 87 (March 23, 1911), 740; Hollander and Barnett, 198–203, 208–11.

31 Corporations Auxiliary Company to United Brewers Association of New York, Oct. 10, 1906 (Mitchell Papers, Box A3-48); Paul Maas to *MMJ*, 16

(February 1904), 117–18; *MMJ*, 16 (April 1904), 298–300; 16 (September 1904), 791; 19 (March 1907), 267–8. One enterprising agency offered its services to the AFL Executive Council to ferrett out other spies, and anyone else the council might want to watch. B. M. Goldowsky to Samuel Gompers, March 20, 1905; ibid., June 3, 1905 (copies in Mitchell Papers, Box A3-47).

32 Ordway Tead, *Instincts in Industry: A Study of Working-Class Psychology* Boston and New York, 1918), 122–4.

33 Edwin E. Witte, *The Government in Labor Disputes* (New York and London, 1932), 84. For discussions of injunction law, see Witte, op. cit.; Felix Frankfurter and Nathan Greene, *The Labor Injunction* (New York, 1930). See also below pp. 160–1, 166–7.

34 *Industrial Commission*, 7, 9, 40. Witte, *Government in Labor Disputes* is one of the few legal studies to stress the importance of local ordinances.

35 *MMJ*, 20 (May 1908), 440.

36 Ibid., 16 (January 1904), 9–10.

37 Quoted in Green, 101.

38 Ralph Easley to John Mitchell, December 8, 1904 (Mitchell Papers, Box A3-10). See also Statement of John Kirby, Jr., in Easley to Morris Hillquit (draft), June 26, 1911 (Mitchell Papers, Box A3-11); National Civic Federation, *The National Civic Federation, Its Methods and Its Aims* (New York, 1905). For usual depiction of the NCF and its rivals, see Thomas C. Cochran, *The American Business Systems* (New York, 1962); Robert H. Wiebe, *Businessmen and Reform: A Study of the Progressive Movement* (Cambridge, Mass., 1962); Weinstein, *Corporate Ideal*. Cf., Foner, *History*, III, 61–110.

39 *Chicago Daily Tribune*, September 30, 1903; *Chicago Record-Herald*, September 30, 1903.

40 Easley to Mitchell, October 3, 1903 (Mitchell Papers, Box A3-10).

41 NCF, "Joint Trades Agreement Conference . . . 1904"; Green, 108–11.

42 Green, 112. Eliot's demands included: no closed shop; no restriction on the use of machinery; no limitation of output; no boycott; no sympathetic strike; and no restrictions on apprentices.

43 See invitations in Mitchell Papers, Box A3-10.

44 Robert F. Hoxie, *Trade Unionism in the United States* (New York and London, 1936), 202–3; Green, 274n; Committee on Collective Bargaining membership list, 1914 (Mitchell Papers, Box A3-11).

45 *MMJ*, 19 (March 1907), 263; 19 (April 1907), 372; 19 (May 1907), 473, 483–4; 19 (June 1907), 591–2; 19 (July 1907), 666–8, 682–3; 19 (September 1907), 891–2; 20 (January 1908), 64–8; 21 (April 1909), 341–2. On the Bucks Stove and Range case, see Philip Taft, *The A. F. of L. in the Time of Gompers* (New York, 1957), 268–71.

46 *MMJ*, 10 (January 1900), 15; Perlman, *Machinists*, 24, 151–4, 174–89, 206.

47 "Biographical," *MMJ*, 16 (May 1903), 402–8. On Ashe, see *MMJ*, 9 (August 1897), 366–9. On O'Connell, see Report of the IAM Delegates to the AFL Convention, *MMJ*, 15 (January 1903), 25–7. The quotation is from *MMJ*, 9 (June 1899), 362.

48 On the SLP, see P. J. Conlon, "His Reason for Swatting," *MMJ*, 10 (September 1898), 593–6; Stuart Reid to *MMJ*, 11 (March 1899), 147–8. On the IWW, see editorial, *MMJ*, 18 (November 1906), 984–5.

49 *MMJ*, 15 (July 1903), 552.

50 H. N. Casson, "Words of Wisdom," *MMJ*, 15 (April 1903), 271; Warren R.

Van Tine, *The Making of a Labor Bureaucrat: Union Leadership in the United States, 1870–1920* (Amherst, Mass., 1973).

51 "Unauthorized Strikes," *International Molders' Journal* (May 1900), 277.

52 Strasser quoted in G. M. Janes, *The Control of Strikes in American Trade Unions* (Baltimore, 1916), 118.

53 International Association of Machinists, *Proceedings of the Fourteenth Biennial Convention* (Davenport, Iowa, 1911), 17.

54 Compulsory arbitration was often discussed between 1900 and 1914. See LaFollette, *Making of America*, VIII; Commons, *Trade Unionism and Labor Problems*, 195–221.

55 Green, 65–9, 81.

56 Easley to Mitchell, n.d. (1902 folder, Mitchell Papers, Box A3-10). It is an interesting commentary on the mores of the age that at the social affairs of the NCF, which the wives of capitalists dutifully attended, the wives of the trade unionists were conspicuously absent.

57 Edward Marshall, "Welfare Work May Conquer Great Labor Problems," *New York Times*, November 17, 1912. See also Green, 272–4; Civic Federation of New England, *Better Workshops*, Bulletin No. 5 (Boston, May 1906).

58 The Socialist leaders of the Brewery Workers used the NCF to arrange negotiations with the National Brewers Association as late as 1904. Easley to Mitchell, February 8, 1904 (Mitchell Papers, Box A3-10).

59 *MMJ*, 15 (January, 1903), 5.

60 Editorial, *MMJ*, 15 (June 1903), 449–50. Two Socialists, A. M. Simons and T. J. Morgan, and two philosophical anarchists, Benjamin Tucker and George Schilling, had participated in the 1899 National Conference on Combinations and Trusts, which gave birth to the NCF. Ralph Easley to Morris Hillquit (draft), June 26, 1911 (Mitchell Papers, Box A3-11). For early Socialist criticisms of the NCF, see Easley to Mitchell, November 2, 1902 (Mitchell Papers, Box A3-10).

61 IAM, *Proceedings of the Twelfth Biennial Convention* (St. Louis, 1907), bound with *MMJ*, 19 (October 1907), 79–80; *MMJ*, 23 (October 1911), 1050.

62 *MMJ*, 16 (August 1904), 735; Eugene Debs, *Unionism and Socialism; A Plea for Both* (Terre Haute, Ind., 1904).

63 *MMJ*, 17 (February 1905), 101–3.

64 On the miners' wage cut and Socialist responses, see E. V. Debs in *Social Democratic Herald*, April 7, 1904 and *Chicago Chronicle*, May 12, 1904; Laslett, 205–7. Mitchell had earlier been roundly attacked by the Socialists of West Virginia for his opposition to a sympathetic strike by miners in 1902. Frederick A. Barkey, "The Socialist Party in West Virginia from 1898 to 1920: A Study in Working Class Radicalism" (Unpublished Ph.D. dissertation, University of Pittsburgh, 1971), 38–44.

65 East Moline was later added, changing the name of the group to "Quad Cities."

66 *Tri-City Workers' Magazine* (January 1906), 11–17. Cf. Stephen Thernstrom's treatment of the aspiration to home ownership as a deterrent to class consciousness, *Poverty and Progress: Social Mobility in a Nineteenth Century City* (Cambridge, Mass., 1964), and his modification of the argument in Laslett and Lipset, *Failure*, 522–3.

67 *Tri-City Workers' Magazine* (February 1906), 13–16; (August 1906), 5–7. My description of the arsenal is based on U.S. Congress, House, *Hearings before the Special Committee of the House of Representatives to Investigate the Taylor and other Systems of Shop Management* (Washington, D.C., 1912), 895–922, 1262.

68 Alifas' employment record is reproduced in *The Taylor and other Systems of Shop Management* 1262–4.

69 *Tri-City Workers' Magazine* (September 1906), 6–7. I am indebted to Neil Basen for bringing this magazine to my attention.

70 Debs, *Unionism and Socialism*, 43–4.

71 H. L. Varney, "The Fallacy of Scientific Management," *MMJ*, 24 (January 1912), 22–4.

72 *Tri-City Workers' Magazine* (December 1905), 5; (September 1906), 1–4. The SP's ringing denunciations of dance halls may have made them as obnoxious to many young workers as the local evangelists.

73 Floyd Dell, "Socialists and Kindergartens," ibid., (February 1906), 7–11. The remarkable similarities of these arguments to those of early nineteenth-century bourgeois educational reformers explains the Socialists' consistent lionizing of Horace Mann and contrasts sharply with recent revisionist critics of educational reform. Cf., Michael Katz, *The Irony of Early School Reform: Educational Innovation in Mid-Nineteenth Century Massachusetts* (Cambridge, Mass., 1968).

74 See Barkey, "Socialist Party in West Virginia"; Henry F. Bedford, *Socialism and the Workers in Massachusetts, 1886–1912* (Amherst, Mass., 1966); Bruce M. Stave, ed., *Socialism and the Cities* (Port Washington, N.Y., 1975). See also Kipnis, 198–201, on the composition of party membership (41% craftsmen and 20% laborers in 1908). For the role of workers in nineteenth-century struggles for public sanitation, see Estelle Feinstein, *Stamford in the Gilded Age, 1868–1893* (Stamford, Conn., 1974).

75 O'Hare speech to IAM Lodge 105, Toledo, in *Toledo Evening News*, June 6, 1903. I am grateful to Neil Basen for this item. Karl Kautsky expressed the same fear and contempt of the "slum proletariat," which was constantly replenished by migrants from the countryside, in *The Class Struggle (Erfurt Program)* trans. William E. Bohn (New York, 1971), 168–70.

76 This tendency is analyzed well in William E. Walling, *Socialism As It Is: A Survey of the World-Wide Revolutionary Movement* (New York, 1912), 350 ff.

77 Robert Hunter, *Labor in Politics* (Chicago, 1915), 179.

78 Barkey, "Socialist Party in West Virginia"; Joseph R. Conlin, "The IWW and the Socialist Party," *Science and Society*, 31 (Winter, 1967), 22–36.

79 James Weinstein, *The Decline of Socialism in America, 1912–1925* (New York, 1967), 44, 52.

80 Sally M. Miller, *Victor Berger and the Promise of Constructive Socialism, 1910–1920* (Westport, Conn., 1973), 47–8, 138 n. 12; Hunter, 181–2.

81 Eg., Hunter, 31–45, 105.

82 Socialist Party, *How to Organize a Socialist Local or Branch* (Chicago, n.d.). Copy in R.G. 28, Post Office, Item 529, Box 13, National Archives, Washington, D.C.

83 "The Ideas on Which Socialism Rests: The Cooperative Commonwealth," *Tri-City Workers' Magazine* (December 1905), 13–15. On the Haywood–Moyer–Pettibone case, see ibid., (March 1906), 19 and (May 1906), passim. Cf., Kipnis, 325 ff. who contends that constructive socialists held aloof from the case.

84 Quoted in Kipnis, 237. On left-wing demands for amalgamation and industrial unionism within the IAM, see IAM, *Proceedings Fourteenth Convention*, 90–2, 137; *MMJ*, 17 (December 1905), 1123, 1125–6; Bruno Ramirez, "Collective Bargaining and the Politics of Industrial Relations in the Pro-

gressive Era, 1898–1916" (Unpublished Ph.D. dissertation, University of Toronto, 1975), 192–6.

85 John H. Griffin, *Strikes: A Study in Quantitative Economics* (New York, 1939), 43. For IAM struggles during these years, see *MMJ*, 21 (April 1909), 341–2; *Proceedings Fourteenth Convention*, 17. On strikes in other industries, see Ch. 4.

86 Weinstein, *Decline of Socialism*, 116–17; Laslett, *Labor and the Left*, 161.

87 [Ludwig Lore,] "Progress Backward," *The Class Struggle*, 2 (September–October 1918), 507–12; Kipnis, 336–7; Green, 144–55; Van Tine, 158.

88 Kipnis, 341–3.

89 Green, 343.

90 Foner, *History*, III, 136–60; Van Tine, 113–60.

91 On the United Metal Workers, see Ramirez, 162 ff.; on the Brewery Workers and the New Orleans strike, see the massive record in the AFL Executive Council minutes, January 5, 1907–January 23, 1908 (Mitchell Papers, Box A3-49); on the Boot and Shoe Workers, see Laslett, 83–5.

92 Frank Morrison to John Mitchell, February 21, 1907 (Mitchell Papers, Box A3-49).

93 Van Tine, 158.

94 IAM, *Proceedings Fourteenth Convention*, 94, 109, 159-60, and passim.

95 Hunter, 12–46; Marc Karson, *American Labor Unions and Politics, 1900–1918* (Boston, 1965), 42–89; Graham Adams, Jr., *Age of Industrial Violence, 1910–15: The Activities and Findings of the United States Commissions on Industrial Relations* (New York, 1966), 168–75, 219–26; Elliott Rudwick, *Race Riot at East St. Louis July 2, 1917* (New York, 1972), 7–15; Foner, *History*, III, 335–66.

96 Hunter, 45–96.

97 Paul Kleppner, *The Cross of Culture: A Social Analysis of Midwestern Politics, 1850–1900* (New York, 1970).

98 Advisory Council of the National Civic Federation (Mitchell Papers, Box A3-9); Taft, *AFL*, 334–41; George H. Nash, III, "Charles Stelzle: Apostle to Labor," *Labor History*, 11 (Spring 1970), 151–74. The quotation is from Charles Stelzle to *MMJ*, 19 (May 1907), 455–7. The Protestant campaign against Sunday work in steel was thoroughly reported in the semimonthly periodical *The Survey*.

99 Bedford, 181–219; Kipnis, 268; Daniel DeLeon, *The Vatican in Politics: Ultramontanism* (New York, 1962), 31–4 and passim; Peter E. Dietz, *Social Service: A Summary Review of the Social Position of Catholicism*, 1 no. 1 (1911), 66, 68; Karson, *American Labor and Politics*, 212–84; Karson, "Catholic Anti-Socialism," in Laslett and Lipset, *Failure*, 164–84.

100 Lore, "Progress Backward." See also Karson, "Catholic Anti-Socialism," and the reply by Henry Browne (Laslett and Lipset, *Failure*, 185–94), labelling the Militia of Christ a "one man show" (p. 186); *International Socialist Review*, 14 (January 1914), 414–15. By 1917–18 the alliance between Gompers and the Catholic Actionists had given way to bitter rivalry. See Lore, 510–15; Taft, *AFL*, 346, 362–3.

101 Dietz, 63. See John A. Ryan, *A Living Wage* (Washington, D.C., 1906), 10–19 and passim for a telling attack on the cult of productivity. For its roots in Catholic doctrine, see Pius IX, *Syllabus of Errors*, in *The Papal Encyclicals in Their Historical Context*, Anne Freemantle, ed. (New York, 1956), 135–52.

102 Dietz, 61, 65. For Dietz's early ideas, see Dietz to Mitchell, April 10, 1911; Mitchell to Dietz, April 12, 1911; and passim file no. 108 (Mitchell Papers, Box A3-14). Dietz was roused to come to the 1909 AFL convention by the news that the executive council had passed a resolution protesting the execution of the Spanish anarchist Francisco Ferrer.

103 Ryan, 132. The phrase "reasonable and frugal comfort" was from Pope Leo XIII, *Rerum Novarum* (New York, 1939), 27.

104 Ryan, 133n.

105 Dietz, 64. At the 1894 convention of the AFL many delegates had spontaneously attacked the prospect of state inspection of their homes. AFL, *A Verbatum* [sic] *Report of the Discussion of the Political Programme* (New York, 1895), 21–5.

106 Quoted in Dietz, 64.

107 Mitchell, *The Wage Earner and His Problems* (Washington, D.C., 1913), 129.

108 Vincent A. McQuade, O.S.A., *The American Catholic Attitude on Child Labor since 1891* (Washington, D.C., 1938). See also Aaron Abell, *American Catholicism and Social Action: A Search for Social Justice, 1865–1950* (Garden City, N.Y., 1960); Pope Pius XI, *Quadragessimo Anno* (New York, 1939).

109 James Cardinal Gibbons, "Organized Labor," in *Wages, Hours, and Strikes: Labor Panaceas in the Twentieth Century*, Leon Stein and Philip Taft, eds. (New York, 1969). The quotations are on pp. 23, 18.

110 Miller, 21; *International Socialist Review*, 14 (March 1914), 562–3.

111 Hilaire Belloc, *The Servile State* (London and Edinburgh, 1913). For Belloc's influence on Ryan, see Patrick W. Gearty, *The Economic Thought of Monsignor John A. Ryan* (Washington, D.C., 1953), 271–2. For his influence on British Guild Socialists and shop stewards, see James Hinton, *The First Shop Stewards' Movement* (London, 1973).

112 "Person Case," IAM, *Proceedings, 1916*, 142–4.

113 The voting data used in the analysis to follow is from *MMJ*, 23 (October 1911), 1025–32. Location of the lodges is from ibid., 1085–97. The political loyalties of convention delegates are determined by their votes for members of the convention's committees (laws, credentials, railroads, etc.). Only 2 of the 353 lodges which consistently supported "progressive" candidates had favored O'Connell in the presidential election, and only 13 of the 241 lodges which voted for right wing committee members had supported Johnston in that election. IAM, *Proceedings, 1911*.

114 See Wayne Roberts, "Toronto Metal Workers and the Second Industrial Revolution, 1889–1914," forthcoming in *Labour/Le Travailleur*; Robert H. Babcock, *Gompers in Canada: A Study in American Continentalism before the First World War* (Toronto, 1974), 126–33; M-Ludovic Maltais, *Les Syndicats catholiques canadiens* (Washington, 1925).

115 See p. 107–8.

116 Weinstein, *Corporate Ideal*; Wiebe, *Businessmen and Reform*; Kolko, *Main Currents*; Ramierez, "Collective Bargaining"; and especially Ronald Radosh, "The Corporate Ideology of American Labor Leaders from Gompers to Hillman," *Studies on the Left*, 6 (November–December 1966), 66–88.

4. The "new unionism" and the transformation of workers' consciousness in America, 1909–22

André Tridon, correspondent of *La Bataille Syndicaliste* in the United States, had little concern for theoretical debates among syndicalists, industrialists, Socialists and "pure and simple" unionists. The "New Unionism," said he, "is the practice which will enable the workers to assume as a return for their labor the full control of the various industries."[1] This emphasis on practice and control suggests that syndicalist tendencies among American workers may have reached far beyond the limited influence of the Industrial Workers of the World, and that the customary image of the IWW as representing conduct and aspirations far removed from the "mainstream" of American labor development may be misleading. To test these implications of Tridon's view this essay will first examine the patterns of working-class behavior in the years 1909 to 1922, then explore the causes of that behavior. Along the way it will try to shed some light on the question widely voiced in "Wobbly" circles in 1911: "Why don't the IWW grow?"

The IWW was born just as a massive upsurge in trade union strength had been brought to an abrupt halt. Between 1898 and 1903 the American economy had enjoyed an extraordinary boom resulting from the reconstruction of urban commercial centers with reinforced concrete and structural steel, the emergence of a host of new industries based on products and processes created in research laboratories of the previous decade, ranging from chemicals to electrical machinery, and an extensive quest for the resources of the tropical world, the value of which was largely revealed by those laboratories. In this setting financial houses sponsored mergers among competing manufacturing firms, which gave birth to most of the twentieth century's leading corporations. The same upsurge generated so strong a demand for labor that skilled workmen had been able to force General Electric, U.S. Steel, International Harvester, the Morgan interests in anthracite and the Big Four meat packers of Chicago, not to mention the smaller employers of the building trades, machine tool industry, boot and shoe manufacture and northern textiles, to deal at least momentarily with numerous craft unions.

The economic downturn of 1903–4 changed this situation dramatically. The great steel corporation, having seriously limited union influence in the 1901 strike, began to pick off union outposts in the South, and Great Lakes shipping and bridge erection, in preparation for dealing the coup de grace to all unions within its writ in 1909. Harvester and the meat packers disposed of union annoyance in 1904, and eastern metal working shops began universally to ignore the rules of the machinists' union and to substitute handymen and specialists for journeymen.[2] Outside the metropolitan centers of the land, all unionism but that of miners was "stopped in its tracks"[3] by Citizens' Alliances and other mobilizations of the local middle classes sponsored by employers' associations to rid their communities of strikes and union restrictions on production.

But the craft unions, checked at flood tide by an aroused Babbittry, had already been tamed in their own conduct by the bitter social conflicts of the 1890s. The quest for binding trade agreements to secure their industrial positions had induced their leaders to suppress sympathy strikes, which had been the mainspring of their growth in earlier decades. Most unions, furthermore, had come to rely on the union label as their primary organizing instrument. By bestowing labels on companies with which they signed agreements, union leaders offered employers a talisman to promote their sales in working-class markets (as with overalls, beer or machinists' instruments) or to distinguish wares of high quality from mass produced articles (as with cigars or shoes). "The union label," observed Brewery Workers' editor W. E. Trautmann, "is practically the manufacturers' label."[4]

It was such unionism which roused the ire of the men and women who assembled in July 1905 to found the IWW. Agreeing that "trade lines have been swallowed up in a common servitude of all workers to the machines which they tend,"[5] the delegates decided to organize workers from the bottom up, enlisting first the unskilled and using their enthusiasm and power to pull the more highly skilled workers into action. This meant that the IWW had to replace the craft unions' meticulous caution with dramatic tactics. It would scorn large strike funds, relying instead on mass appeals for aid, on the workers' own spirit of sacrifice and on short strikes. It would reject all reliance on negotiations, labels, written contracts, trade autonomy and benefit funds, and it would summon the workers to leave the decrepit "American Separation of Labor" and enlist in the new revolutionary union.[6]

In the ensuing four or five years little came of these great hopes. The IWW seemed determined to devour itself in internecine bickering. Leaders of the AFL union which had borne the most intense raids from the IWW, the Machinists, could assure their members by the end of 1906 that the rival organization had reached the end of its career. What "went up like a rocket," they crowed, "came down like a stick."[7] In fact, the most massive struggle of the period, set off in 1907 when thirty-six unions of the New Orleans Dock and Cotton Council closed the port of the Crescent City to help the Brewery Workers challenge a jurisdictional award of the AFL, had borne many attributes of an IWW battle – a general strike based on the power of the "unskilled," Black–White unity explicitly and decisively asserted, Marxist leadership and bitter worker hostility to the AFL – but the Wobblies had played no greater part in it than the organization of some support meetings.[8]

Strike decade

Despite its peculiar attributes of being set in the deep South and engaging strikers more against the AFL than against capital, the New Orleans strike did portend things to come. In the last quarter of 1907 the economy was struck by a crisis of such severity that the average level of unemployment for the ensuing year was 16.4 percent of the nation's nonfarm employees.[9] Then between July 1909 and the summer of 1910 the economy revived vigorously, before sinking back into the doldrums for all of 1911. With the upturn came the beginning of a decade of strikes of unprecedented scale and continuity.

In New York a militant nucleus of workers enrolled in the Ladies Garment Workers broke sharply with the union label tradition by calling general strikes, first of the city's entire shirtwaist industry then of cloak and suit manufacture. Strikers at the Pressed Steel Car Company near Pittsburgh called in IWW organizers to assist them. The great armaments works of Bethlehem Steel was brought to a halt when blast furnace laborers quit work in sympathy with machinists, who had struck to protest Sunday work.[10]

In Philadelphia, efforts by the city government to break the streetcarmen's union provoked in quick succession a strike of motormen, violent crowd action against scabs, which saw 298 cars wrecked and more than 500 people arrested, a sympathy stoppage which spread from the knitting mills of the Kensington district across the city, and ultimately a general strike involving 146 thousand workers at its peak and directed by the AFL's Central Labor Union for twenty days.[11] The Socialist editors of the *New York Call* saw in this upsurge a challenge to the established practices of the union movement and the electoral orientation of their party alike:

> Such strikes as that of McKees Rocks, the shirtwaist makers' strike of this city, and now the Philadelphia strike are witnesses of the incapacity of the conservative and "constructive" labor leaders, as well as of the fighting spirit which animates the working masses . . . The working masses are just as ready to fight the capitalists by means of the strike as by means of the ballot.[12]

The direct, mass-involvement challenge to managerial authority and contempt for accepted AFL practice workers exhibited in 1909–10 were to remain the outstanding characteristics of American labor struggles, not episodically but continuously for the next dozen years. That most large strikes of the epoch ended in total defeat for the workers testifies both to the audacity of the strikers' pretentions and to their willingness to act in defiance of warnings from experienced union leaders that chances of victory were slim. In fact, large-scale strikes erupted whenever the level of unemployment fell off sufficiently to give the strikers a ghost of a chance of success. The critical level of unemployment seems to have been as high as nine percent of the nonfarm labor force. At any jobless rate below that level, the ratio of strikers to industrial workers shot up.[13]

From mid-1910 until the first quarter of 1912, however, the economy sagged consistently and unemployment rose above the 13 percent mark, despite a short-lived false recovery early in 1911. Major strikes were few, though one of them, that of the shopmen on the Illinois Central Railroad, was to be a major landmark in the history of American syndicalism. No great strikes were staged against wage reductions, largely because major corporations followed the lead of U.S. Steel in scrupulously avoiding wage cuts. They sought rather to reduce unit costs of production by the widespread promotion of new efficiency schemes and to capitalize on heavy unemployment by "the weeding out of the less efficient workman."[14] Socialist party votes surged upward and party members captured leading positions in the Machinists and the Mine Workers, but direct action in basic industry was at a minimum.[15]

Even before the first clear signs of revival in 1912, the woolen mills of Lawrence were closed by the IWW's famous strike against one group of companies which had assumed that the state of the labor market would allow them to reduce wages (in conjunction with a small reduction of hours mandated by law). The textile workers' revolt spread across New England and New Jersey during the ensuing eighteen months, focusing its fire increasingly on the new stretch-out and premium pay schemes.

By April 1913, *Iron Age* complained that the country was gripped by an "epidemic of strikes."[16] Most of the walkouts were brief, spontaneous, and local and were sparked by unskilled workers, like those at Studebaker and Firestone Rubber. Republic Steel avoided trouble by raising its common labor rate for the first time since May 1910 from seventeen cents to nineteen and a half cents an hour. In New York the most wretchedly paid garment workers, the ten thousand women who sewed kimonos, wrappers, and other "white goods," staged a fierce and successful strike for union recognition.[17]

By the end of 1913 both the prosperity and the workers' militancy had subsided. *Iron Age* commented that "a year of blight" had opened with the "most buoyant activity ever known," and closed in an atmosphere of business uncertainty.[18] Unemployment stood at brutally high levels for a year and a half, and strikes were largely confined to long-unionized sectors, such as coal mines and the building trades.

Then came the Allies' war orders, and with them all economic inhibitions to direct action were removed. The "munitions strikes," as they were called by the U.S. Bureau of Labor Statistics, swept out of New England across the whole northeastern part of the country in the hot summer of 1915. Metal trades replaced building trades as the most strike-prone occupations. Small and middling-sized towns, the scene of the Open Shop Drive's earlier triumph, replaced big cities as the location of most work stoppages. Moreover, of the 179 strikes of machinists recorded for 1915, only 43 had union support.[19] In the ten-day closing of the whole complex of firms controlled by Westinghouse in the East Pittsburth area, the Machinists and other AFL unions were repudiated by the forty-thousand strikers, despite the fact that the tumultuous strike had been initiated by tool and die makers. The most prominent spokesmen of the strikers had Socialist party, Socialist Labor party, and IWW affiliations.[20]

Despite the uneven impact of the war orders on the economy and the persistence of serious unemployment through 1916, the strike fever spread to many other industries. For the seven years following 1915, the ratio of strikers to all industrial and service employees remained constantly on a par with the more famous strike years of 1934 and 1937. The declaration of war had only a minor impact on this militancy. In each year of American participation more than a million workers struck, more, that is, than had ever struck in any year before 1915. The soaring cost of food, and especially government orders diluting wheat flour with corn meal, added fuel to the fire. Food riots flared in March 1917, when New York women attacked grocery stores and marched on the Waldorf-Astoria Hotel demanding bread. In Philadelphia troops killed one woman and wounded nine others, breaking their occupation of the city's market place.[21]

The 6,205 recorded strikes between April 6, 1917 and November 11, 1918 tended to be short and took on an outlaw quality more than ever in the face of the AFL's official pledge not to strike. With unemployment down to 1.4 percent, workers improved their incomes as much by moving from job to job as they did by striking. It was common for workers to accept six to eight jobs in a single day of searching, then to report to the most promising one. An annual factory turnover rate "of 1,600 to 2,000 percent was by no means phenomenal," observed Professor L. C. Marshall.[22] On the other hand, the most ambitious claims of workers, the 8-hour day and control over their conditions of work, could not be obtained by individual action. They provoked the most intense, and the most chronic, collective conflicts.

The second decade of the twentieth century was the decisive period in the battle for the 8-hour day, which American workers had been waging since the 1860s. At the start of the decade only 8 percent of the country's workers had regular schedules of 48 hours a week or less. Almost 70 percent of them worked more than 54 hours weekly. By 1919, however, 48.6 percent had the 48-hour week, and less than 26 percent still put in more than 54 hours.[23] The machinists of Trenton, whose strike for a 9-hour day in 1914 had been drowned in the unemployed of Philadelphia, shut their city's machine shops for three months at the end of 1915 to demand an 8-hour day. When their employers yielded to the union, they found "practically all" of the strikers had found jobs elsewhere.[24] According to the National War Labor Board, 1,026,703 workers had achieved the 8-hour day between 1915 and 1917 alone, before the board instituted its "basic 8-hour day." Most dramatic of all was the accomplishment of the silk, cotton and woolen mill hands of the North. In 1910 the state of Massachusetts had legislated a 58-hour week for textile workers, the first reduction since the law of 1874 had established the 60-hour week. Nine years later the 48-hour week was the norm in all three industries.[25]

Such gains cannot be understood simply as the logical fruit of technological progress and rising productivity. In fact, there is evidence to suggest both that output per man-hour declined during the war years and that some restoration of longer hours accompanied rising productivity in the twenties.[26] A survey by the National Industrial Conference Board of five major industries in 1919 and 1920 found employers overwhelmingly

Table 2. *Strike trends in the United States, 1900–25*

Year	Strikes and lockouts (1)	Workers involved (000) (2)	Strikers as % of all workers (3)	Index of control strikes (4)	Unemployed as % of nonfarm employees (5)
1900	1,899	568	4.9	182	12.6
1901	3,012	564	4.7	320	10.1
1902	3,240	692	5.6	328	8.6
1903	3,648	788	6.2	375	9.0
1904	2,419	574	4.3	296	12.0
1905	2,186	302	2.2	249	9.5
1906	629[a]	74[b]	5.1[b]	—	3.0
1907	680[a]	94[b]	6.3[b]	—	6.0
1908	315[a]	28[b]	1.9[b]	—	16.4
1909	452[a]	65[b]	4.1[b]	—	11.6
1910	604[a]	218[a]	11.4[a]	—	11.6
1911	511[a]	112[a]	5.8[a]	—	13.0
1912	575[a]	138[a]	7.0[a]	—	9.0
1913	567[c]	337[c]	24.4[c]	—	8.2
1914	1,204	—	—	81	14.7
1915	1,593	640	3.7	109	15.6
1916	3.789	1,600	9.2	225	9.1
1917	4,450	1,227	6.9	312	8.2
1918	3,353	1,240	6.8	220	2.4
1919	3,630	4,160	22.5	269	2.4
1920	3,411	1,463	7.8	214	8.6
1921	2,385	1,099	5.7	144	19.5
1922	1,112	1,613	8.3	93	11.4
1923	1,553	757	3.8	150	4.1
1924	1,249	655	3.3	121	8.3
1925	1,301	428	2.1	133	5.4

Notes: [a] Massachusetts, New York and New Jersey figures. [b] Massachusetts and New York only. [c] New York and New Jersey only.

Sources: The number of strikes and lockouts (1) and the number of workers involved (2) are from Florence Peterson, *Strikes in the United States, 1880–1936* (U.S. Department of Labor, Bulletin No. 651), 21; U.S. Bureau of the Census, *Historical Statistics of the United States, Colonial Times to 1957* (Washington, D.C. 1960), 99; Massachusetts Bureau of Statistics of Labor, *Reports, 1901–16*; New York Department of Labor, *Bulletin No. 66* (November, 1914); New Jersey Bureau of Industrial Statistics, *Reports, 1901–16*; U.S. Census Bureau, *Census of Manufacturers, 1914 Abstract* and *Census of Manufactures, 1919 Abstract*. No strike data was gathered by the federal government from 1906 through 1914.

The number of "all workers" on which column (3) is based is the number of "manual and service workers" minus the number of "private household workers," from *Historical Statistics,* 74. Annual figures were estimated from the decade figures of the census.

The index of control (4) is the ratio of the total number of strikes each year for recognition, union rules, sympathy and miscellaneous, to the number of such strikes in 1886, taken as 100. The data used is from Peterson, 33, 39.

Figures on unemployment (5) are from Stanley Lebergott, *Manpower in Economic Growth* (New York, 1964), 512.

of the opinion that the more mechanized an industry was, the more *difficult* it was for employers to compensate for reduction of hours by increases in hourly output, and consequently the greater the resistance of employers to such reductions.[27] Certainly the intense opposition of metal trades firms to demands for the 8-hour day in the strikes of 1916 (when some 600 strikes were called on May 1 alone) indicated their full agreement with the editorial resolve of *Iron Age*, "that the unparalleled situation which has made victory in Europe turn not only upon sheer tonnage in steel projectiles, but upon the metal-cutting capacity of American machine tools, must not be allowed to settle for years to come so important an issue as the 8-hour machine shop day."[28]

Control strikes

Every bit as provocative of conflict as the battle for the 8-hour day, but far less richly rewarded in long-term effects, was the effort by workers to establish collective control over their conditions of work. A measure of control struggles other than those for eight hours may be constructed by lumping together such strike issues as enforcement of work rules, union recognition, discharge of unpopular foremen or retention of popular ones, regulation of layoffs or dismissals, and actions of sympathy with other groups of workers. An index of the frequency of these control strikes since 1881 reveals that they became especially prominent in three periods: 1901–4, 1916–20, and 1934–41.[29]

The control strikes of 1901–4 basically involved the titanic and mostly unsuccessful effort of the craft unions to secure a firm hold within the congealing struture of monopoly capitalism. Many similar efforts appeared in the 1916–20 period, when unions like the United Brotherhood of Carpenters and Joiners and the International Association of Machinists took advantage of the buoyant labor market to renew their efforts to operate in the old way. Much more distinctive and significant were the extensive efforts of workers both inside and outside the old unions to exert new forms of collective control. Even the recognition struggles of older unions, however, could trigger new forms of struggle. Five city-wide general strikes plagued the government between September 1917 and April 1918: in Springfield, Illinois; Kansas City, Missouri; Waco, Texas; and two in Billings, Montana. The Billings strikes were called to aid embattled building tradesmen; Kansas City's was to help laundry workers, and the others were in support of streetcar motormen and conductors.[30]

In the four years following the armistice, control strikes persisted at high levels, while the phrase "workers' control," seldom heard before that time, became a popular catchword throughout the labor movement. Union membership in the United States was two and a half times the level of 1910, an increase not far below the threefold rise for the world's twenty leading industrial nations as a whole.[31] The Machinists union alone had grown from 54,000 members under predominantly conservative leadership in 1910 to 331,450 members under a Socialist administration by 1919.[32] Both the United Mine Workers, now over 400 thousand strong, and the increasingly unified coalition of sixteen unions among the 1.85 million railway workers had committed themselves officially to immediate nationalization of their particular industries, with future direction to be shared by the employees and consumer groups. When the railroad brotherhoods and shopcraft unions tested the sentiment of their members on the so-called Plumb Plan in 1920, 90 percent of the workers voting favored a strike to make congress enact the nationalization scheme.[33]

Among the 4,160,348 workers who participated in strikes in 1919 every conceivable type of demand was raised: wage increases to catch the soaring cost of living, reductions of hours to forty-four a week in the needle trades and forty in metropolitan building trades, recognition of unions and shop committees, joint negotiation with councils of related unions in particular plants, ship-yards or communities, defiance of governmental decrees and, on July 4–9, freedom for Tom Mooney. In Seattle the committee directing the city's general strike declared:

Labor will not only SHUT DOWN the industries, but Labor will REOPEN, under the management of the appropriate trades, such activities as are needed to preserve public health and public peace. If the strike continues, Labor may feel led to avoid public suffering by reopening more and more activities.
UNDER ITS OWN MANAGEMENT.
And that is why we say we are starting on a road that leads – NO ONE KNOWS WHERE![34]

The new mood among workers shattered the Socialist party and subjected the AFL to extreme stress. As J. B. S. Hardman noted: "the war emphasized the power of money, of industry, the significance of leadership, of direct action. And the Socialist party had nothing to offer but advice to use the franchise intelligently."[35] Samuel Gompers, in turn, organized an "All-American" committee of labor leaders to stage rallies against "bolshevism, I.W.W.ism and red flagism in general."[36] Editorially he warned his flock: "History records few ideas more tragic and fantastic than the idea of government by direct action . . . The strike itself is a weapon too sacred and too valuable to be used for any other than its legitimate purpose."[37]

In 1920, consequently, 7.4 percent of the strikes and 58 percent of the strikers were without union sanction. The insurgent strike of 60 thousand Illinois coal miners and another of 25 thousand railroad switchmen were the best known of these conflicts.[38] They also marked a return to the center of the American labor scene of the alliance of railroad workers and coal miners which had been the germ of most nineteenth-century mass strikes.[39] But the upward spiral of unemployment, starting in the summer of 1920 and rising to 20 percent through 1921, put a damper on this insurgent behavior.

The main thrust of official union efforts during the 1921–2 depression was to preserve contracts and work rules, even at the expense of wage reductions.[40] Workers, in turn, tended to close ranks around their organizations and hence to strengthen the hand of incumbent leaders. In 1922 less than one-tenth of one percent of the 1.613 million strikers were out without union authorization. Yet the year began with almost forty thousand packing house workers on strike and progressed to a summertime state of war in American basic industries. The strikes were not numerous, but they were huge, protracted, desperate battles. Fully 400 thousand railroad shopmen, 600 thousand coal miners and 60 thousand textile workers struck in vain attempts to preserve union organization against the employers' American Plan offensive.[41]

In summary, then, direct action had been, not the exclusive property of the IWW, but the main theme of a dozen years of fierce class conflict in America. During those years a secondary theme of workers' control had recurred incessantly and become increasingly explicit. It is small wonder, therefore, that avowedly syndicalist groupings of workers were numerous, some of them inside the AFL. The Cloth Hat and Cap Makers and the Sheet Metal Workers of New York put no faith in trade agreements or union labels and bestowed absolute power on shop committees, co-ordinated by executive boards of avowed revolutionaries.[42] The Jewelry Workers, sparked by an alliance of Jewish Socialists and Italian syndicalists, boasted their shop autonomy and the direct action which had won them a 44-hour week as early as 1916.[43] Another Italian–Jewish axis gave similar orientation to the local of the Structural Iron Workers which dealt with New York's ornamental iron shops.[44]

All these unions were made up of skilled craftsmen and dealt with very small employers. A Parisian syndicalist would have understood them well.[45] But all of them stood outside the world of modern large-scale industry, where the direct action currents of these twelve years were concentrated. The more significant appearance of New Unionism *within* basic industry was attributed by Vice-President P. J. Conlon of the Machinists to the spread of new managerial practices which, he claimed, stimulated a response of "sabotage, syndicalism, [and] passive resistance" on the workers' part. "We did not hear of any of these things," he argued, "until we heard of scientific management and new methods of production."[46]

Conlon's view merits careful examination because American manufacturing had, in fact, been drastically transformed since the 1890s not only in its financial structure and market relationships by the consolidation of competing firms and the formation of ubiquitous trade associations, but also in the internal organization of the production process itself. The cutting edge of the internal reform was described by Frederick Winslow Taylor as "the deliberate gathering in on the part of those on management's side of all of the great mass of traditional knowledge, which in the past has been in the heads of the workmen, and in the physical skill and knack of the workman, which he has acquired through years of experience."[47]

Worker response to "rationalized industry"

Although the particulars of the process varied substantially from one industry to another, employers in every major industry sought to develop an engineering staff, academically educated for its new role, which could plan and direct the flow of production on the basis of systematic research in both the properties of materials used in production and the logical sequence of productive operations, then assign each worker a very specific task in that sequence, based on time and motion studies, and finally, induce the worker to perform that task as assigned by a carefully structured system of incentive payments. By this innovation, the power of the craftsmen which had rested on their superior knowledge of their work relative to their employers was undermined, and the traditional dualism of craftsmen operating the machinery while laborers fetched and carried was remodeled into a continuum of specialized machine tenders performing functions which required only minor variations in training and agility, and all of which were directly under the detailed supervision of a swarm of managerial officials.[48]

Three important consequences for workers flowed from the combination of corporate consolidation and the adoption of new efficiency schemes. The first was the divorce between the technical and social systems of control in the factory, which Roethlisberger and Dickson were to discover in the famous Hawthorne experiments.[49] Some degree of worker restriction of output remained, but on a guerrilla basis – as defiance of management's will and instructions, as sabotage. The small informal work group persisted, not as an agency of explicit control, as it had been under craft unionism, but as a submerged, impenetrable obstacle to management's sovereignty. The steel mill laborers of Whiting William's gang had "not the slightest interest in what [their work] means or how it affects the operations of the mill around them . . . It is all just a matter of doing as little work as the boss will allow." Their favorite saying was, "what the hell!"[50]

Secondly, the more thoroughly business rationalized itself, the more extreme became the chaos of working-class life. Even the frail safeguards of employment stability that union rules and standard rates had represented were swept away, while the urgent need of heavily capitalized corporations to operate only at full capacity made job tenure increasingly spasmodic for many workers. Hence weavers could be ordered to run twelve looms in place of eight because, "there's plenty waitin' at the gates for our jobs."[51] Henry Ford could enforce any tempo of work he wished because, when he announced the famous five-dollar day in January 1914, ten thousand men rioted at the plant gates, fighting each other for the jobs.[52] At a national conference on unemployment that year, the secretary of the Chicago Unemployment Commission reported that conditions were no worse than usual. That was the tragedy, he continued, unemployment was now chronic and endemic to the economy.[53] The typical unemployed male, a conference the next year concluded, was neither the casual laborer nor the craftsman, but the specialist, whom scientific management had spawned. In New York only 21 percent of the unemployed had been in the United States fewer than five years. Fifty-five percent of them had been here more than ten years.[54] The jobless were not marginal men, but an indispensible part of "rationalized" industry.

Third, the oligopolistic power of the new corporation provided it with a new capacity to administer prices on the basis of long-range planning for company development. Simultaneously, the rapid growth of the urban population reversed the nineteenth-century trend of constantly falling food prices. These two factors contributed to an upward drift in the cost of living, which averaged 2.4 percent annually from 1896 through 1912. With the coming of the war the rate of increase soared upward.[55] As a result, even though major corporations increasingly adhered to a policy of maintaining stable wages through crisis periods, thus avoiding mass revolts against wage cuts, real earnings were, in fact, constantly falling.

Every period of relatively full employment, therefore, was marked by strikes of lower paid workers over wages.

The combined impact of these three developments generated two distinct currents of working-class struggle, which often tended to fuse during and after the war years: one arising from the craftsmen and the other from operatives and laborers. The more skilled workers took advantage of every period of low unemployment to attack certain elements of the new managerial methods directly. During the war they mounted a widespread revolt against premium pay systems, dilution of skills and the stop watch, especially in metal-working plants where, Taylor had boasted, little overt protest had greeted the introduction of those devices.[56] Anxious to maintain uninterrupted war production, the National War Labor Board had even agreed to the abolition of incentive pay systems in some large companies, at the very time top AFL leaders were consummating their celebrated reconciliation with the Taylor Society.[57] Numerous strikes for job classifications with standard rates directly challenged the individualized wage rates which employers had come to believe were inevitable reflections of the variety of machine tending tasks and necessary inducements to individual exertion. The board consistently refused to support such sweeping changes in company practices as the demand for classifications entailed.

Furthermore, the enormous expansion of tool room work which attended the shift from the use of all-around machinists to specialized operators in metal works made the manufacture of jigs and fixtures itself a production line function, carried on in large plants by hundreds of men, who were called tool makers but who had very heterogeneous work assignments and earnings (ranging from thirty-eight to ninety cents per hour). Consequently in the munitions strikes the "tool makers" were the stormy petrels. Their demand for a standard tool room rate was the most difficult issue for government agencies to mediate. Ostensibly a wage demand, it challenged the basic fabric of the new managerial methods.

Bridgeport, Connecticut, where some 120 local firms subcontracted for the Remington Arms Company, which directly employed fifteen thousand men and women in a twenty-one building plant erected in the first eight months of 1915, was a seething cauldron of such conflicts from the summer of 1915 onward. Strikes for the 8-hour day, wage increases and overtime pay, abolition of premiums, equal pay regardless of sex on all jobs where women were substituted for craftsmen, an end to discrimination and intimidation against union members, secure draft deferments and recognition of shop committees were endemic to this boom town.

The preeminence of tool makers in these actions brought the city's District 55 of the IAM under the leadership of an erstwhile Wobbly, Samuel Lavit, and his radical colleagues. The refusal of the National War Labor Board to uphold their demand for seven standardized job classifications (where there were more than 250 known wage rates) provoked a total strike at Remington and most contractors in September 1918 that was broken only when President Wilson personally ordered all who failed to return to work barred from any war employment for a year. A city-wide council of shop delegates, created by the government to ease the crisis atmosphere, quickly fell under the leadership of Lavit, and was repudiated by the employers. By January 1919 when the local machinists staged rallies against layoffs, their leaders cast off the nonpolitical guise they had carefully assumed through America's participation in the fighting. Louise Bryant, just returned from Russia with John Reed, was the featured speaker, and union petitions demanded "co-operative ownership and democratic management of industry."[58]

The Bridgeport struggles, with their clear emphasis on control questions, were led by skilled workers, in fact by a craft union (the IAM). The second current of workers' activity, however, that which arose from laborers and operatives, was prompted primarily by wage questions, that is to say, by the rising cost of living. The resistance of these workers to speedup and management's authority tended to take the form of continuous, covert, self-organization by small informal groups at work.[59] On the other hand, the very occurrence of strikes among them shattered the myth of immigrant docility and revealed that the new industrial discipline had promoted a sense of raw injustice and common cause among, as well as within, the various ethnic communities of foreign born. The experience of immigrant machine tenders, furthermore, made both the craft divisions of the AFL and its traditional commitment to self-help appear ludicrous.[60]

Consequently, revolts of immigrant operatives offered a fertile field for the work of revolutionary activists, provided those activists could circumvent the Socialist Party's official fixation on electoral activity.[61] The mass picketing and endless succession of huge rallies which characterized such strikes lent themselves to an energizing sense of collective power and invited revolutionary rhetoric. When, for example, two thousand Lithuanians, Poles, and Hungarians walked out of the pipe threading, finishing and furnace departments of National Tube in Pittsburgh in 1912, the leadership of their daily meetings and parades quickly fell to Fred Merrick, a local Socialist journalist, and several of his party comrades. More than a thousand strikers marched across a bridge over the Monongahela to stand outside the company office, while Merrick and their committee negotiated the settlement.[62]

As this pattern of action recurred time and again, some well-tested and charismatic radicals became veritable folk heroes: William Z. Foster, William D. Haywood, Arturo Giovanitti and especially Carlo Tresca, one man who actually incarnated the conservative's fantasy of the agitator who could start an uprising with a speech. During the strikes of immigrants local authorities went to extraordinary lengths to exclude such men from the mill towns and to dominate the mass meetings themselves. In Ipswich, Massachusetts, the local citizens of standing mobilized vigilante forces to control rallies of Greek and Polish cotton-mill strikers in 1913, jailed all the Socialist and Wobbly activists who came to town and lured native workmen back to their jobs with patriotic appeals. In the strike of Bayonne oil refinery workers, Sheriff Kinkead literally seized command, first by flamboyantly jailing eighty Bergoff detectives and the company superintendent on riot charges to gain credibility with the strikers while his deputies discretely lured Frank Tannenbaum and other Wobblies onto company property, beat them brutally and expelled them from town, then persuaded a mass meeting to accept a settlement he had worked out with Standard Oil.[63] In Passaic in 1919 police officers sat on the platform and censored speeches, while a representative of the Department of Labor denounced the strike leaders sent by the Amalgamated Clothing Workers and cajoled strikers into the AFL. When Anthony Capraro, a leader of the 1919 Lawrence strike, succeeded in smuggling Tresca into the city past the police dragnet, the police retaliated by taking Capraro into the countryside and beating him within an inch of his life.[64]

Such repression, however, does not provide a sufficient explanation of the IWW's failure to grow apace with the rising militancy of industrial workers. Parodoxically, the greater the scope and intensity of struggles in the Northeast grew, the more exclusively the IWW's attention became riveted on timber and agricultural workers of the South and West. Conversely, individual Wobblies of industrial areas collaborated ever more closely with mill town locals of the Socialist Party, which were charting their own courses in direct action without guidance (or even in the face of hostility) from their party's national executive.[65]

Two reasons for the small role of the IWW as such in the New Unionism suggest themselves. First, it became increasingly apparent that the immigrant machine tenders wanted something more from their organization than oratory and strike leadership. As their aspirations to regulate working conditions and shorten hours grew stronger, their desire for durable, open, recognized unions grew with them. The enthusiastic responses of immigrant packing house workers and steel workers to William Z. Foster's organizing committees revealed this desire clearly.[66] The steady growth of the language federations of the Socialist Party, from 15,340 members in 1912 to 23,000 in 1915 and 56,680 by 1919 and the great effectiveness of the Ladies Garment Workers among Jews in New York and of the United Shoe Workers among Italians in Lynn and Poles in Chicago – both unions being led by militant Socialists – bore testimony to the appeal of revolutionary leadership coupled with business-like organization among foreign-born workers.[67] After 1916, however, the lodestone of the leftward movement among immigrants clearly became the Amalgamated Clothing Workers. So effective was the fusion of Jewish and Italian workers on which that union and its satellite, the Amalgamated Textile Workers, rested that by 1919 even Giovanitti and Tresca had put the IWW behind them and were devoting all their energies to the Amalgamated.[68]

Second, the contempt of the Wobblies for craft unions all too easily became contempt for the more skilled workers. "I do not care the snap of my finger whether or not the skilled workman joins this industrial movement," Haywood had said in 1905. "When we get the unorganized and unskilled laborer into this organization, the skilled worker will of necessity come here for his own protection."[69] This contempt in turn explains the absence of any reference to "workers' control" at the founding convention of the IWW, aside from the recurring theme that under socialism workers would assume direct management of their industries.[70] As the munitions strikes revealed, fights for the deliberate collective regulation of production were most likely to arise from the ranks of workers who had exercised such regulation in the memorable past, that is, from craftsmen. Despite the fact that the progress of scientific management had ruled out the possibility of their restoring control in its traditional form (the journeyman machinist, pledged to union rules, making the product his way), the machinists of Bridgeport had formulated by the summer of 1918 their own clear alternative to the way management directed the factories: a plan based on the 8-hour day, standard job classifications, and shop committees energized by a militant machinists' union. This counterplan, distilled from countless strike meetings, provided the substance behind the rhetoric of their 1919 appeal for "collective participation of the workers in the control of the industry."[71] Without such widely shared aspirations and collectively formulated plans, Louis Fraina had argued six years earlier, syndicalism easily degenerates into a "slavery to means," a fixation on militant tactics, or even a cult of violence.[72]

The potential significance of craftsmen's struggles had been grasped, however, by the North American Syndicalist League, and the shopmen of the Illinois Central Railroad and Harriman lines provided their favorite case in point. These workers had been noted both for the prevalence of Socialist politics among them and for their craft exclusiveness. Their lodges cast overwhelming votes at the 1903 IAM convention for resolutions favoring the cooperative commonwealth and against resolutions to admit handymen to the union.[73] Here were political Socialists of the type any good syndicalist would mock. Yet in 1911, the very year the bloc of Socialist Party candidates swept the elections for top offices in the IAM, these shopmen launched a strike which was to last for four years and pit them as insurgents against the union's new leaders.

The spur was the spread of time study and incentive pay to railroad car shops, which had long been strongholds of traditional unionism. When organized craftsmen in the Illinois Central's two largest shops (Chicago and Paducah, Kentucky) observed new timecards and stopwatches appearing around them, they began on their own initiative to protest to local superintendents through joint committees of the several trades. Meeting top-level resistance from the railroad, the shopmen convened an unofficial meeting in Memphis, where they formed a "system federation" to speak jointly for locals of the machinists, steamfitters, carmen, sheet-metal workers, boilermakers, blacksmiths, painters, laborers and (cruelest blow of all to the company) clerks.

A parallel movement spread out of Kansas City along the Union Pacific and other lines controlled by the Harriman interests, which the Illinois Central linked to Chicago and New Orleans. Together the new systems federations demanded the abolition of premium pay schemes, time study, personnel records, and dilution of skills. When the railroads involved refused to deal with the unions except through the separate national offices of the different crafts, as they had done in the past, the federations called a strike of more than sixteen thousand workers, to which the seven national unions gave reluctant support.[74]

The railroads deluged the strikers with injunctions and drew strikebreakers from the heavy ranks of unemployed, and from the "clerks, druggists, soldiers, street car drivers, motormen . . . [and] young men that wanted to learn a trade," in towns along their lines.[75] Gunplay blazed around the tracks and shops for four years, 553 strikers were jailed and

1,069 lost their homes before the unions officially called off the strike, over the angry protests of its leaders.[76] Subsequently Illinois Central executives complained that clerks who had returned to work showed a marked aptitude "in removing and concealing records, in removing cards from cars, and in exchanging cards on cars so that the utmost confusion resulted from their action."[77]

The strike had revealed a readiness among some craft unionists of long standing to fuse all grades of workers in open confrontation with scientific management. William Z. Foster of the newly established Syndicalist League used the strike to illustrate the foolishness of the IWW's dual unionism and the significance of a "militant minority" among unionized workmen. Max Dezettel, James Cannon and Earl Browder were three of the league's supporters in Kansas City, a storm center of the conflict and the cradle of the Communist Party in the West.[78] The strikers themselves pushed their unions into a convention at Kansas City in 1912, where they created a Federation of Federations to coordinate the efforts of all railway shopmen and to agitate for a general strike over the whole western railroad district.[79]

In short, both the control struggles of skilled workers and the wage strikes of laborers and machine tenders had opened new vistas to millions of workers by 1920. In fact, the basic challenges to which employers responded with the American Plan were those of preventing the convergence of the two currents of working-class activity and defusing control demands with an appearance of worker participation in management. But the transformation of consciousness which generated these challenges by enrolling five million into unions and infusing into their ranks a widespread aspiration to direct the operation of railroads, mines, shipyards and factories collectively, was itself the product of a decade of continuous struggle, the new forms of which resulted from management's reorganization of industry. Only when that transformation was well under way, and only when the strong unionization of workers in basic industries it made possible had been achieved, did the challenge Joseph Schlossberg hurled to the 1920 convention of the Amalgamated Clothing Workers become meaningful: "It is now our responsibility to establish order in the industry in the place of the chaos created by the employers when they had things their own way."[80]

Notes

1 André Tridon, *The New Unionism* (New York, 1914), 17.
2 David Brody, *Steelworkers in America: The Nonunion Era* (Cambridge, 1960),

50–79; Luke Grant, *The National Erectors' Association and the International Association of Bridge and Structural Ironworkers* (Washington, 1915); Robert Ozanne, *A Century of Labor-Management Relations at McCormick and International Harvester* (Madison, 1967), 44–70; David Brody, *The Butcher Workmen, A Study of Unionization* (Cambridge, 1964); Clarence E. Bonnett, *Employers' Association in the United States: A Study of Typical Associations* (New York, 1922); Jacob H. Hollander and George E. Barnett, *Studies in American Trade Unionism* (New York, 1912), 109–52.

3 President C. W. Post of the Citizens' Industrial Alliance, quoted in Selig Perlman and Philip Taft, *History of Labor in the United States, 1896–1932* (New York, 1935), 136.

4 *Proceedings of the First Convention of the Industrial Workers of the World, Founded at Chicago, June 27–July 8, 1905* (New York, 1905, hereinafter cited as *IWW Proceedings*), 123. See also Marguerite Green, *The National Civic Federation and the American Labor Movement, 1900–1925* (Washington, 1956); James Weinstein, *The Corporate Ideal in the Liberal State, 1900–1918* (Boston, 1968); Philip S. Foner, *History of the Labor Movement in the United States* (4 vols., New York, 1947–1965), III, 32–110.

5 "Manifesto," in *IWW Proceedings*, 4.

6 Vincent St. John, *The IWW, Its History, Structure and Methods* (Chicago, 1919); Foner, IV, 36–9, 114–71.

7 *Machinists' Monthly Journal*, 18 (December 1906), 1108–11. Hereinafter cited as *MMJ*.

8 Oscar Ameringer, *If You Don't Weaken* (New York, 1940), 194–223; James Leonard to Frank Morrison, June 2, June 6, June 9, July 7, July 14, September 1, September 29, 1907, John Mitchell Papers, Box A3-49, Catholic University of America, Washington, D.C.; *New Orleans Daily Picayune*, July 13, 1907; Foner, III, 250–3.

9 *Iron Age*, 92 (December 4, 1913), 1294; Stanley Lebergott, *Manpower in Economic Growth* (New York, 1964), 512.

10 Louis Levine, *The Women's Garment Workers* (New York, 1924), 144–95; Melvyn Dubofsky, *When Workers Organize: New York City in the Progressive Era* (Amherst, Mass., 1968), 49–66; John N. Ingham, "A Strike in the Progressive Era: McKees Rocks, 1909," *The Pennsylvania Magazine of History and Biography*, 90 (July 1966), 353–77; U.S. Congress, Senate, *Report on the Strike at the Bethlehem Steel Works*, Senate Document 521 (Washington, D.C., 1910).

11 Perlman and Taft, 343–8; Edward Levinson, *I Break Strikes! The Technique of Pearl L. Bergoff* (New York, 1935), 89–104.

12 Editorial, *New York Call*, March 7, 1910.

13 See Table 2, Ch. 4.

14 Editorial, *Iron Age*, 93 (April 23, 1914), 1018–19. See also ibid., 88 (September 21, 1911), 607; Judge Gary's speech, ibid., 87 (January 19, 1911), 208–10.

15 James Weinstein, *The Decline of Socialism in America, 1912–1925* (New York, 1967), 93–119; John H. M. Laslett, *Labor and the Left: A Study of Socialist and Radical Influences in the American Labor Movement, 1881–1924* (New York, 1970), 161–4, 214–18.

16 *Iron Age*, 91 (April 17, 1913), 954.

17 Melvyn Dubofsky, *We Shall Be All: A History of the Industrial Workers of the World* (Chicago, 1969), 286–7; *Iron Age*, 92 (September 11, 1913), 572; Levine, 227–31.

18 *Iron Age*, 93 (January 1, 1914), 13.

19 *Monthly Labor Review*, 2 (April 1916), 13–26.

20 Dianne Kanitra, "The Westinghouse Strike of 1916," (unpublished M.A. paper, University of Pittsburgh, 1971).

21 *International Socialist Review*, 16 (April 1917), 582–7; Joseph T. Makarewicz, "The Impact of World War I on Pennsylvania Politics, with Emphasis on the Election of 1920," (unpublished Ph.D. dissertation, University of Pittsburgh, 1972).

22 Leon C. Marshall, "The War Labor Program and Its Administration," *Journal of Political Economy*, 26 (May 1918), 429.

23 *Monthly Labor Review*, 17 (December 1923), 82–5.

24 Bureau of Industrial Statistics of New Jersey, *Thirty-Ninth Annual Report* (Camden, 1916), 225; ibid., 1914, 227–40.

25 Alexander M. Bing, *War-Time Strikes and Their Adjustment* (New York, 1921), 60–1, 178n, 181; Susan M. Kingsbury, *Labor Laws and Their Enforcement, with Special Reference to Massachusetts* (New York, 1911), 90–125.

26 Robert Ozanne, *Wages in Practice and Theory: McCormick and International Harvester, 1860–1960* (Madison, Wis., 1968), 108–11.

27 Paul H. Douglas, C. N. Hitchcock, and W. E. Atkins, *The Worker in Modern Economic Society* (Chicago, 1923), 361–2.

28 *Iron Age*, 96 (October 14, 1915), 884–5.

29 See Table 2, Ch. 4.

30 Bing, 30n.

31 Frank Tannenbaum, *The Labor Movement: Its Conservative Functions and Social Consequences* (New York, 1921), 147n.

32 Mark Perlman, *The Machinists: A New Study in American Trade Unionism*, (Cambridge, 1961), 33, 51.

33 Douglas, Hitchcock and Atkins, 562–3; Nationalization Research Committee, United Mine Workers of America, *How To Run Coal* (New York, 1922); Glenn E. Plumb and William G. Roylance, *Industrial Democracy: A Plan for Its Achievement* (New York, 1923); William Z. Foster, *The Railroaders' Next Step* (Chicago, 1921); John G. Randall, Jr., *The Problem of Group Responsibility to Society* (New York, 1922), 227.

34 History Committee of the General Strike Committee, *The Seattle General Strike* (reprinted as Root and Branch pamphlet 5, Charlestown, Mass., 1972), 4.

35 J. B. S. Hardman, ed., *American Labor Dynamics, in the Light of Post-War Developments* (New York, 1928), 21. cf., Weinstein, *Decline*, 177–233.

36 *The Tailor*, April 8, 1919.

37 "Direct Action Loses," *American Federationist* (October 1919), 962–4.

38 Sylvia Kopald, *Rebellion in Labor Unions* (New York, 1924), 50–177. The percentage figures of insurgent strikers are my own.

39 Jeremy Brecher, *Strike!* (San Francisco, 1972), 69–96, 243–4.

40 Vertrees J. Wyckoff, *The Wage Policies of Labor Organizations in a Period of Industrial Depression* (Baltimore, 1926); Royal E. Montgomery, *Industrial Relations in the Chicago Building Trades* (Chicago, 1927), 233–309.

41 *Monthly Labor Review*, 14 (May 1922), 183; ibid., 16 (June 1923), 231–9.

42 Interviews with Max Zuckerman, Gen. Secy., Cloth Hat and Cap Makers of America, March 3, 1919 and David Brodsky, Pres. Local 137 Sheet Metal Workers, March 11, 1919, David J. Saposs Papers, Box 22, State Historical Society of Wisconsin, Madison.

43 Interview with Samuel E. Beardsley, Organizer Local Union No. 1, Jewelry Workers Union, February 19, 1919; D. J. Saposs, "Jewish Unions," typescript (Saposs Papers, Box 21).

44 Interviews with Harry Jones, Secy.-Tres., International Association of Bridge

and Structural Iron Workers, January 23, 1919, and Sol Broad, Business Agent, Jewish Local, IABSIW, March 6, 1919 (Saposs Papers, Box 22).

45 See Peter N. Stearns, *Revolutionary Syndicalism and French Labor: A Cause without Rebels* (New Brunswick, 1971), 19–33.

46 U.S. Commission on Industrial Relations, *Final Report and Testimony*, 11 vols., 64th Congress, 1st session, Senate Document No. 415 (Washington, D.C. 1916, hereinafter cited as CIR), 1, 874.

47 Frederick W. Taylor, "Testimony," 49, in Taylor, *Scientific Management. Comprising Shop Management. The Principles of Scientific Management. Testimony before the Special House Committee* (New York, 1947).

48 See Ibid.; Robert F. Hoxie, *Scientific Management and Labor* (New York, 1915); Hugh G. J. Aitken, *Taylorism at the Watertown Arsenal: Scientific Management in Action, 1908–1915* (Cambridge, 1960).

49 F. J. Roethlisberger and W. J. Dickson, *Management and the Worker: Technical Vs. Social Organization in an Industrial Plant* (Cambridge, 1934).

50 Whiting Williams, *What's on the Worker's Mind, By One Who Put on Overalls to Find Out* (New York, 1921), 20.

51 Leon Stein and Philip Taft, ed., *Workers Speak: Self Portraits* (New York, 1971), 30.

52 *Iron Age*, 93 (January 8, 1914); Keith Sward, *The Legend of Henry Ford* (New York, 1968), 52–60.

53 *American Labor Legislation Review*, 4 (May 1914), 225.

54 Ibid., 5 (November 1915), 486–7. See also Don D. Lescohier, *The Labor Market* (New York, 1919).

55 Lebergott, 524, 528.

56 CIR, 1, 772–3.

57 Eg., National War Labor Board, Administrative Files Box 54 (General Electric); Docket No. 22 (Bethlehem Steel), Record Group 2, National Archives, Washington, D.C. On the reconciliation, see Milton J. Nadworny, *Scientific Management and the Unions, 1900–1932* (Cambridge, 1955).

58 National War Labor Board, Case File 132, Record Group 2, National Archives, Washington, D.C. On the Remington plant, see *Iron Age*, 96 (October 14, 1915), 296–303.

59 See Stanley B. Mathewson, *Restriction of Output among Unorganized Workers* (New York, 1931).

60 William M. Leiserson, *Adjusting Immigrant and Industry* (New York, 1924), 169–233.

61 Paul Buhle, "Debsian Socialism and the 'New Immigrant' Worker," in *Insights and Parallels: Problems and Issues of American Social History*, William O'Neill, ed. (Minneapolis, 1973), 249–77.

62 *Survey*, 28 (July 6, 1912), 487–8, (August 3, 1912), 595–6.

63 J. S. Biscay, "The Ipswich Strike," *International Socialist Review*, 14 (August 1913), 90–2; Bureau of Industrial Statistics of New Jersey, 1915, 210–31.

64 Interview with Matthew Pluhar, Pres. Industrial Textile Workers Union, Passaic, April 3, 1919 (Saposs Papers, Box 21); Nat Hentoff, ed., *Essays of A. J. Muste* (Indianapolis, 1967), 71–3.

65 Foner, IV, 462–72; Frederick A. Barkey, "The Socialist Party in West Virginia from 1898 to 1920; A Study in Working Class Radicalism," (unpublished Ph.D. dissertation, University of Pittsburgh, 1971), 106–56, 180–6.

66 William Z. Foster, *The Great Steel Strike and Its Lessons* (New York, 1920); William M. Tuttle, "Labor Conflict and Racial Violence: The Black Worker in Chicago, 1894–1919," *Labor History*, 10 (Summer 1969), 408–32.

67 Buhle, 267–8; Levine, 233–41; Interview with C. P. Dean, Business Agent Joint Council No. 9, United Shoe Workers of America, December 24, 1918 (Saposs Papers, Box 21).
68 Interviews with David Wolf, Gen.-Treas., Amalgamated Clothing Workers of America, February 27, 1919 and Frank Blanco, Gen. Organizer, ACWA, March 29, 1919 (Saposs Papers, Box 21); Hentoff, 59–83.
69 Quoted in Foner, IV, 37.
70 The only explicit reference to workers' control was in Haywood's speech to the ratification meeting. *IWW Proceedings*, 579.
71 Petition for the Creation of National Labor Agencies, National War Labor Board, Case File 132, Record Group 2, National Archives, Washington, D.C.
72 Louis Fraina, "Syndicalism and Industrial Unionism," *International Socialist Review*, 14 (July 1913), 25–8.
73 *MMJ*, 15 (July 1903), 590–1.
74 CIR, 10, 9697–10048; Carl E. Person, *The Lizard's Trail. A Story of the Illinois Central and Harriman Lines Strike of 1911 to 1915 Inclusive* (Chicago, 1918); William Z. Foster, *Pages from a Worker's Life* (New York, 1939), 146–8; *MMJ*, 1911–16.
75 CIR, 10, 9918.
76 Ibid., 10, 9877–8.
77 Ibid., 10, 9705.
78 *The Agitator*, May 15, 1912; Ibid., April 15, 1912; William Z. Foster and Earl C. Ford, *Syndicalism* (Chicago, n.d.); Theodore Draper, *The Roots of American Communism* (New York, 1957), 308.
79 Person, 42–63.
80 Quoted in Evans Clark, "The Industry Is Ours," *Socialist Review*, 9 (July 1920), 59.

5. Whose standards? Workers and the reorganization of production in the United States, 1900–20*

During the first two decades of the twentieth century both managers and workers in America's large-scale factories sought to reorganize the human relationships involved in industrial production. The authority of foremen and the autonomy which skilled craftsmen had customarily exercised in the direction of their own work and that of their helpers came under attack from two directions at once, as the scale and complexity of industrial enterprises grew.[1] From one side, the craftsmen themselves developed increasingly collective and formal practices for the regulation of their trades, both openly through union work rules and covertly through group-enforced codes of ethical behavior on the job. The rapid growth of trade union strength in most sectors of the economy between 1898 and 1903, the eagerness of workers to undertake massive strikes to obtain or preserve union recognition, such as the coal strike of 1897, the steel and machinists' strikes of 1901, and the meat packing strike of 1904, and the revival of sympathetic strikes all increased the ability of skilled workers to impose their union work rules and standard rates (minimum wages) on their employers.[2]

From the other side, the owners and managers of large enterprises developed more direct and systematic controls over the production side of their firms. By the end of the 1890s many metalurgical, textile, and machinery-making companies had erected new plants, which were well adapted to the unemcumbered flow of materials through successive operations, introduced large numbers of specialized machines, developed careful methods of cost accounting, and experimented widely with systems of incentive pay, which, the managers hoped, would entice their workers to greater exertion.[3] After 1900 a veritable mania for efficiency, organization, and standardization swept through American business and literary circles.[4]

The scientific management movement of Frederick Winslow Taylor and his disciples was the articulate and self-conscious vanguard of the businessmen's reform effort. Although fewer than thirty factories had been thoroughly reorganized by Taylor and his colleagues before 1917, the essential elements of their proposals had found favor in almost every industry by the mid-1920s. Those basic elements were as simple as they were profound: (1) centralized planning and routing of the successive phases in fabrication, (2) systematic analysis of each distinct operation, (3) detailed instruction and supervision of each worker in the performance of his discrete task, and (4) wage payments carefully designed to induce the worker to do as he was told.[5] All of these points undermined the traditional autonomy of the craftsmen, and the last three were incompatible with the wage scales and work rules of trade unions. As its impact spread, therefore, the scientific management movement not only clashed frontally with the growing power of trade unionism, but also exposed basic weaknesses in the craft-based structure of American unionism and inspired many workers to experiment with new forms of struggle.

Three aspects of the battle to reshape work relations at the beginning of this century will be examined: management's standardization of tasks, the conversion of laborers into machine tenders, and the controversy over incentive pay schemes and job classifications. Special attention will be devoted to the metal-working industries, where these issues appeared first. The struggles of munitions workers in Bridgeport, Connecticut, will be used to illustrate the innovations which appeared during these years at the initiative of workers.

Standardization of tasks

"It is only through *enforced* standardization of methods, *enforced* adoption of the best implements and working conditions, and *enforced* cooperation that this faster work can be assured," wrote Taylor. "And the duty of enforcing the adoption of standards and enforcing this cooperation rests with the *management* alone."[6] The quest for systematic control by the management of all aspects of the production process, which Taylor described, arose in part from its needs for more thorough cost accounting, interchangeable parts, and integration of the various departments of large-scale manufacturing.[7] On the other hand, it also involved the destruction of work practices which had grown up over the last half of the nineteenth century, and through which skilled workmen had exercised considerable discretion in the direction of their own work and that of their helpers. Iron molders, iron rollers and heaters, glass blowers, bricklayers, coal miners, machinists, jiggermen in potteries, stitching-machine operators and lasters in shoe factories, mule spinners, and other craftsmen not only enjoyed broad autonomy in their own work, but also defended that autonomy by their own codes of ethical work behavior. The operation of more than one machine by one man, undermining a fellow worker's position, employing more than one helper at a time, suffering any supervisor to watch one work, turning out more production than the stint set by the group, and, among carpenters, machinists, and others, accepting any piecework form of payment, were all seen as "hoggish" and "unmanly" forms of conduct, unbecoming a true craftsman.[8]

Taylor denounced the craftsmen's code as "soldiering" (restriction of output), but, as he was keenly aware, skilled workers were able to direct their portions of any production process and to defend work patterns which they considered honorable and rational, because their knowledge of their own tasks was superior to that of their employers. The first step in reform, said Taylor, was "the deliberate gathering in on the part of those on the management's side of all of the great mass of traditional knowledge, which in the past has been in the heads of the workmen, and in the physical skill and knack of the workman, which he has acquired through years of experience."[9] The best technique for "gathering" the craftsmen's knowledge into the engineer's head was time and motion study, which Taylorites called "the basis of all modern management."[10]

To the craftsman, therefore, time study symbolized simultaneously the theft of his knowledge by his employers and an outrage against his sense of honorable behavior at work. Hugo Lueders, a machinist at the Watertown arsenal, spoke for thousands of his colleagues, when he said that he had no objection to improved planning of production. "The men would welcome any system," he said. "They want it bad." But, he added quickly and emphatically, "as far as having a man stand back of you and taking all the various operations you go through, that is one thing they do not care for."[11] The molders where he worked agreed among themselves that none would work under the clock. A machinist at the Rock Island arsenal, who was seen measuring the bed of a planer for standardized bolts and clamps, was ostracised by his workmates. Time-study men at Pittsburgh's American Locomotive Company were attacked and beaten by workers in 1911, despite the fact that they had been introduced into the plant with the consent of the unions. The appearance of time clocks and work tickets at the Norfolk Navy Yard in 1915 led to a mass walkout and a union rally "in emphatic protest." Five years earlier machinists at Starrett Tool had resolved to treat such clocks "as part of the furniture." The mere suspicion that time study was to be introduced into the repair shops of the Illinois Central Railroad was enough to forge a united front of all the shop crafts and precipitate a strike in 1911, which lasted four bloody years.[12]

Time study, like incentive pay, was introduced most easily in nonunion shops, where each worker could be induced to accept the new ways separately. When the National Metal Trades Association launched its open-shop drive against the machinists' union in 1901, it demanded "full discretion" for employers "to designate the men we consider competent to perform the work and to determine the conditions under which that work shall be prosecuted." Its declaration of principles added: "We will not permit employees to place any restriction on the management, methods, or production of our shop, and will require a fair day's work for a fair day's pay."[13]

Where unions were effectively excluded from the plant, many craftsmen acquiesced in time study and learned to grasp at incentive pay, as the only means available to improve their incomes. In remarkable contrast to the machinists of American Locomotive in Pittsburgh, who threw their premium pay envelopes into trash bins to demonstrate their contempt for the new system, those of United Shoe Machinery in Beverly, Massachusetts, lined up to volunteer for premium pay contracts and crossed streets to avoid meeting union members. In the machine shops of Bethlehem Steel, Taylor's disciple Henry Gantt observed to his satisfaction that the lathe operators, in ardent pursuit of bonuses, lost their scruples against hurrying the helpers and crane men, not to speak of themselves.[14]

In such factories, the stint, by which craftsmen had openly and deliberately regulated output in former times, had been abolished. But extensive studies of nonunion factories in the 1920s revealed that it had survived in a new form. Everywhere Stanley B. Mathewson looked in that decade he found that the restriction of output which "Taylor discovered [still] obtains today," while "payment plans, designed as incentives to increase production . . . turn out to be incentives to restriction." In fact, he observed, "the mere intimation that the time-study man is to make his appearance will often slow up a worker, a group or a whole department."[15] This is not to say, however, that scientific management had changed nothing. The customary craftsman's stint had been an overt and deliberate act of collective regulation by workers who directed their own productive operations. The group regulation which replaced it was a covert act of disruption of management's direction of production. The stint had become sabotage.

The scientifically managed factory appeared to employers to be under rational engineering control. But to craftsmen of the prewar generation that plant resembled a bedlam: arbitrary and pretentious men in white shirts shouted orders, crept up behind workers with stopwatches, had them running incessantly back and forth to time clocks, and posted silly notices on bulletin boards. Incentive pay in any form impressed machinists as a "vile, insidious disease," which "encourages greed, is immoral in its tendencies, and does more to create discord and make a perfect hell of a harmonious shop or factory of our craft, than all the evils that escaped from Pandora's box."[16] Taylor's famous paper *Shop Management* was widely read by union machinists. In fact, it was their main source of information on their employers' intentions. Their response to it was angrily summed up by Nels Alifas, a machinist from Davenport, Iowa:

Now we object to being reduced to a scientific formula, and we do not want to have the world run on that kind of a basis at all. We would a good deal rather have the world run on the basis that everybody should enjoy some of the good things in it, and if the people of the United States do not want to spend all of their time working, they have a right to say so, even though the scientific engineers claim that they can do five times as much as they are doing now. If they don't want to do it, why should they be compelled to do it?[17]

Laborers and machine tenders

By the end of the First World War the most numerous group of workers in the major metal-working industries (auto, electrical equipment, farm machinery, and machine tools) was made up not of craftsmen, but of specialized machine tenders. A survey of the automobile industry in 1923 found that only 9 percent of the workers were in skilled trades, such as machinists or die sinkers, and less than 9 percent were common laborers. On the other hand, almost 18 percent worked on assembly lines and 47 percent were machine tenders. "The ability to meet ('to hit') and maintain a constant pace," noted a contemporary observer, "to be able to eliminate all waste and false motions; to follow without wavering printed instructions emanating from an unseen source lodged in some far off planning department – these constitute the requirements of a successful machine tender."[18]

The "dilution" of skilled trades (to borrow the splendid British expression) involved both placing men and women with little prior training at the controls of machine tools and creating a large supervisory force to direct their work. In Taylor's view this innovation provided promotions for both the skilled workers who became foremen and the laborers who operated the machines. In fact, there were workers who experienced improvements in their status and earnings as a result of the dilution of crafts, and such workers were unlikely to battle for restoration of the old ways. The new art of welding with oxyacetylene torches, for example, had been part of the general skill which a machinist acquired during his apprenticeship, but during the war many women were trained exclusively as welders in railroad car shops and other metal works. To the women involved, most of whom had previously been garment and textile workers, the welder's job represented a considerable improvement in their economic status, which they were prepared to defend. The machinists, however, saw the women's presence as an intolerable erosion of their trade and an unwelcome intrusion by women into shops which had previously been male preserves. They reacted furiously, and often violently, against the women welders in their midst.[19]

It was the rapid expansion of the metal-working industries, however, which accounted for both the widespread conversion of unskilled laborers into machine tenders and the improvement in earnings which the new positions often represented for them before 1920. During the war decade the number of journeymen and apprentice machinists listed in the U.S. census actually grew by 8 percent annually, from 460 thousand to 841 thousand. In the next decade, however, that growth turned to a decline of 2 percent per year (to 656 thousand in 1930). On the other hand, the number of machine operatives in the auto and farm equipment industries alone swelled by almost 40 percent each year between 1910 and 1920 (from 26 thousand to 129 thousand) and continued to grow, though at a much slower rate, through the twenties. This change was not the result of the introduction of new machine tools. Although there was extensive retooling by American industry after the crisis of 1907–9, the new lathes, boring mills, milling machines, and radial drills were no simpler to operate than the old. The simplification resulted from prefabricated jigs and fixtures and from the detailed instruction and supervision given to those who repeated the same standardized operations again and again on those machines.

Ironically the same dilution also created a new skilled trade, that of tool and die maker. "Cheap men need expensive jigs," said Taylor's associate Sterling Bunnell, while "highly skilled men need little outside of their tool chests."[20] Nowhere was the truth of this observation more evident than in the wartime production of artillery shells, where tens of thousands of inexperienced men and women manipulated form tools, jigs, dies, and taper fixtures, which had been fabricated in the tool room. In 1900 the category "tool and die maker" had not existed in the national census of occupations. In 1910 there were nine thousand of them listed, and by 1920 there were 55 thousand, a growth of more than 50 percent per year during the war decade. In many wartime strikes the practitioners of this new skill proved to be the most militant and the most innovative of the workers involved.

The process of converting skilled workers into tool makers or supervisors, so that production itself could be assigned to untrained operatives, performing minutely subdivided tasks, was carried to its ultimate development in Ford's Highland Park plant. Ford's circumstances were unique. So great was the demand for the company's Model T's that 90 percent of the one thousand or more cars which came off its final assembly lines each day were shipped immediately to dealers. Consequently, it was possible to commit fifteen thousand men and women to fabricating a single product in a plant which was characterized not only by large and small chain-driven assembly lines, but also by thousands of machine tools especially designed for making a single cut on a single part (and capable of nothing else).

To perform such jobs, the company had "no use for experience." In the words of one engineer: "It desires and prefers machine-tool operators who have nothing to unlearn, who have no theories of correct surface speeds for metal finishing, and will simply do what they are told, over and over again, from bell-time to bell-time."[21] On the other hand, outfitting the machine tools which those novices could operate required a staff of 240 tool makers, 50 tool-fixture draftsmen, and 105 pattern makers, for whom nothing was "scamped and hurried." No fewer than 255 overseers in the machine shops alone watched over the machine tenders, with absolute authority to fire any of them at will.[22]

Such conditions obviated the need for incentive-pay schemes, so everyone in the plant was on hourly rates. They also produced staggering rates of labor turnover. Company officials had discovered that to maintain an average force of thirteen thousand during the prosperous times between October, 1912 and October, 1913, they had to hire 54 thousand men (an annual turnover rate of 416 percent). They introduced elaborate personnel checks and a system of periodic wage increases based upon the recommendations of foremen, and later a personnel department to which a worker might appeal his discharge, in order to reduce this separation rate. The campaign of the Industrial Workers of the World at the gates of Detroit's auto plants and the strikes which that organization led in the tire industry and at smaller auto plants added to the company's anxiety. Consequently, in January, 1914, the company proclaimed an 8-hour day and five-dollars-a-day pay for all those employees who were over twenty-two years of age, contributed to the support of others, and were pro-nounced "acceptable." A staff of 100 "sociologists" examined the habits, home lives, and attitudes of workers to discover who was "acceptable," and by the end of March, 1914, 57 percent of them were receiving the magical five dollars. Later in the year Ford introduced classes in the English language, which foreign-born employees were required to attend, and subsequently it celebrated the graduation of the first such group with an "Americanization Day" festival, featuring a parade of more than six thousand Ford workers.[23]

Small wonder there was always a crowd outside the gates of the High-land Park plant looking for work, and a riot had broken out among job-seekers the day after the five-dollar day had been announced to the press. The fact remains, however, that Ford's policies were unique, even within the automobile industry. No other firms could undertake mass production of a single item on so lavish a scale. On the other hand, there is no doubt that unskilled workers throughout the land did enjoy substantial im-provements in their incomes between 1909 and 1920, even if they did not rush off to Detroit. Those gains were the consequences of rapid economic growth, which enabled laborers to move from job to job in-cessantly in search of better incomes, and to undertake wage strikes with increasing frequency and effectiveness.[24] They were not benefits which flowed from managerial reform.

In fact, during the war years, when workers in munitions and other industries most often struck and won the most significant advances in their earnings (relative to those of more skilled workers, as well as in absolute terms), they also challenged management's efforts to systematize and intensify their work. The experience of the Brighton Mills of Passaic, one of the very few textile mills to be reformed by Taylor's colleagues before the war, illustrates this development. Henry Gantt boasted in 1914 that his introduction of functional foremanship and the task-and-bonus plan had stimulated new "habits of industry" among the weavers and accomplished miracles of production. All of the weavers he studied had either conformed to the new output standards or quit. In April 1916, however, the weavers struck the Brighton Mills, demanding an end to Gantt's innovations.[25]

Conflict over the pace of work raged with special intensity in shell turning. As early as 1910 a preview of the wartime disputes in that line

of work had been offered by the workers of Bethlehem Steel. The operatives in Machine Shop No. 4, where the strike began, complained that
the premiums paid to lathe operators and their foremen had created
unbearable chaos. The eagerness of foremen to maximize their own
bonuses had led them to monopolize the crane men and other laborers
for the use of the shell-turning lathes, charge work on which there was
no bonus up to shell-turning time, and, worst of all, to order the shell
turners into work one Sunday after another. The strike began when one
lathe operator feigned illness on a Saturday in order to avoid being told
to come in on Sunday. He was caught in the act and fired. All the
machine shop's workers then went on strike.[26]

The frenzied atmosphere of the war years reproduced this type of
situation time and time again. At the Westinghouse works of East Pittsburgh the workers' demands in the strikes of 1914 and 1916 and in the
acrimonious negotiations of 1915 and 1917 consistently involved efforts
to abolish premium pay and to ease the pace of work. Workers could
stay home from work more safely as jobs became more plentiful, and at
Bethlehem Steel an average of 20 percent of the force was missing each
day by the fall of 1918. After those workers had struck several times,
the National War Labor Board ordered Gantt's task-and-bonus system
abolished, on the grounds that it had had a "serious detrimental effect
upon the production of war materials."[27]

To the eyes of leading figures in American business, output per hour
was declining during the war years at the very same time that the number
of hours regularly worked each week were falling.[28] This trend not only
injured the war effort, they claimed, it also threatened their plans for the
postwar world. The 1916 convention of the National Metal Trades Association was warned by its president, James A. Emery, that the current
war of arms would be followed swiftly by a war of economic competition.
Only by resisting union interference and efforts to reduce working hours
could American business prepare itself for the "world contest of peace
succeeding that of war." "It is no hour for watered capital or watered
labor," Emery declared, "but for management trained to the moment and
operatives conscious that harmonious co-operation and intelligent self-
interest can alone insure the joint industrial success of employer and
employee."[29]

In short, the war crisis itself intensified the struggle for power within
the factory, increased labor's ability to impose its standards and resist
those of the employer, and greatly increased the appeal of scientific
management to industrialists. It also forced the apostles of scientific man-

agement to wrestle with the problems of industrial psychology, personnel management, and "Americanization" of immigrants, in addition to the more familiar questions of standardizing tasks and wage systems. Although the transformation of immigrant laborers into machine tenders and the rapid increase in the number of supervisors and tool and die makers had initially weakened the position of craft unions in the metal-working industries, the unskilled operatives came to assert themselves with increasing militancy, and sometimes undid the once-successful work of efficiency experts. The day of reckoning came, of course, in the postwar depression of 1920–2. Then union strength in basic industries toppled like a house of cards, and the wages of all workers plummeted downward (especially those of the unskilled). Weekly hours of work were lengthened again, and productivity per worker rose rapidly. Only then did the standards of scientific management, now in harness with the new concerns of personnel management, carry the day.[30]

Incentive pay

More controversy arose around the payment systems associated with scientific management than over any other single aspect of the new managerial practice. Although the workers' hostility to incentive pay posed a less fundamental challenge to scientific management than did open protests against the stopwatch and job standardization, it often gave rise to large and protracted conflicts because it reflected both their sense of moral work relations and their urgent concern with what they earned. Moreover, struggles arising over this issue contributed to the growing desire of American workers for their own standards and also produced new styles of organization among them, which were perceived as a dangerous challenge to the authority of the employers and of the existing trade union leadership alike.

Conflicts over piecework had been endemic in the metal trades during the late nineteenth century, in America as well as in Europe. The widespread experimentation of employers with the various types of premium payments and differential piecework rates during the 1890s heralded the dawn of scientific management. The International Association of Machinists was intransigent in its opposition to all forms of payment by results, as is evident from its famous constitutional provision adopted in 1903 that no member of the union might "operate more than one machine or accept work by the piece, premium, merit, task, or contract system, under penalty of expulsion."[31] Often during the decade after that rule was adopted, officers of the union sought authorization from their members to negotiate with employers concerning terms which might safeguard the workers in return for union acceptance of the new pay schemes, but the elected delegates to convention after convention adamantly refused to allow their leaders to make any compromise on the question whatever. In response, the owners of most machine shops around the country simply declared their enterprises "open shops." They were supported by the National Metal Trades Association, which announced as one of its basic principles: "Employees will be paid by the hourly rate, by premium system, piecework, or contract, as the employer may elect."[32]

To the advocates of scientific management, however, the decisive question was not simply what form of wages would best induce workers to meet the norms set by time-and-motion study. The crucial point was that wages had to be individualized – the tasks and performance of each worker had to be evaluated separately, if that worker was to be persuaded to toil at maximum efficiency. "Class wages" were denounced by Taylor and Gantt as slovenly management practice. Companies which boasted of "scientific wages" were typified by the H. H. Franklin Company of Syracuse, which fixed wages on "a purely individualistic basis," through periodic evaluations of each worker's output, attendance, spoiled work, "co-operation and conduct factor," and fourteen other variables of behavior.[33] The task-and-bonus, differential piece rate, Halsey–Towne, Bedaux and other wage plans were all designed to make each employee stand alone in this relationship to the company. From the point of view of their advocates, the trade union tradition of the "standard rate" for each craft was an abomination.[34]

By 1909 many more machinists and operatives were paid according to some "scientific" scheme than were covered by IAM standard rates. Beginning with the strikes at the Pressed Steel Car Company in McKees Rocks that year and Bethlehem Steel the next, however, the demand that straight hourly pay rates be substituted for premium and bonus schedules became an increasingly common feature of workers' protests. As we have seen, a relentless attack on incentive wages infused the joint struggles of tool makers and machine tenders at Westinghouse Electric from 1914 through 1917. A few miles away at the huge Mesta Machine Company 300 machinists, helpers and tool makers struck late in 1918 for demands which by then had become commonplace: end the premium system, establish standard rates, accept the 8-hour day, and recognize a shop committee. Cancellation of government contracts made it easy for the company to fire its dissidents, but six months later 720 workers walked out at the same plant for the same demands.[35] Throughout 1918 and 1919 the General Electric Company's plants in Schenectady, Lynn, Pittsfield, Erie, and Fort Wayne were wracked by a series of strikes over the same issues. Workers' delegates sent from each of those cities to present their cases to the National War Labor Board in Washington used their visits to the capitol to keep each other informed and to spread sympathetic strikes.[36]

Three characteristics of these numerous strikes deserve attention. First, in this instance it was the workers who were demanding standardization. The idea of job classifications for large industrial enterprises was not proposed by management reformers, but resisted by them. When the War Labor Board ordered General Electric to abolish bonus payments and accept minimum wages for different classes of work, the company refused to obey the award. Similarly in Bridgeport, the officials of Remington Arms contended that a "standard wage . . . would destroy discipline," and that "the right to classify must be exercised by those directly responsible for maintaining production."[37]

On the other hand, the demand for classifications was not simply a return to craft traditions. Wartime strikers were seeking not one standard rate (as had been the time-honored machinists' demand) but a graduated scale of standards, which recognized the variety of skill levels created by modern management while it opposed the individualization of earnings. The workers clearly disliked the idea of a vast array of wage rates. Usually in metal works they proposed six or seven rates including a catch-all category for operatives whose machines were set up by other, more skilled workers, and a minimum for unskilled labor. The high turnover of workers and the rapid dilution of skills during the war made the establishment of such classifications urgent for the workers. Moreover, their proposals often appealed to the bureaucratic mentality of the functionaries of government agencies and received some support from that quarter.

Second, the workers' new types of wage demands appeared together with new forms of organization, which modified or even abandoned the craft orientation of the unions. The earliest manifestation of this development was the appearance of "system federations" among railroad workers. These alliances of the unions of craftsmen in the repair shops with those of the clerks and the laborers were widely formed by activity at the base as early as 1910–1911, and were closely linked to the struggle against the stopwatch and premium pay. During the war shop committees flourished, both on the workers' own initiative and on that of government agencies. They quickly became a battleground where employers' efforts to shape them into employee representation plans (or company unions) clashed with the efforts of imaginative local trade unionists to use them as militant tribunes of the union members and nonmembers within the firm alike.[38]

Most impressive of all were the local metal trades councils, which were formed in factories and shipyards to coordinate the struggles of the different trades. Although such councils had existed before the war, their role had been rather perfunctory. During 1917 and 1918, however, they displayed considerable local initiative and often preempted the role once played by the national trade unions in the formulation of demands and the leadership of strikes. The independence of the councils disturbed the national officers of the unions involved as much as it did the employers. In 1919 the leaders of the AFL moved vigorously to tame the metal trades councils, which had proven themselves very effective in the electrical, machine tool, automobile, and shipbuilding industries. A special conference of the metal trades department of the AFL decreed in February of that year "that no local metal trades council can order a strike unless the local unions affiliated first have received sanction or permission from the internationals," and that "any attempt on the part of any local council to force any sympathetic strike in any locality is a violation of our general laws."[39]

Third, manufacturers viewed proposals that they recognize these new workers' organizations with undisguised hostility. To be sure, the National War Labor Board and other government agencies tried to preserve industrial peace by dealing with workers' delegates and supporting many of their demands. But Loyall A. Osborne of Westinghouse expressed the dominant mood of the business world, when he wrote to former President W. H. Taft concerning the policies of the NWLB, on which they both served:

It is quite natural that you should approach these questions in a different frame of mind than do we, for you have not for years, as we have been, fighting the battle for industrial independence. You have not had constantly before you as part of your daily life evidences of bad faith, restriction of output, violence, disregard of obligations and irresponsibility that has [sic.] ever been the characteristic of their [the workers'] organizations.[40]

A brief filed by the manufacturers of Bridgeport to the NWLB summed up the response of metal trades' employers to labor's demands by restating the essence of the new managerial practice. It insisted upon: (1) complete and exclusive control of production by the employers, (2) the rewarding of each individual employee according to his or her merits,

(3) full freedom for management to evaluate those merits, and (4) settlement of all disputes by the management and the employee directly concerned, without the intervention of outside agencies, trade union or governmental.[41] The employers' resolution not to yield on these principles intensified at the close of the war, when they faced strong deflationary pressures. Although the government quickly dismantled its regulatory agencies, it fostered corporate self-regulation through trade associations. At the same time, the Republican Party was returned to power (in the congressional elections of 1918 and the presidential election of 1920) largely by its success in championing consumers' desires for lower prices. By the time of the depression of 1920–2 manufacturers' associations and government leaders were working in harmony to eliminate "waste in industry," reduce labor costs, and roll back prices.[42]

In short, although incentive-pay plans represented only one element of scientific management, and one, moreover, which had less direct impact on the worker's status than the standardization of tasks, the new style of supervision, or time-and-motion study, overt conflicts between the efforts of workers and those of employers to reorganize work relations often focused on methods of payment. This fact is not surprising – one endures work in search of pay. On the other hand, disputes over forms of payment crystalized the struggle over power at the point of production. The American Federation of Labor at its 1920 convention turned management's own rhetoric against it with the claim that the "workers are appalled at the waste and ignorance of management, but they are too frequently denied the chance to offer their knowledge for use." The remedy, the AFL resolved, was to replace "autocratic management" with "conference boards of organized workers and employers" as a means of "promoting the democracy of industry through the development of cooperative effort."[43]

On the Left, numerous activists of the Socialist Party, the Socialist Labor Party, and the Industrial Workers of the World derived from the workers' new forms of struggle a vague but attractive formula of "mass action," which promised to reconcile their earlier ideological differences over "parliamentary" versus "direct" action and to guide the working class toward the overthrow of capitalism.[44] All of them agreed that the workplace itself was the decisive battleground of revolutionary struggle and that the councils formed by workers in the midst of industrial conflicts were the embryonic forms of a future socialist regime. The cataclysmic experience of the war itself confirmed the wisdom of these mutually exclusive conclusions to their adherents on the Left and the Right and laid the basis for postwar divisions in the American workers' movement, comparable to those which their European counterparts then experienced.[45] It was the new level of workers' activity which all parties involved in these debates were trying to interpret from their own vantage points.

Bridgeport

Craftsmen's resistance to standardization, the new importance of machine tenders and tool die makers, the conflicts over the intensification of work and wage classifications, the employers' determination not to allow the vagaries of full employment to loosen their grip on their factories or impede managerial reform, the workers' new forms of organization, the gospel of "mass action" and the encounter between local revolutionaries and the newly powerful leadership of international unions were all evident in the munitions center of Bridgeport, Connecticut. A brief look at the events which unfolded there may serve to illustrate the preceding general arguments.

The state of Connecticut had been a center of brass, watch, armaments, and machine tool production since the eighteenth century. Bridgeport's good harbor, its ready access to the brass of Waterbury, and its location on Long Island Sound close to New York City had made it an ideal site for the manufacture of sewing machines, motor boats, typewriters, turret lathes, and gramaphones by the early twentieth century. It was here that the Remington Arms and Ammunition Company elected to build a factory in less than eight months of 1915 which could employ more than fifteen thousand workers. The company was a subsidiary of the Midvale Steel and Ordinance Company, on whose board of directors sat representatives of the Chase National Bank, the National City Bank of New York, International Nickel, Baldwin Locomotive, the Guarantee Trust Company, and Midvale Steel, as well as Percy A. Rockefeller himself.[46]

Incentive pay and time study prevailed throughout the machine shops of this city by 1910, and the machinists' union was so weak there that its Lodge 30 could not even send a delegate to the 1903 convention. By 1911 it had revived somewhat, and it cast its vote solidly with the Socialist bloc, which won control of the IAM that year. But it was only with the war orders of 1915 that the union grew in strength and, by threatening a strike, persuaded the Remington Arms Company to grant its workers an 8-hour day in August 1915. Huge contracts from the Russian government for cartridges, shells, machine guns, and other accouterments of modern warfare led Remington Arms to install thousands of specialized machine tools and employ men and women with little previous machine-shop experience. The older firms of Bridgeport soon became subcontractors for the new giant, making parts and especially tools, jigs, and fixtures. Hundreds of tool and die makers, of varying degrees of expertise, found employment in them.

Until the summer of 1917 most of the city's industrial conflict took place in the older companies, especially the American Graphophone Company, as those plants tried to fend off the growing power of the unions by discharging and blacklisting their members. In February, 1917, however, a strike of Remington Arms' metal polishers against a reduction of their piece rate for polishing bayonets was actively supported by more than one thousand machinists in the factory, despite the opposition of the local leadership of the IAM to any sympathetic action. In the union elections which occurred soon afterwards two prominent militants replaced the incumbent conservative leaders: Edwin O'Connell as President of Lodge 30 and Samuel Lavit as business agent of the city's District 55 of the IAM.

Lavit had formerly been active under several pseudonyms in the IWW, and he had served one and a half years in prison for his activities during the 1913 Paterson silk strike. He soon became Bridgeport's most famous citizen, loyally supported by an ever-growing circle of machinists and regularly denounced by the local press as a German agent and the source of all the city's troubles. "Samuel Lavit," announced the *Bridgeport Times* in a typical report, "surrounded by the usual crowd of henchmen, appeared at his usual haunts in the German cafes and wined and dined in a most lavish fashion."[47]

Under the leadership of Lavit and O'Connell, all of Remington Arms's machinists walked out in sympathy with the company's metal polishers in July 1917 when those craftsmen protested the employment of women to perform roughing and other less skilled polishing work. In the meantime, the machinists had drawn up a list of their own demands and circulated it to all the employers of the city. The 8-hour day, freedom to join unions, recognition of shop committees, and six standard wage classifications, ranging from tool maker to specialist and helper, were the basic demands. When Remington Arms responded with a reduction in piece rates for grinders and screw machine operators, it set off a wave of work stoppages, which lasted through most of September and October.

By January 1918, the organized machinists of Bridgeport had developed an effective style of struggle, in the face of heavy labor turnover, ever-spreading dilution of the craft, and draconic use of military conscription by the city's draft board to tame the restless workers. The proper strike procedure which was prescribed by the constitution of the IAM (involving negotiations with the management and a three-fourths affirmative majority of the union's members before a strike might be called) was ignored by the Bridgeport members. Stoppages in that city were sudden, usually brief, involved only one or two departments in most instances, and often ended with the strikers returning to work without a formal settlement, as abruptly as they had left.

Lavit loudly proclaimed his loyalty to the war effort, while his followers used strikes to bring government mediators running to the offices of their employers to plead for concessions. The only newspaper openly critical of the war was a Hungarian-language journal, which the government suppressed early in 1918. The Bridgeport *Labor Leader*, edited by Lavit himself, coupled patriotic stories from the front with acclaim for the endeavors of German revolutionaries and admonitions that a scientific organization of production could be established only by "the Cooperative system of production for use through industrial democracy." Its regular column, "Men and Matters" reprinted news items from the Socialist Labor Party's official organ, *The Weekly People*.[48] Four locals, including a new "Polish Lodge No. 782" and a very active Ladies' Auxiliary, developed under the aegis of District 55 of the IAM, and in each of more than seventy metal working plants in the city a shop committee carried grievances to the management.

The relative calm of early 1918 was shattered on Good Friday, when Remington Arms's tool makers walked out in a rage at the news that they were not to receive time-and-a-half for working that day. They assembled in their union hall, where they drew up a new set of demands. In addition to overtime pay on holidays, they called for a standard rate for their trade and others for machinists and operatives, equal pay for women who did equal work, the "free right to fraternize and co-operate for their mutual benefit," and a thirty-day extension of draft exemptions for anyone who changed jobs.[49] The campaign for these objectives reached its climax in May, when a strike began among subcontractors, then was dramatically joined by seven hundred tool makers and machinists from Remington Arms. A promise from the Ordnance Department to arbitrate the dispute sent everyone back to work.[50]

On June 8 the Labor Adjustment Board of the Ordnance Department agreed to six minimum wage classifications, covering tool makers, machinists and the more highly skilled specialists, but it said nothing about the less skilled operatives. When the large American and British Arms Company rejected the award, its employees began holding "a continuous meeting," and finally organized a public rally where some three thousand workers, heavily infiltrated by agents of the military intelligence, vowed to join the strike. All metal factories of the city were shut down, when the National War Labor Board announced it would take up the situation at once, if the strikers would return to their jobs.

Back they went, and throughout July their delegates presented arguments to the officials of the NWLB. The question of job classifications quickly became the central issue of the controversy. The IAM expanded its demands to seven standard rates, among them rates for machine operatives, and a minimum of thirty-five cents per hour for "women's jobs." In other words, the craft union had adapted its standard rate principle to cover all metal workers in the city. So sharp was the disagreement within the NWLB itself over the question that, for the first time in its career, the board engaged an umpire to resolve the dispute among its own members. Loyall Osborne of Westinghouse personally presented the employers' case. The "thousands of hourly rates" in Bridgeport, he argued, were "incentives to self-interest," with which the government had no right to interfere. Above all, he added, it was outrageous to propose that machine tenders doing a wide variety of work be given a single rate.

In its award on August 28, the board decided "against changing the method" of payment "now in operation." It did grant extensive wage increases on a sliding scale, the largest going to the lowest-paid workers on a percentage of their present earnings. It also granted a minimum wage of thirty-two cents an hour for the two thousand women on piecework and decreed an 8-hour day. Finally, it called for government-supervised elections of shop committees, which should be recognized by every employer, and for a city-wide committee of six workers' representatives and six employers, to hear appeals from disputes in any factory of the city. The Bridgeport employers and the Board alike evidently hoped to isolate the militant machinists' lodges by offering large wage increases to the unskilled workers who did not belong to the union and by establishing government-supervised shop committees, which would be far more broadly representative of the workers than the craft unions and presumably less militant than the existing unofficial committees.[51]

The skilled machinists were enraged by the award, but it confronted them with a difficult strategic problem. To react with a successful strike they would need to enlist the active support of the unskilled operatives and also to violate the no-strike pledge of their international union. Both acts would bring them into conflict, not only with their employers and government, but also with the leaders of the IAM. The contradiction inherent in their position quickly became evident.

A huge Labor Day rally, bedecked with large placards denouncing bloated profiteers, was addressed by both President William Johnston of the IAM, who reminded his members of their patriotic duty to continue production, and the future Communist leader Ella Reeve Bloor, who evoked roars of enthusiasm with her denunciation of the NWLB's award, the capitalist war, and the imprisonment of Eugene V. Debs. By the time the board tried to conduct its shop committee elections the following week, more than five thousand workers were already on strike. They demanded that President Woodrow Wilson seize the factories and enforce the earlier ordinance department ruling, and they refused to return to work without classified standard wages. When a national officer of the IAM, addressing another rally the following Sunday, threatened to revoke each local's charter if they did not return to work, the strikers bellowed, "take it!" and passed resolutions calling for a national convention of the union to depose its officers, if they outlawed the strike.[52]

It was not President Johnston but President Wilson who outlawed the strike. On September 13 he addressed a letter to the Bridgeport machinists, ordering them back to work. "If you refuse," said the president's proclamation, "each of you will be barred from employment in any war industry in the community in which the strike occurs for a period of one year . . . and the draft boards will be instructed to reject any claim of exemption based on your alleged usefulness on war production."[53]

The strikers quickly returned to their jobs, and in the ensuing calm the city's Board of Education created a network of community associations, under the personal direction of Harrison Streeter of the Committee on Public Information and President Wilson's daughter Margaret, to promote industrial peace and warn "against German propaganda." The schools were "thrown open to the workers in the munitions plant for the selection of committees to deal on their behalf with the employers," announced a CPI news release, labeled "for Social Democratic League – European Circulation."[54]

When the workers elected their six representatives to the city-wide arbitration panel, however, Lavit himself and two other strike leaders were among those chosen. The employers refused to deal with them. Moreover, District 55 launched a local American Labor Party in the November elections, running candidates for every local office "for the express purpose," according to their platform, "of exercising their political rights as an instrument of industrial emancipation thus paving the way for an autonomous Industrial Republic (shop control in the factories, mines, mills, and other establishments wherein workers are employed)."[55] The phraseology of this declaration was clearly borrowed from the Socialist Labor Party.

The Bridgeport Central Labor Union, which was dominated by cautious members of the Socialist Party, refused to endorse the electoral effort. More important, the new party was too tightly bound to the local IAM (to which every one of its candidates belonged) to attract many voters. Undaunted by its small poll, the *Labor Leader* enthusiastically endorsed revolutionary proposals from other lodges of the IAM, especially that of Micrometer Lodge 460 in New York, to which Ella Reeve Bloor belonged, for a convention to reconstruct the IAM on industrial union principles.

When cancellation of government contracts in December 1918 brought heavy unemployment to the city, Lavit's organization staged a rally of nearly four thousand workers, under close scrutiny from the police, who prohibited a parade and limited the number of speakers. At this point Lavit could still share the platform with Andrew McNamara of the IAM's leadership and attorney Louis Waldman of the Socialist Party. Petitions to Congress were circulated, calling for "National Labor Agencies" to protect collective bargaining, extensive public works to absorb the unemployed, and the "abolition of competition, criminal waste and profiteering in industry and substituting co-operative ownership and democratic management of industry and securing to each the full product of his toil." At the IAM hall Louise Bryant's new book *Six Red Months in Russia* was on sale, and Miss Bryant herself addressed a second rally of the unemployed on the Soviet solution to their problem.[56]

In short, a continuous struggle by the munitions workers of Bridgeport against the huge Remington Arms Company and its scores of local subcontractors had evolved from a craft-based effort of machinists and metal polishers to enforce their union scales and work rules into a confrontation involving several thousand men and women, who were attempting to establish collective bargaining and their own scheme of wage classifications in the face of unrelenting opposition from their employers. The intensity and persistence of this battle brought the city's district of the IAM under the leadership of Lavit, O'Connell, and their colleagues, who never opposed the war effort, but did use their position to popularize the Socialist Labor Party's conception of "an autonomous Industrial Republic" based on "shop control" as the true way to operate industry scientifically. They also used the lodges of the IAM to coordinate both city-wide strikes, involving nonmembers as well as union members, and the activities of the government-sponsored shop committees. They even won election to the city's arbitration board, which had been designed to combat their influence.

On the other hand, the war's end virtually closed the Remington Arms plant and left older firms of the city determined to rid themselves promptly of the radical menace which had grown up in their midst. Although the National War Labor Board strove to strengthen the shop committees it had created, the city's manufacturers treated that agency with undisguised scorn as the date approached for the closing of its local office, in March 1919. The city-wide arbitration board never functioned, and in its absence only the role of the IAM prevented the shop committees from becoming simply company unions, or collapsing altogether.[57]

Consequently, the hostility of the international officers of the IAM toward the leaders in Bridgeport became increasingly important in the local balance of power. President Johnston warned in May against the "growing tendency" of lodges to disregard the laws of the IAM, especially when they were connected with shop committees and metal trades councils, and he insisted that he would enforce his union's regulations no matter what the price. Hardly two months later a wave of strikes swept across the older Bridgeport firms, bringing out 22 thousand workers by the beginning of August. When Lavit applied to the international union for strike funds, the executive board replied by accusing Lavit of admitting anyone to the IAM, regardless of trade, and it suspended him from office. The board charged that the membership of Lodge 30 had fallen from four thousand to fourteen hundred under Lavit's misleadership and that he pulled men "on the street under promises of benefits who were not members of the IAM" or connected with the trade, "in conjunction with an organization known as the W.I.I.U." The charge referred to the union arm of the Socialist Labor Party, formerly known as the Detroit IWW. "We are at this time," concluded the board's circular, "fighting Lavitt [sic.], the I.W.W. group, the private detective group, the manufacturers' association group, all in one."[59] When Lodge 30 continued to support Lavit, its charter was revoked.[60]

By August 10 the Bridgeport strikes had collapsed, and the city had set out on the short road back to open-shop status. Lodge 30 was restored the next spring, in the safe hands of "good members," but its influence within the city remained negligible.[61] In the meantime, within a month of his suspension from union office, Lavit was arrested in Newport,

Rhode Island, and charged with having driven across the state boundary with a male friend and two young women "for immoral purposes," in violation of the Mann White Slave Act. The Mayor of Bridgeport and a federal agent offered him the choices of facing prosecution or leaving the city. On August 30 the *Bridgeport Times* printed the banner headline: "Sam Lavit quits town."[62]

Conclusions

Throughout the first two decades of the twentieth century both organized workers and management reformers were attempting to reform work relations. Over the demise of customary factory management, based on the autonomy of the skilled craftsman and the personal authority of the foreman, there developed a bitter battle of standards. Scientific management and trade-union rules sought to transform industrial practice in mutually exclusive ways. The conflict reached its greatest intensity during periods of abundant employment after 1909, when scientific management spread rapidly through metal-working industries and became increasingly concerned with personnel relations. Simultaneously, the level of strike activity rose rapidly, and large numbers of workers took part in devising forms of organization which transcended older craft union lines. The workers formulated their own plans counter to those of management, particularly in the realm of payment schemes. These developments intensified the employers' determination to restore the "open shop" and contributed significantly to the ideological controversies which divided the labor movement.

Notes

* This essay originally appeared in a somewhat different form and in French as "Quels Standards? Les ouvriers et la réorganisation de la production aux Etats-Unis (1900–1920)," *Le Mouvement Social*, 102 (Janvier–Mars 1978), 101–27. Research for the study was assisted by a fellowship from the John Simon Guggenheim Memorial Foundation.
1 For three different views of the role of foremen and craftsmen in late nineteenth-century industry, see Daniel Nelson, *Managers and Workers: Origins of the New Factory System in the United States 1880–1920* (Madison, Wis., 1975); Benson Soffer, "A Theory of Trade Union Development: The Role of the 'Autonomous' Workman," *Labor History*, 1 (Spring 1960), 141–63; David Montgomery, "Workers' Control of Machine Production in the Nineteenth Century," *Labor History*, 17 (Fall 1976), 485–509.
2 David A. McCabe, *The Standard Rate in American Trade Unions* (Baltimore, 1912); Jacob H. Hollander and George E. Barnett, *Studies in American Trade Unionism* (New York, 1912); John R. Commons, et al., *History of Labour in*

the United States, 4 vols., (New York, 1918–1935), IV, 41–123; Fred S. Hall, *Sympathetic Strikes and Sympathetic Lockouts* (New York, 1898).

3 Nelson, 34–54.

4 See Samuel Haber, *Efficiency and Uplift: Scientific Management in the Progressive Era, 1890–1920* (Chicago, 1964); Milton J. Nadworny, *Scientific Management and the Unions, 1900–1932* (Cambridge, 1955); Robert F. Hoxie, *Scientific Management and Labor* (New York, 1915); Robert F. Wiebe, *Businessmen and Reform: A Study of the Progressive Movement* (Cambridge, 1962); Monte A. Calvert, *The Mechanical Engineer in America, 1830–1910: Professional Cultures in Conflict* (Baltimore, 1967).

5 F. W. Taylor, *The Principles of Scientific Management* (New York, 1912); Taylor, "Shop Management," *Transactions of the American Society of Mechanical Engineers*, 24 (1903), 1337–1456; Nelson, 55–78.

6 Taylor, *Principles*, 83.

7 David S. Landes, *The Unbound Prometheus: Technological Change and Industrial Development in Western Europe from 1750 to the Present* (Cambridge, 1969), 290–326; Nelson, 3–33.

8 The best single source on these practices is U.S. Commissioner of Labor, *Eleventh Special Report*, "Regulation and Restriction of Output" (Washington, D.C., 1904).

9 U.S. Congress, *Hearings before the Special Committee of the House of Representatives to Investigate the Taylor and Other Systems of Shop Management* (Washington, 1912), 1393.

10 R. T. Kent, "Micro-Motion Study in Industry," *Iron Age*, 91 (January 2, 1913), 37. For differing assessments of time study among Taylor's colleagues, see Nelson, 65–6.

11 *Taylor Hearings*, 1000.

12 Hugh G. J. Aitken, *Taylorism at the Watertown Arsenal: Scientific Management in Action, 1908–1915* (Cambridge, 1960), 137–50; *Taylor Hearings*, 228–30, 895–922, 1236–50, 1660–9; *Iron Age*, 95 (April 29, 1915), 954–5; David Montgomery, "The 'New Unionism' and the Transformation of Workers' Consciousness in America, 1909–1922," *Journal of Social History*, 7 (Summer 1974), 523–4.

13 "Regulation and Restriction of Output," 197.

14 U.S. Commission on Industrial Relations, *Final Report and Testimony*, 11 vols., Senate Document No. 415, 64th Congress, 1st session (Washington, D.C., 1916), 1, 879–80; G. C. Kilbonny to *Machinists Monthly Journal*, 15 (September 1903), 826–7; Henry L. Gantt, "A Practical Application of Scientific Management," *Engineering Magazine*, 41 (April 1911), 8.

15 S. B. Mathewson, *Restriction of Output among Unorganized Workers* (New York, 1931), 54, 71, 153. See also John Macy, *Socialism in America* (Garden City, N.Y., 1916), 170; Mike Davis, "The Stop Watch and the Wooden Shoe: Scientific Management and the Industrial Workers of the World," *Radical America*, 8 (January–February 1975), 69–96.

16 Editorial, *Machinists Monthly Journal*, 9 (May 1897), 139.

17 Commission on Industrial Relations, *Report*, 1, 944.

18 Charles Reitell, "Machinery and Its Effects Upon the Workers in the Automobile Industry," *Annals, American Academy of Political and Social Science*, 116 (November 1924), 37–43. The quotation is on p. 39.

19 Taylor, "Shop Management," 1422; Maurine Greenwald, "Women Workers and World War I: The American Railroad Industry, A Case Study," *Journal of Social History*, 9 (Winter 1976), 157, 169–71.

20 S. H. Bunnell, "Jigs and Fixtures as Substitutes for Skill," *Iron Age*, 93 (March 5, 1914), 610–11.

21 Horace L. Arnold and Fay L. Faurote, *Ford Methods and Ford Shops* (New York, 1915), 41–2.

22 Ibid., 6, 8, 38, 46. The quotation is on p. 6.

23 Ibid., 46, 61; Keith Sward, *The Legend of Henry Ford* (New York, 1948), 32–8; Alfred D. Chandler, Jr., *Giant Enterprise: Ford, General Motors, and the Automobile Industry* (New York, 1964), 34–45; *Iron Age*, 93 (January 1, 1914), 48–51, (January 8, 1914), 150–1; (January 29, 1914), 306–9; L.A., "The Automobile Industry," *International Socialist Review*, 13 (September 1912), 255–8; Nelson, 144–50.

24 See "strike decade" section, Ch. 4.

25 Henry L. Gantt, "The Mechanical Engineer and the Textile Industry," *Transactions of the American Society of Mechanical Engineers*, 32 (1910), 499–506; *Taylor Hearings*, 592–605; Henry L. Gantt, *Work, Wages, and Profits*, 2nd ed. rev., (New York, 1919), 9; New Jersey Bureau of Industrial Statistics, *Thirty-Ninth Annual Report* (Trenton, 1917), 244.

26 U.S. Congress, *Report on the Strike at the Bethlehem Steel Works*, Senate Document No. 521, 61st Congress, 2d session (Washington, D.C., 1910), 35; Gantt, "Practical Application," 1–8.

27 Examiner in charge to E. B. Woods, October 28, 1918, National War Labor Board Administrative File B 56, Record Group 2, National Archives; NWLB Docket No. 22, "Findings in re. Machinists, Electrical Workers, et al, versus Bethlehem Steel Company . . . July, 1918," Record Group 2, National Archives, Washington, D.C.

28 See section on "strike decade," Ch. 4.

29 *Iron Age*, 97 (May 4, 1916), 1075.

30 See J. B. S. Hardman, *American Labor Dynamics in the Light of Post-War Developments* (New York, 1928); Robert H. Zieger, *Republicans and Labor, 1919–1929* (Lexington, Ky., 1969); Vertrees J. Wyckoff, *Wage Policies of Labor Organizations in a Period of Industrial Depression* (Baltimore, 1926).

31 "Regulation and Restriction of Output," 103. On payment plans in Europe, see Peter N. Stearns, *Lives of Labor: Work in a Maturing Industrial Society* (New York, 1975), 214–19.

32 "Regulation and Restriction of Output," 197; Mark Perlman, *The Machinists: A New Study in American Trade Unionism* (Cambridge, 1961), 24–26, 43.

33 Taylor, "Shop Management," 1342; Gantt, *Work, Wages, and Profits*, 58–60; G. D. Babcock, "Fixing Individual Wage Rates on Facts," *Iron Age*, 97 (June 8, 1916), 1375–9.

34 See McCabe, *Standard Rate*.

35 Department of Labor, Mediation and Conciliation Service files 33/37, 33/202, 33/374, 33/2849, 170/487, Record Group 280, National Archives, Washington, D.C.

36 NWLB Administrative Files B 54, Record Group 2; Department of Labor Mediation and Conciliation Service files 33/403, 33/1702, Record Group 2, National Archives, Washington, D.C.

37 On GE, see NWLB Administrative Files B 54, Record Group 2. On Bridgeport, see "Brief Submitted by Remington Arms Union Metallic Cartridge Company, July 12, 1918," 18–19, NWLB Case File 132, Box 21, Record Group 2, National Archives, Washington, D.C.

38 Commission on Industrial Relations, *Report*, 10, 9697–10048; Carl E. Person,

The Lizard's Trail. A Story of the Illinois Central and Harriman Lines Strike of 1911 to 1915 Inclusive (Chicago, 1918); Alexander M. Bing, *War-Time Strikes and Their Adjustment* (New York, 1921), 160–4.

39 *Machinists Monthly Journal*, 31 (March 1919), 233.

40 Osborne to Taft, May 31, 1918, Records of the NWLB, E 15, Administrative Files, National Archives, Washington, D.C.

41 "Brief Submitted by Manufacturers other than the Remington Arms and U.M.C. Companies," NWLB Case File 132, Box 20, Record Group 2, National Archives, Washington, D. C.

42 Zieger, 17–50, 109–43; Federated American Engineering Societies, *Waste in Industry* (New York, 1921).

43 Quoted in Commons, *Industrial Government*, 371–2.

44 Karl Dannenberg, *Reform or Revolution, or Socialism and Socialist Politics* (New York, 1918); Charles E. Ruthenberg, *Are We Growing Toward Socialism?* (Cleveland, 1917); *The Rank and File vs. The Labor Skates, with Official Statements of the Communists and I.W.W. and the One Big Union Advocates in Regard to Industrial and Political Action in America* (n.p., 1920).

45 See James Weinstein, *The Decline of Socialism in America, 1912–1925* (New York, 1967), 177–257.

46 *Iron Age*, 96 (October 14, 1915), 908; ibid., 96 (July 22, 1915), 201–3.

47 *Bridgeport Times*, May 10, 1918; NWLB Case File 132, Record Group 2, National Archives, Washington, D.C. On Lavit, see R. M. Wade to W. B. Wilson, n.d., Department of Labor Mediation and Conciliation Service file 33/567, and file 33/347, Record Group 280, National Archives, Washington, D.C.

48 NWLB Case File 132; W. H. Lamar to George Creel, March 4, 1918, file 49506, Record Group 28, National Archives, Washington, D.C.; *Labor Leader*, January 10, 13, 17, 1918.

49 Department of Labor Mediation and Conciliation Service File, 33/1116.

50 "Transcripts of Proceedings, District 55 . . . " NWLB Case File 132, Box 22, Record Group 2, pp. 100–5.

51 "Transcripts of Proceedings, District 55"; "Brief submitted by Remington Arms Union Metallic Cartridge Company," NWLB Case File 132, Box 21; "Transcript, Executive Session of Board, Washington, D.C. August 16, 1918," NWLB Case File 132, Box 20, Record Group 2.

52 Department of Labor Mediation and Conciliation Service files 33/1116, 33/1819, Record Group 280; "Collective Bargaining," typescript in C. P. Sweeney files, Record Group 2; Ella Reeve Bloor, *We Are Many* (New York, 1940), 146–7; A. Winter to W. Jett Lauck, September 10, 1918, NWLB Administrative Files, B 56, Record Group 2.

53 "Letter from the President of the United States to Striking Employees at Bridgeport, Conn.," September 13, 1918, Record Group 2.

54 *National Plan of Community Organization and Local Community Constitution* (n.p., n.d.); "Hello, Uncle Sam," typescript, September 10, 1918; "Collective Bargaining," C. P. Sweeney files.

55 *Labor Leader*, October 24, October 31, November 7, 1918.

56 Ibid., Dec. 19, 1918, January 2, 9, 16, 1919; "Petition for the Creation of National Labor Agencies," NWLB Case File 132, Box 22, Record Group 2.

57 A. Winter to E. B. Woods, March 19, 1919, W. G. Aborn to E. B. Woods, March 8, 1919, NWLB Case File 132, Box 20, Record Group 2.

58 *Machinists Monthly Journal*, 31 (June 1919), 511–12.
59 Connecticut Bureau of Labor Statistics, *Twenty-Ninth Report* (Hartford, 1920), 57–66; *Machinists Monthly Journal*, 31 (September 1919), 857.
60 *MMJ*, 31 (September 1919), 853, (October 1919), 953.
61 Ibid., 32 (July 1920), 645.
62 Ibid., 32 (April 1920), 317; *Bridgeport Times*, August 30, 1919. Lavit soon returned to Bridgeport and became active in the Republican Party. In 1951 Republican leaders proposed his name as a candidate for mayor, to oppose the Socialist incumbent, but Lavit declined to run. Bridgeport *Post*, November 4, 1951, December 18, 1958 (obituary). I am indebted for this information to Ms. Cecelia Bucki.

6. Facing layoffs

Co-author: Ronald Schatz

Overwork and unemployment have been indispensable and inseparable characteristics of economic life under capitalism since its inception. No American worker who came of age before 1940 could have failed to be keenly aware of the relationship between the two. The first fifteen years of this century were marked by rapid economic growth and a relentless increase in productivity per worker, yet in only one of those years did the annual rate of unemployment fall below 6 percent of the industrial labor force. In nine of those years it rose above 10 percent. Long before and long after that period a "slack season" came every year in construction, clothing manufacture, lumbering, coal mining, and other industries, and in meat packing easily half again as many people could find employment during the first three days of any week as in the last three. From time to time the entire economy was plunged into crisis: during 1903–4, 1908–9, 1913–14, and 1920–2 one out of every five or six wage earners faced grim weeks or months without a job. And, of course, memories of the hungry thirties haunt older workers to this day.

The more recent, protracted experience of Americans with relatively high levels of employment, unemployment compensation, and welfare systems (which were forced by popular struggles of the 1930s and 1960s to be noticeably more accessible to those in need than anything experienced by earlier generations) has served to dull our memories of the techniques formerly used by workers to cope with unemployment of both the routine and catastrophic varieties. Even the sharp economic slumps of 1949–50, 1953–4, and 1957–9 failed to generate a significant revival of the types of self-organized activity at the base which had been characteristic of earlier crises. On the other hand, the severity of the current levels of unemployment and the prospect that much higher levels of joblessness than have been customary in the last thirty-five years are likely to be with us for a long time to come have made it important to recall various ways in which workers used to cope with layoffs and widespread unemployment in their ranks.

Workers' styles of adaptive struggle have changed in response to changes

139

in managerial practices, the government's role, and the strength and structure of unionism. The depression of the 1930s itself marked an important watershed in all these developments, and hence in the evolution of workers' practices. That decade saw the rise of seniority systems to govern layoffs in mass-production industries, unemployment compensation to ease the burden of short-term joblessness, and extensive relief programs, financed by the federal government to get the angry unemployed off the streets. All those developments modified the forms of workers' actions in the face of widespread joblessness.

Seniority

Seniority itself emerged from the confluence of twentieth-century managerial practice with the demands of workers in depression-born industrial unionism. Few nineteenth-century workers harbored any sense of long-term attachment to a particular company. The tie to one's trade was far stronger than that to one's place of work. When, for example, the Massachusetts Bureau of Statistics of Labor surveyed 230 shoe operatives, textile hands, machinists, carpenters, and others in 1878, it found that 65 percent of them had been in the same occupation for more than ten years, but only 15 percent had been that long with the same firm.[1] The extraordinary rates of geographic movement, which Stephan Thernstrom and other historians have lately made so familiar to us, had their counterpart in rates of job turnover which dwarf anything to be found today. When major corporations first became seriously concerned about turnover, during the rather flush period between early 1910 and late 1913, they found that separations averaged slightly over 100 percent of the number of people on company payrolls each year, and that more than two-thirds of the workers leaving quit on their own initiative. The Ford Motor Company's 415 percent turnover rate of 1912–13 dwarfed its 1969 rate of 25 percent. Major efforts were undertaken to secure the stability of trained workers after that period, and especially during the 1920s. Pensions, stock options, insurance, home financing, and other benefits were awarded in return for long service with the company. Consequently the median quit rate in manufacturing fell to 30 percent per year by 1929, and then in the face of the depression below 15 percent in 1936 and 1937. By 1949–50 the average annual turnover for all occupations had reached the all-time low of less than 10 percent.[2]

Of course, workers usually quit when plenty of other jobs were available. When economic downturns made it necessary to lay off large numbers of employees, however, many companies learned to sack relatively new and unskilled workers wholesale (their turnover rates being incurably high in any case), while transferring more skilled and experienced men and women into the unskilled jobs, or instituting a general reduction of their hours, so as to spread the available work within the favored group. Most glass works, located as they were in small towns which could have met huge welfare costs only by increasing taxes on the mills, cut hours rather than dismissing older men, even after mechanization had broken unions. Westinghouse retained almost all the workers at its vast East Pittsburgh plant who had more than ten years service during the worst of the early 1930s. Ford and General Motors in those same years devised preferential lists of skills, which the NRA's automobile labor board easily converted into departmental seniority rules in 1934.[3]

These company practices had two important effects. First, they allowed the employers to assume the initiative in worksharing, for which workers had often fought before. Despite the fact that this initiative was applied selectively (favoring leaders of local ethnic lodges, activists in the Democratic and Republican machines, officers of veterans organizations, etc., and throwing workers older than fifty out wholesale), they often succeeded in earning the intense gratitude of people who had been saved from layoff by these means. Secondly, as workers' attachment to a particular place of work grew stronger, a new tendency developed (to a remarkable degree in the 1930s) for people who had lost their jobs to stay where they were and wait to be recalled. As late as the bitter depression of 1920–2, more than half of the Slavic and Black workers of Allegheny County left the region, just as their nineteenth century counterparts would have done. What was new after 1929 was not the vagrancy but the relative lack of it, the large numbers of people who did not move to another town in search of work. Of course, the universality of the crisis reinforced the sedentary impulses which new management practices had nurtured. It was, however, this new tenacity which provided the basis for the rapid rise of unemployed organizations, irresistible pressure on legislatures for unemployment compensation, and struggles demanding that particular companies restore jobs, most notably the Ford Hunger March of 1932.

It was out of this setting that workers' demands for the regulation of layoff and recall by seniority became a central feature of the emerging industrial unionism. Before the 1930s the seniority principle was seldom found in union rules or contracts, as they applied to layoffs. The peculiar characteristics of each occupation had shaped its workers' demands. Seniority clauses were unknown in coal miners' unions down to World War

11. Such schemes as two weeks of work for half the miners, followed by two weeks for the other half, remained commonplace. Anthracite miners, whose industry was clearly expiring during the thirties, did raise a contract demand for seniority in layoffs in 1940, but failed to get it. Like garment and construction workers, miners had previously sought to safeguard themselves against arbitrary dismissals by a combination of the closed shop and a standard rate (minimum wage), which would deny the employer any economic advantage from dismissing union members or better paid men or women first. As seasons of steady work drew to a close, workers in all three of these groups customarily slowed down. For contract miners and clothing workers in piecework, this custom amounted to a self-instituted work-sharing scheme. Garment workers still practice it today.[4]

The closed shop, combined with a union hiring hall, provided workers with the best possible control over who got recalled to a job when work picked up again. Just such a hall was especially important to longshoremen, sailors, and construction workers, whose jobs changed constantly and for whom seniority never had much meaning. In the San Francisco strike of 1934 a rotary hiring hall was the central demand of the longshoremen. Of course, such hiring control could be used effectively to exclude Blacks, as was done by Brooklyn's Local 968 of the International Longshoremen's Association in 1949–50, but it could also be used to secure the position of at least a minimal quota of Blacks, as it was in New York's retail stores by Local (later District) 65 during the same period.

Layoffs themselves were dealt with by unionized workers as they arose. Tapestry weavers in Philadelphia's many shops fabricating upholstery textiles drew lots to determine who would leave and, where possible, exchanged surplus members among shops under union control. Seniority was used by them only to decide which weaver got which loom. The locals in the beef-killing and sheep-killing sections of Chicago packing houses during the period of peak union strength (1903) actually waged a successful struggle to prevent any layoffs at all, then demanded a raise in piece rates to compensate for their scanty work late in each week. Machinists in Chicago's militant District 8 of the IAM demanded "seniority and proficiency to govern" in recall from layoffs in 1900, though they made no mention of the layoffs themselves. Many railroads of that period followed the pattern of the machinists' agreement covering repair-shop workers of the Atcheson, Topeka, and Sante Fe, which stipulated that "when reductions in force are necessary, seniority, proficiency and married men be given the preference of employment." Much more common in the machinists' trade, however, was the clause: "Should a reduction of expenses become necessary, it shall be made in a reduction of hours, unless otherwise agreed upon by both parties."[5]

Closed shop, standard rate, work spreading, and (where possible) a union-controlled hiring hall, then, were the most common techniques by which organized workers regulated layoffs before 1930. Organized and unorganized workers alike slowed down, when the word from the shipping room and office clerks had it that a layoff was in the offing. Seniority clauses did appear occasionally. As early as 1886 the Knights of Labor put one in an agreement with the large E. S. Higgins Carpet Weaving Company after a strike against discriminatory dismissals. In fact, strike settlements served to popularize the idea of seniority. Early in the twentieth century the demand of unions that employers should fire all scabs and reinstate all strikers was often compromised after long struggles by reinstating all employees (old and new) in order of seniority. During World War I the National War Labor Board used that formula regularly in its mediation of strikes. The first widespread general application of the seniority principle, however, appeared on the railroads under government administration in 1918 and 1919. Unionized railroad shop crafts managed to keep seniority even after the disastrous strike of 1922. Locomotive engineers, however, were often successful in avoiding unemployment by urging the railroads to lay off firemen instead of themselves, and put the engineers temporarily to stoking the firebox.[6]

It was, therefore, with the industrial unions of the 1930s that the seniority rule became so basic a part of American life that many workers today find it difficult to imagine any other principle as just. Nothing was more obvious to the workers of the 1930s than the insecurity of their jobs. As soon as they organized in any form, they demanded an end to arbitrary employers' control over layoff and recall. The power of foremen to pick and choose which worker should stay and which should go was challenged by a determined struggle to impose a clear, objective standard on layoffs. Seniority clauses were demanded and won by the new unions in rubber, oil, steel, textiles, electrical machinery, auto, and urban transportation.[7] Often these clauses were not far removed from what the companies had already been doing in practice, but they eliminated the arbitrariness which had characterized that practice when it rested entirely on the companies' initiative. The gain was of enormous importance to older workers especially, and it provided a major component of the complex formula by which the second generation of Eastern and Southern Europeans secured a recognized position in American economic life.

Unemployment relief

Regulating layoffs, however, was only one facet of workers' efforts to cope with unemployment. The other was the struggle to put food on the tables of those who were already out of work. This effort assumed too many different forms under constantly varying circumstances to allow anything like a full account here. At times workers' parties and unions staged massive public rallies demanding relief from municipal authorities, as they did in New York City in the winter of 1873–4, or marched in force into bourgeois neighborhoods to dramatize the workers' hunger, as they did in Chicago in 1884. In other instances unions whose members could afford high dues, like cigar makers and printers, paid benefits out of the unions' treasuries to unemployed members.

It was probably the first nine months of the Crisis of 1893 which witnessed the most impressive variety of efforts by unions to aid the jobless. In Danbury, Connecticut, locked-out hat workers went to the town meeting and voted themselves and other unemployed people fifty thousand dollars in relief (which the selectmen subsequently refused to pay). In Chicago a series of militant demonstrations organized by the unions forced Mayor Carter Harrison and the city council to appropriate funds for relief and public work directly to a union-controlled Labor and Temporary Relief Committee. In Denver, which teemed with unemployed miners from mountain camps of the region, the city's Trades and Labor Assembly established Camp Relief, which provided shelter and clothing in a tent colony run completely by its own inhabitants, and the Maverick Restaurant, which fed 550 people a day.[8]

All these efforts ultimately collapsed from lack of funds, and relief work in each community was taken over by church and civic reform groups, which had the confidence of wealthy contributors. It was only appropriate, therefore, that the IWW aimed its unemployed struggles of 1913 and 1914 directly at public charities and churches. Its most famous efforts involved direct action to clean up relief shelters and the invasion of Catholic churches during mass to demand some Christian charity on the spot.[9] The unemployed movements of the early 1930s resorted to both self-organized mutual assistance and pressure on charities and public agencies, but they enjoyed little of the assistance from city central labor bodies which had been evident in the 1890s.

The final phase of the depression of the thirties, which began with the severe downturn of the fall of 1937, forced the young unions of the CIO to act quickly and imaginatively on both fronts: control of layoffs and relief to the unemployed. On the latter, the unions themselves assumed many of the functions which unemployed councils and leagues had exercised before 1935. Dealing with layoffs, they coupled the new seniority principle with older working-class practices, often in highly imaginative ways, which suggested that the two forms of regulation could be combined effectively by workers who had both ingenuity and audacity.

It is important to recall how perilous was the plight of the new unions. Hardly had the first contracts of CIO unions been negotiated when the economic upswing, which had nurtured labor's militancy and effectiveness in 1935 and 1936, collapsed. In the last quarter of 1937 the steel industry suffered the largest production drop in its history (roughly 70 percent), and its total payroll was cut in half. In St. Louis, a center of light electrical manufacturing, the United Electrical Workers found half its members unemployed throughout 1938, and most of the others working only part time. That year was one of many lost strikes, and companies like General Motors, Philco, and Maytag sought to withdraw what recognition they had extended to the CIO. The traditional union device of controlling layoffs through the closed shop was denied to the new industrial unions by the adamant resistance of the corporations. Court rulings against sit-down strikes and an ominous rash of "labor peace bills" in state legislatures made veterans of the labor movement fear that a repetition of the disasters of 1920–2 was at hand.

On the other hand, hundreds of thousands of the workers who were being laid off from mass-production industries were already union members. In the UE "out-of-work stamps" were issued for five cents a month (regular dues were one dollar a month), and those who paid such dues were treated as full-fledged members, with voting rights at local meetings. Local secretaries were urged by the international officers to keep laid-off members informed of all meetings and developments in their locals. Many locals assisted unemployed members in obtaining relief and in fighting any bureaucratic obstacles they might encounter in welfare agencies.[10] At its 1939 convention the UE resolved to battle in each district for the right of workers to be placed on relief automatically, as soon as they were certified as unemployed by union officers, thus circumventing any investigation by welfare agencies. Indeed, in some industrial centers, like Pittsburgh and Tarentum, Pennsylvania, CIO unions had won the power to place their unemployed members on relief rolls by early 1938.[11]

Moreover, UE locals waged a major and often highly effective effort to place their unemployed members quickly on the payrolls of the WPA and to defend their rights and earnings there. In Dayton, Ohio, the UE established a WPA Auxiliary to assist its needy members. The new auxiliary quickly expanded its endeavors to try to organize all workers in the area's WPA, to press workers' grievances with WPA officials, and to campaign for higher wages on WPA work. It had a steward system and an educational committee. According to K. M. Kirkendall, a well-known leader of the UE in Dayton, the auxiliary was "spreading the gospel of unionism to many people who never had the opportunity to organize before the axe fell and cut them away from private employment."[12]

Jobless union members were thus forged into a link between the in-dustrial workers of the community as a whole and the new industrial unions. Similar activities were undertaken by UE locals in St. Louis, where Henry Fiering, financial secretary of Local 1108, who had himself been fired from Century Electric after a strike in April 1937, helped place 700 laid-off workers from that company on WPA jobs or relief during the following year. Nor were such activities confined to the UE. As early as 1935 the Trotskyist-led Local 574 of the Teamsters had created an effective Federal Workers' Section, which took over many of the functions formerly performed by the Trotskyists' unemployed or-ganization in Minneapolis. Numerous locals of the Steel Workers Or-ganizing Committee set up relief committees for their unemployed members, who were exonerated from all dues and assisted in getting relief by staff representatives.[13]

Clearly the activities of the Steel Workers were more in the form of a service to the members, as was typical of that organization, while those of the Teamsters and UE took the form of mobilization of the members. The difference between waiving all dues and requiring a nickel a month is symbolic of the contrast. But both forms of activity represented a new style of unemployed struggle, which was significantly different from that of the early 1930s. The struggles of the early thirties had been largely community-based, highly spontaneous in their actions, and organized by the various revolutionary parties. Those of the late thirties were shaped in the mold of industrial unionism and directly attached to the new unions.

The new characteristics became most evident in the WPA strikes of the summer of 1939. Early that year the new conservative majority in Congress had ordered all WPA offices to trim their rolls, to require a loyalty oath of WPA employees, to close down all nonmanual relief work such as theater projects and historical records surveys, which could not find state sponsorship, and, most drastic of all, to lay off for one month everyone who had been on the rolls for more than a year and a half.[14] The response in Minneapolis typified the new role of unions in the unemployed movement. The strike was called by a United Organizational Committee, which consisted of five representatives from each of the following groups: the AFL Central Labor Union, the city's Building Trades Council, the Federal Workers Section of the truck drivers' local (now numbered 544), the Workers' Alliance (a united front of the older unemployed organizations), and the county CIO Council. All projects of the WPA were picketed, and the committee demanded that the WPA administrator for the state close them down. The walkout was widespread, but fiercely resisted by the new Republican administrations of the city and state, which had ousted their Farmer-Labor predecessors through campaigns dominated by imflammatory red-baiting and anti-Semitism the previous fall. The projects were kept open; police fired into one crowd of pickets, killing a bystander; and 163 strikers were indicted by a grand jury.[15] A union-led strike of unemployed workers who had been taken on by government relief projects could have occurred only in the setting of the new managerial, governmental, and union practices.

Just as the heavy unemployment of 1938–9 drove many unions into unprecedented involvement in the struggles of the unemployed, so too did it stimulate flexible and innovative efforts to control layoffs. Several locals in the building trades used their control over hiring to prevent employers from taking advantage of the heavy unemployment to rid themselves of workers who had slowed down with age. The painters' and electricians' unions in New York fixed quotas of the minimal numbers of workers over 55, whom contractors were obliged to hire for every job, as did the electricians in Cleveland and Cincinnati. The Fur and Leather Workers, through a protracted strike in the New York market in 1938, sharply limited the employers' ability to discharge "inefficient" workers at the end of each season and lengthened their formally recognized work-sharing period.[16] All these accomplishments represented novel applications of traditional union controls over hiring.

Although the Steel Workers Organizing Committee had won a weak seniority clause from U.S. Steel, it authorized each local in that company and elsewhere to deal with the new layoffs as it wished. Some of them cut the work week drastically – to as little as twenty hours. Others permitted large layoffs, while battling for unqualified application of the seniority principle. Usually younger workers fought for the first approach and older workers for the second, and many locals were badly split over the question. These conflicts stimulated the desire of the union's leadership to return control to management's hands, provided it could be limited by clearly formulated seniority rights in the contracts. But U.S. Steel and other firms in the industry fought adamantly to make "merit ratings" prevail over seniority in selecting who was to be spared in layoffs, and thus kept local initiative very much alive until the war years, when the War Labor Board introduced the complex seniority systems, which lasted until the recent consent decree.[17]

When UE locals wrestled with the terrible choices involved in workers' efforts to control layoffs, they came up with a wide variety of answers. At the big Westinghouse Local 601, to take but one example, the union had contended vehemently for an unqualified seniority principle before 1937, but the stunning impact of the new dismissals led it to demand a general reduction of hours in order to share the remaining work. As short time in many departments dragged on month after month, however, everyone in the local became uneasy over what the union's paper called this "tremendous sharing of misery," and local activists came increasingly to share the fear of countless Americans at the time that unemployment at very high levels had become a permanent part of American life, instead of the cyclical affliction it had formerly been.

Consequently, Charles Newell, whom the local had elected its business agent, argued that the union should abandon its work-sharing policy, insist on layoffs by strict seniority, and couple that policy with a militant battle for massive expansion of employment by the public sector. Yet Newell himself was openly anxious over the dangers inherent in that approach. He explained:

It is the tendency of the employed workers to disown the unemployed workers, to refuse giving them any help, and even to try to exclude them from the union and deprive them of the right to vote. This represents the gravest danger to both.

There is nothing that makes me angry as does the sneer or taunt one of our more conservative members may make towards our unemployed workers, accusing them of being too radical, etc. One can expect it from [Westinghouse Board Chairman] A. W. Robertson, but not from other workers.[18]

Although Local 601 still did not have a contract with Westinghouse, it had already wrung control over layoffs away from the foremen. Now it had to devise a complex formula to solve its own dilemmas, and in August 1939 it wrested agreement to that plan from the company. The first response to lack of work was to be a reduction of hours in the division affected. If average hours fell below thirty-six a week in any division for more than four weeks, everyone in the division with less than a year's service was to be dropped. If they fell below thirty-four hours, as many people as necessary with less than five years were to be transferred to other jobs or laid off. No reductions below thirty-two hours would be allowed. Representatives of any division threatened by such a development would negotiate an alternative with the company. Rehiring options were to go first to any employee who had been transferred off his or her job, then to those who had been laid off, according to plant-wide seniority.[19]

These elaborate arrangements deserve close attention because they reveal not only the thoroughness with which workers could thrash out their own agonizing problems, but also that, even after seniority had become enshrined as the basic principle governing layoffs in mass-production industry, that principle could still be subjected to significant modification in order to avoid a paralyzing division between the older and newer workers. Seniority and contracts both had their place in workers' struggles, but it was equally dangerous to sanctify either device.

Seniority and Black unemployment

The dangers became especially evident during the next sharp downturn of the economy, that of 1949–50. By that time some kind of seniority formula (plant, divisional, departmental, "with ability to do the job," or whatever) had become standard practice in most basic industry. On the other hand, large numbers of Black workers had first obtained jobs in those industries during World War II. Strict application of seniority, therefore, threatened to wipe out the gains of Black workers and sharply pit unemployed Blacks against White workers, who remained on the job with union protection. In this setting Black organizations launched a powerful campaign for state and federal fair-employment-practices commissions, and the Communist Party warned that "seniority today, in its effects upon the Negro people in a period of generally declining employment, acts in the interests of the employers."[20]

Alone among the predominantly White organizations which had any influence in the unions at the time, the CP called for a revitalization of older methods of combating layoffs, as part of a many-faceted struggle to secure the unity of White and Black workers. Although the political conditions of the period guaranteed the defeat of its program, it did contain several ideas which are very much worthy of review, at a time like the present when layoffs threaten the position of women workers and Blacks alike.

First, where a union controlled hiring to any degree, the CP called upon it to make a deliberate effort to place Blacks on any jobs that came open, regardless of their seniority, much as the New York building trades had done on behalf of older workers during the thirties. In Local 65 and in the United Office and Professional Workers this was actually done, and both unions dealt with occupations with high turnover. Those unions established the rule that at least one out of every four workers placed on jobs had to be Black. Numerous shop meetings were held to thrash out, and where necessary defend, this policy. Because Black office workers were then very few, the UOPWA encouraged Blacks who were not members to use its hiring halls.

Second, the program called for battles on the job to open more skilled jobs to Black workers and to secure their positions there by plant-wide rather than departmental seniority rules. Third, it called for work sharing through shorter weeks and other time-honored practices, in order to hold newer members on the job. Finally, it advocated the automatic awarding of two to five years seniority to all Blacks, to compensate for the many decades in which they had been barred from employment in the industries altogether. All these efforts were to be placed in the context of a general campaign for government measures to restore full employment, just as George Meany would advocate today; but in sharp contrast to Meany, the Communists' leaders of that time warned: "The general struggle for jobs for workers as a whole should not be permitted to submerge the special struggle for jobs that must be conducted in relation to the Negro workers. The achievement of the 30-hour week will not end discrimination. Sharing work alone will not solve the special problem of the Negro workers."[21]

For the most part the Communists' program was howled down in the unions as "Jim Crow in reverse," "super-seniority," and a diabolical effort to pit race against race. The inviolability of seniority became the basic argument used against the program by union leaders, rank-and-file White workers, and employers alike. The greatest degree of success was scored in battles over upgrading and over the use of job-dispatching powers to combat the decline of Black membership through layoffs.

It would be foolish to mechanically apply any of yesterday's techniques for wrestling with today's unemployment problems. But it would be even more foolish to treat the seniority principle and other established collective-bargaining arrangements as insuperable obstacles to the emergence of new, imaginative styles of struggle. As those new styles emerge, they are certain to contain recognizable features of the older methods.

The tradition of work sharing, for example, has largely receded from workers' consciousness today. Any reduction of hours below forty now quickly reaches the point where the take-home pay of the workers is less than they would get on unemployment compensation. Moreover, the lure of consumerism drives workers to seek long hours of overtime and moonlighting in order to meet their bills. On the other hand, whenever signs of a layoff appear, a widespread aversion to overtime quickly materializes. Even workers who have been on an overtime binge for years then mobilize peer-group pressure against the acceptance of overtime, while shop mates are out of work. When they discuss the struggle at union meetings, some of the workers invariably castigate the effects of installment-buying capitalism on their own lives. It is precisely in situations of this type that the workers' initiative can carry them beyond the seniority formula ideologically as well as organizationally, with tactics well attuned to their own peculiar circumstances.

Whatever changing forms social evolution may impart to struggles over unemployment, however, the most significant moments of working-class unity have occurred when workers have fought simultaneously for control of layoffs and for organization of the unemployed. Only this two-front battle could have effectively combated the employers' ability to divide the workers into privileged and underprivileged segments. Even during such struggles potent forces of division remained present. Some workers wrote to the *People's Press* and the *U.E. News* during 1938 and 1939 arguing that women should give up their jobs in favor of men with families, and Charles Newell testified to the contempt and fear in which some employed union members held the unemployed. But it is only in the context of the battle on both fronts, whether it be coordinated by unions, community-based groups, or some collective form not yet dreamed of, that workers can prevent their own cherished formula for seniority from being used against them with devastating effect. Conversely, only such a struggle might effectively demand a general reduction of working time and put an end to the installment mania, which has made workers willing slaves in the production of wares that fashion changes or flimsy construction render obsolete as soon as they have been bought.

Notes

1 Massachusetts Bureau of Statistics of Labor, *Report* (1879), 104–5.
2 Sumner H. Slichter, *Union Policies and Industrial Management* (Washington, D.C., 1941), 100–1; Magnus Alexander, "Waste in Hiring and Discharging Men," *Iron Age*, 94 (October 29, 1914), 1032–3; Special Task Force to the Secretary of Health, Education, and Welfare, *Work in America* (Cambridge, Mass., 1973), 38–40.
3 Harry A. Millis, *How Collective Bargaining Works* (New York, 1942), 723–34, 765–6, 581, 617–20.

4 An excellent survey of union rules related to layoffs may be found in Slichter, 98–163.

5 Gladys Palmer, *Union Tactics and Economic Change: A Case Study of Three Philadelphia Textile Unions* (Philadelphia, 1932), 34; John R. Commons, *Trade Unionism and Labor Problems*, First Series (Boston, 1905), 229–30; *Machinists Monthly Journal*, 12 (March 1900), 196; Mark Perlman, *The Machinists: A New Study in American Trade Unionism* (Cambridge, Mass., 1961), 248, 258.

6 New York Bureau of Statistics of Labor, *Report* (1886), 254–8; Millis, 327, 351–7.

7 See the tables on contract layoff provisions in Slichter, 105–7.

8 Carlos C. Closson, Jr., "The Unemployed in American Cities," *Quarterly Journal of Economics*, 8 (January 1894), 168–217, 257–8.

9 Philip S. Foner, *History of the Labor Movement in the United States*, 4 vols. (New York, 1947–65), IV, 435–61.

10 *U.E. News*, February 25, June 3, June 10, July 22, August 5, 1939.

11 Ibid., May 20, 1939; *People's Press* (National Edition), January 29, 1938.

12 *U.E. News*, February 25, June 6, 1939.

13 Ibid., July 29, 1939; Farrell Dobbs, *Teamster Power* (New York, 1973), 78–96; Millis, 528. See also Philip S. Foner, *The Fur and Leather Workers Union* (Newark, 1950), 512–13.

14 Joint Resolution of June 30, 1939, 76th Congress, 1st session, *U.S. Statutes at Large*, 53, part 2, 928–36.

15 *U.E. News*, October 28, 1939.

16 Slichter, 55n; Millis, 212–13; Foner, *Fur and Leather Workers*, 522–3.

17 Millis, 554–62.

18 *U.E. News*, April 29, 1939.

19 Ibid., August 26, 1939; Millis, 767.

20 Hal Simon, "The Struggle for Jobs and for Negro Rights in the Trade Unions," *Political Affairs*, 29 (February 1950), 33–48. The quotation is on p. 37. See also John Williamson, "Defend and Extend the Rights of Negro Workers," ibid., 28 (June 1949), 28–37.

21 Simon, 42.

7. American workers and the New Deal formula*

Two motion pictures and a Broadway musical dealing with ordinary Americans earning a living have recently appeared. That is remarkable. "Blue Collar," "F.I.S.T.," and "Working," despite their evasions and equivocations, all ventured into a domain which is as unfamiliar in the mass media as it is familiar in life – daily work. They portrayed a world of authority, competition, conflict, agony, sociability, and solidarity. One of the films ("F.I.S.T.") even went so far as to depict company executives as the workers' enemies and to attribute the hero's popularity with his union's members and his persecution by the U.S. Senate to the fact that he fought the employers vigorously and consistently.

It has been somewhat more usual for the mass media to portray the oppression and struggles of working people in the distant past – say, in the day of the "Molly Maguires," "Roots," or "Mulberry Street"– though not much even of that has been encouraged during the last thirty years. What labor history we are offered, in the classroom or literature as well as on the movie and television screens, appears as a story of progress: "out of the sweatshop"; "out of the jungle"; "then and now." We can thus admire the pithiness but avoid the sting of George McNeill's ninety-year-old description of the wage earner's status: "When at work, he belongs to the lower orders, and is continually under surveillance; when out of work, he is an outlaw, . . . the pariah of society, homeless in the deep significance of the term."[1]

A favorite belief among historians, and a myth sustained by the labor movement itself, is that Franklin D. Roosevelt changed all that. Though Calvin Coolidge may have affirmed, "the business of America is business," the New Deal curbed the "economic royalists," championed the "ill-fed, ill-clad, and ill-housed" third of the nation, and brought "industrial de-mocracy" to the workplace. It thus seems somewhat peevish to write, as these essays have done, of powers which working people have lost in this century, of popular values antagonistic to acquisitive individualism which have been snuffed out, of workers' regulation of hiring, work arrangements, and dismissal which have been vanquished in the name of progress, and of continuing traditions of working-class struggle, which have been far broader in scope than the union bargaining sanctioned by government and "public opinion."

Yet every worker knows that she or he remains "under surveillance" on the job and a "pariah" without one. Old timers' stories of yesteryear vary savage descriptions of their plight with accounts of work experiences, which would simply be inconceivable under today's more rigorous and systematic work regime. On occasion the latent brutality of the "surveillance" still flares up and receives official sanction – as when an arbitrator's award rejects the demand of a hospital worker for disciplinary action against a supervisor who hit him, on the grounds that only management can decide what conduct is or is not permissible for its personnel.[2] More often it is simply built into the routine of work assignments. "The machine dictates. This crummy little machine with buttons on it," a switchboard receptionist told Studs Terkel: "You come in at nine, you open the door, you look at the piece of machinery, you plug in the headpiece. That's how my day begins. You tremble when you hear the first ring. After that, it's sort of downhill – unless there's somebody on the phone who is either kind or nasty."[3]

The subject of work and alienation has, to be sure, enjoyed a renaissance of literary treatment in the past decade.[4] Far less attention has yet been devoted to the other side of the coin: the workplace as the locale of the workers' concerted challenge to the authority of management and to the social values which support that authority. As the essays in this volume have argued, American workers share an opaque but potent heritage of on-the-job struggles to control terms under which they labor for a living – a heritage which has evolved in conjunction with the development of industrial capitalism itself.

In the latter part of the nineteenth century those struggles were most sharply manifested by the autonomy of craftsmen and their moral code, by union "legislation," and by the mutual support through which workers strove to regulate what they earned and how they earned it. The growing concentration of employers' might in large-scale enterprises and in anti-union associations curbed open manifestations of the craftsmen's dignity and militancy, while new technology sapped their foundations. The way was thus paved in the early twentieth century for the workers' decisive confrontation with the widespread use of specialized machinery and assembly lines, scientific management, and ubiquitous "sociological" and personnel departments.

Those years were marked by strike activity on an unprecedented scale, especially between 1910 and 1913 and between 1916 and 1922. Not only did workers doggedly resist the employers' efforts to introduce stop-watches and incentive pay, they also frequently formulated their own counter-proposals for industrial reorganization. On one level these included standard pay classifications, union control over reductions in the work force, the 8-hour day, and, above all, management's consent to treat with the workers' elected delegates on all questions affecting the operation of the works. On another level, the unions of coal miners and railway workers, speaking from positions of unprecedented strength, demanded public ownership of their industries with a large managerial role for the employees, and conventions of the Amalgamated Clothing Workers openly debated ways to assume the management of the men's clothing industry.[5]

The erosion of craftsmen's autonomy placed all workers "at the bottom level of a highly stratified organization," as the Hawthorne experiments discovered, with their routines of work, cultural traditions, and personal interactions "at the mercy of technical specialists."[6] The further that process advanced, however, the more questions of power, which had always been inherent in conflicts over control, came to occupy the center of the stage. In the extreme case of the assembly line, where the tasks of each individual were designed in accordance with engineers' calculations of what could be performed in the time the line took to pass his or her work station, the only issue remaining unsettled was the speed at which the line as a whole was to move. The answer to that question was determined solely by the workers' capacity for resistance. There is no "technical" imperative to specify whether Lordstown's line should yield 25, 50, 75, or 120 Vegas per hours. Its tempo simply measures the relative strengths of the two parties which confront each other over the pneumatic wrenches, spot welders, and spray guns each day.

With unions, without unions, and often in spite of unions, members of the most diverse work groups, from the immigrants of the 1890s to "the new breed of young workers" today, have devised ways to curb management's appetite for more output. Cornelia Parker found young women without a union in a Brooklyn candy factory winning and keeping a holiday on Saturday afternoon simply by ignoring their overseers' orders to resume work after lunch.[7] Stanley B. Mathewson revealed ingenious individual and collective tricks for frustrating speed-up in the factories of the late 1920s.[8] Labor spies in auto plants of the thirties found that the daily discussion of how many parts to put out each shift provided one of the main topics of workers' conversations.[9] Today's steelworkers, whose international union has announced agreement after agreement with the companies to improve productivity, speak of the "endless sabotages," which "go on every day" in the mills. Bringing the work flow of a modern establishment "to a crunching halt," observed one steelworker, is both easy and commonplace for those who are familiar with the intricacies of their machinery. He added, significantly: "The men don't usually talk about this stuff; communication is carried on through undercurrents and understanding. . . . The only way the foreman can survive – the only way he gets a fair amount of work done in his zone – is to understand this communication-by-sabotage."[10]

It is equally true, however, that the outcome of everyday workplace struggles is profoundly influenced by the larger power relationships within which foremen and work groups confront each other. Militants of the World War I epoch, who endeavored to consolidate diverse groups of workers into metal trades councils, system federations, national organizing committees, and industrial unions, were keenly aware that to dream of workers' control without the ability to articulate group demands and impose them on the employers was an exercise in fantasy.[11] West coast longshoremen, who in more recent decades before the advent of containerization, were able to exert almost full control over the complex and critical question of their work assignments, could do so only because they had successfully fought for union hiring halls in the 1930s.[12]

The very shop floor militancy which so disturbs corporate executives and union officials alike in the 1970s could not assume the open and chronic form which makes it notorious without the presence of union and legal defenses against arbitrary dismissal. To see the role of unions in this setting as *nothing more* than disciplinary agents for management, therefore, is a facile and dangerous form of myopia.[13] In fact, to understand and appreciate the significance of workplace struggles, the whole network of social controls surrounding the workplace must be considered.

Four sources of employers' control

To think only in terms of work relations, job dissatisfaction, embattled supervisors, and union bureaucrats is to ignore the centerpiece of the game: the awesome power which a company wields over its employees. This suzerainty has four roots. The first is the company's ownership of the means of production, which enables it to determine who is to be hired and fired, as well as what means and manner of production are to be utilized. Most of the workers' struggles chronicled in these essays have involved efforts to assert the employees' wishes on precisely these points. All such attempts, however, have unavoidably encountered the other three roots of business' hegemony, which are considerably less amenable to influence by direct action.

The second source of company power over employees is the context of the profit mechanism and market pricing in which all firms operate. Although this context serves to limit companies in relation to each other, it operates even more significantly to minimize the gains which workers can obtain through trade union action. Sumner Slichter observed in 1940 that in the absence of great outbursts of union enthusiasm the pressure of business competition will always make the unionized sector of any industry tend to shrink. The experience of northern textile workers earlier in the century illustrates his point painfully. Between 1909 and 1922 they had won extraordinary improvements in their wages and hours, only to discover in the ensuing decades that their factories closed down, as the industry moved south.[14]

Similarly steelworkers in the late 1970s know that their employers not only face serious international competition, but have decided to respond to the steel market's glutted condition by eliminating one-fifth of the country's productive capacity by 1982, thus freeing investment capital for more rapid automation of steel manufacture and especially for reinvestment in iron ore and coal production for export.[15] For the economy as a whole the sectoral distribution of investment, which so critically affects the number and types of jobs available, is ultimately decided by gambling – with huge blocs of capital in the stock exchange.

The third bulwark of corporate power is to be found in the systematic integration of the firm's internal line of command into the country's enormous educational establishment. The cult of the expert and the myth of complexity do not simply float in our intellectual atmosphere; they are incorporated into the way in which we are educated from our first confrontation with reading and writing "skills" to the ultimate professional training of the favored few. "Training a worker," wrote Frank Gilbreth in 1912, "means merely enabling him to carry out the directions of his work schedule."[16] That is precisely the conception of education's purpose which has provided the criterion against which the success or failure of public schooling has most often been measured in this century.[17]

Of more direct relevance to this argument is the interlocking of the industrial chain of command with higher education, which has received a penetrating analysis by David F. Noble in his book *America by Design*.[18] The process, as Noble describes it, began in the engineering schools of the nineteenth century, whose students were instructed, for instance by Henry R. Towne, that the "dollar is the final term in every engineering equation," or by Charles F. Scott of Westinghouse and Yale, that they had to learn "to work first for the success of the corporation" and "to subordinate their own ideas and beliefs to the wishes and desires of their superiors," if they would "really be efficient."[19]

The experience of business, academic, and military cooperation in the training of officers and testing of soldiers for placement during World War I laid the basis for extension of such coordination of higher education with business from engineering into the liberal arts curriculum. These developments culminated, Noble shows, with the formation of the American Council on Education, which described itself as "the General Staff organization of education." Its director, Charles R. Mann, asserted in 1927 that the main challenge facing the council was to "decide how education can be organized to meet industrial specifications." Toward this end it solicited information from business on the prerequisites for filling various jobs, as a means of providing "mutually intelligible communication between industrialists and schoolmen." It also established a Committee on Standards, which soon asserted itself as the central accrediting agency for the nation's colleges and universities. In 1948 the council's various testing programs were merged to form the Educational Testing Service, which has reigned as the highest arbiter of standards and qualifications in American higher education ever since.[20]

In short, the current drive by corporations and foundations to establish professorial chairs of "private enterprise" in American universities is really gilding the lily.[21] The academic and industrial systems have been inseparable for half a century.

The fourth root of employers' power, and in a sense its ultimate bastion of defense, is the coercive authority of the government. The centralized instruments of violence, which society has endowed with legitimacy (police, courts, prisons, and armies), have historically inserted themselves into American work relations in countless ways, among the most important of which have been the repression of jobless and alien workers, the use of armed force against strikers, police surveillance of workers' organizations, and the issuance of court injunctions against strikes and boycotts. Although there is not the space here for a detailed and nuanced assessment of the role of legitimate coercion, it is crucial to note that it has not been an occasional or episodic affair (the Red Scare, McCarthyism, Watergate, etc.), but has always been present in one form or another. It is also important to realize that in the 1930s the government's role in industrial relations assumed a significantly new shape.

In the late nineteenth century the state's coercive force was used most frequently against the unemployed and against strikers. Forty states followed the lead of New Jersey between 1876 and 1896 in declaring it a criminal act to "rove about" without employment or visible means of support. In the city of Buffalo alone 21,735 men were sentenced to hard labor in the penitentiary for terms of up to six months on this charge between 1891 and 1898, while almost as many more drew lighter sentences for "vagrancy."[22] Given the facts that most nineteenth-century workers experienced at least some unemployment every year, and that in hard times the only conceivable alternative to roving about in search of work (other than stealing or dying of hunger) was to underbid another desperate worker for his job, it is evident that the same society which made unemployment inevitable also made it illegal.[23]

Between 1910 and 1930 such local coercion of "tramps" was supplemented, and to some degree replaced, by federal deportation of superfluous or undesirable aliens. Although the deportation of alien radicals swelled abruptly to the level of 314 people in 1920 and 446 in 1921, routine deportations of friendless and jobless aliens became inexorably more and more numerous. In a period when at least half of the workers in heavy industrial centers were foreign born, the number of people deported annually by the government rose from 2,124 in 1909 to 19,865 in 1933 (when another 10,347 aliens were simply "required to depart").[24] As William Preston observed, such deportees were not radicals, and thus were without any organized legal defense. Only 15 percent of the aliens so arrested in the 1920s "could raise bail or obtain counsel."[25] They were shipped home as unobtrusively as tramps had been incarcerated in the 1890s. Both types of police action strongly reinforced the authority of employers by imposing legal sanctions on those who, willingly or unwillingly, stepped out from under the discipline of the job.

Military intervention in major strikes, from that of the Lynn shoe-workers in 1860 to the Ludlow Massacre of 1914, is so familiar a subject as to require little comment.[26] What is important to note is that by 1920 soldiers patrolled the scene in virtually every large strike. The four great strikes of 1922 ran the army and national guard ragged, as did those of 1933–4. The army was prepared for such activity, however: In 1920 it had developed "War Plans White" to cope with major and minor domestic disturbances.[27]

Nevertheless, the figure who became familiar to the most strikers was not the soldier with rifle and bayonet, but the policeman with billy club, horse, and pistol. Local ordinances governing trespass, disorderly conduct, and disturbing the peace have always weighed more heavily on the day-to-day atmosphere surrounding picket lines than the more famous and majestic federal statutes. How police applied those ordinances was largely determined by the power balance of local politics. Politically influential workers of smaller nineteenth century towns were often able to remove police commissioners, who had been overly zealous in arresting and beating strikers. The professional metropolitan forces, however, proved themselves implacable foes of strikers over the passing years. Moreover, by the 1920s every sizeable city had its Red Squad, devoted to investigating and suppressing revolutionary activities, and many strikes seemed to fall into that category between the general collapse of labor militancy in 1923 and the strike wave of 1934.[28]

Finally, by the 1920s almost any strike, whatever the political affiliations of its leaders, was likely to face some sort of court injunction. Court orders forbidding boycotts and sympathetic strikes had first appeared in the 1880s and then become widespread during the open-shop drive of the early twentieth century. A series of Supreme Court decisions between 1917 and 1922 gave such judicial orders the sanction of the highest court in the land and increased both the uniformity and the anti-union quality of their subsequent impact. As a result of those decisions, mass picketing could be forbidden, yellow dog contracts were legally enforceable, and injunctions might forbid union organizers from recruiting workers who had signed one of those pledges never to join a union.[29]

In short, by the 1920s the federal government, through its military, police, and judicial agencies, had placed itself alongside state and municipal authorities, squarely in the center of American industrial relations.[30] To be sure, the tight governmental repression of union activity, working-class radicalism, and immigrant behavior, which characterized that decade, only partially explains the remarkable contrast between the labor militancy evident before 1923 and the labor peace of the following ten years. Corporate welfare schemes, generally known as the American Plan, were widely instituted in such prosperous and oligopolistic industries as autos, rubber, chemicals, and electrical machinery. Of all the new benefits which those industries offered their workers, the most important was job security, coupled with job privileges determined by seniority with the firm. Such security was made possible for senior employees, in spite of the spasmodic and uneven growth of the economy, by the employment of a flexible reserve of Black and Mexican workers in the bottom labor grades of companies with necessarily unstable labor requirements.[31]

Productivity per worker soared between 1923 and 1929, even though real wages rose on the average more slowly than they had during the preceding period of numerous strikes and heavy turnover. Workers who had relatively secure jobs eagerly grasped the consumer credit which had become easily available, and purchased cars, homes, gas and electric stoves, ice boxes, and other domestic comforts. Given such compensation for the stifling regimentation of work, it is not surprising that experiments by industrial psychologists at Western Electric's Hawthorne Works should have reintroduced the concept "alienation" into the literary lexicon, at the very time Dean Dexter S. Kimball of Cornell University's School of Engineering (and manager of General Electric's Pittsfield plant) declared: "production is increasing so rapidly that one can predict the near end of all poverty in America."[32]

The New Deal formula

The collapse of "the Coolidge Prosperity" in 1929 produced a celebrated surge of trade union and political activity among workers and forced the government to assume a vastly expanded role in the economy and in industrial relations. Its new policies fixed the legal and political parameters of workers' control struggles to the present time, but as those policies evolved over the ensuing decades, they became less and less beneficial and more and more restrictive for workers. They had three basic ingredients of concern here: state subsidization of economic growth, the encouragement of legally regulated collective bargaining, and the marriage of the union movement to the Democratic Party.

The federal government injected steadily increasing sums of money into the economy in an effort to revitalize and then to sustain its growth. As early as the conference on unemployment convened by President Harding in September 1921, official wisdom had conceded that countercyclical investment policies were necessary to keep a modern capitalist economy from collapse. The economists and engineers assembled there, however, had hoped that the initiative of enlightened corporate policies might suffice to supply such investment.[33] Although the policy makers of the New Deal were equally determined to preserve the matrix of private ownership, markets, and profits, they concluded that the stimulative expenditures had to come from the public treasury and to be supplemented by legislative efforts to stabilize prices, reduce competition, and feed the unemployed. The contradictions resulting from that effort were to unfold over the next forty years.

Though New Deal programs fed millions of needy Americans, they failed abysmally to restore full employment. Although the gross national product had risen by 1937 to a level roughly equal to that of 1929, the next year found 10.4 million people out of work – some nine million more than in 1929. Orders for war production, which began to flow freely in 1940, not only restored economic growth and abundant employment, but went on to provide the solid core of governmental purchases from that day to this. Equally important, the shape of economic development since World War II (the electronic-computer boom, the sprawling world of suburbia and shopping malls based on private automobiles, the virtual disappearance of the small farmer, and so forth) has been determined by the interaction of government policies and private business decisions. Despite the mounting public concern for the lethal pollution of the environment and the depletion of natural resources, which such growth has entailed, postwar experience has convinced everyone that if a capitalist economy even so much as slows down its wild growth, layoff slips fill the time-card racks of America's factories and offices.

Since the middle of the 1960s both the willingness and the ability of the government to combat unemployment by high levels of spending have become dubious. The production of modern armaments is so capital intensive that relatively few jobs are generated by hefty appropriations for that purpose, while the drain on research and development of resources resulting from such priorities has seriously retarded expansion in other sectors of the economy. Years of alternating between expansionist fiscal policies to combat unemployment and restrictive ones to curb inflation have left us with both evils rising at once. In fact, the official rate of unemployment has not fallen below 5 percent since the advent of President Nixon's "new economic policy" of 1971–3 to (in the famous words of one of his aides), "zap labor." At times it has risen to the vicinity of 10 percent.

Although wage and price controls were part of Nixon's program and have often been proposed subsequently, the ability of multinational corporations to redirect their cash flows and administer prices has made a mockery of the efforts of European and American governments alike to regulate their national economies. Moreover, for more than ten years the substantial growth in American economic output and productivity has failed to produce any increase in the real earnings of workers. Whatever improvements in take-home pay American workers have enjoyed in the present decade (in terms of real purchasing power) have come as the result of temporary tax cuts or the addition of more family members working. Any correlation which may ever have existed between worker productivity and the enjoyment of material comforts has clearly been dissipated.[34]

Second, during the New Deal the federal government not only reduced its repressive activity toward immigrants, strikes, and unions sharply, it actively encouraged the development of collective bargaining between companies and unions. Workers themselves took the initiative in building unions, but the government played an important role in shaping the outcome of their activity. In a few industries, notably coal and clothing, important groups of employers quickly acquiesced before whirlwind organizing drives of AFL unions, because they hoped that union standardization of labor costs might ease the ruinous competition among them. Elsewhere, however, employers tended to follow the examples of steel and auto in furious resistance to the unionization of their workers. In this setting, strikes were usually violent, and the government rushed soldiers and implacably antiradical "mediators" to the scene, while it sought to compromise with the industries' company union schemes, in hopes of minimizing disruption of economic recovery.[35]

Between the spring of 1936 and the summer of 1937, when what economic growth the decade was to bring was at full flood, workers in the auto, steel, rubber, electrical, and other industries broke through their employers' defenses with sit-down strikes, mass picketing, and company union take-over. The impact of this success on work relations was abrupt and dramatic. "Quickie" strikes forced managers to revise piece rates and pay for "down time," to slow assembly lines, to correct unsafe or unhealthy conditions, and to sack unpopular foremen. For example, in the two months *after* a CIO strike had forced Goodyear Rubber Company to recognize the union and establish a 36-hour week in all production departments, there were fifteen sit-down strikes in the company's Akron plant. Newly unionized workers there openly enforced lower production quotas, barred anti-union literature from the plant, ousted unpopular foremen and protected popular ones against company discipline, and during one dispute imprisoned twenty supervisors and members of the company's hated "flying squadron" in one room of the plant.[36]

The power which unionizing workers won on the job at this time was far more significant to them and to their employers than whatever wage gains they won. Shop stewards and committee men and women, backed up (often physically) by the employees in the departments they represented, translated the inextinguishable small-group resistance of workers into open defiance and conscious alternatives to the directives of the management.[37] Union contracts, where they were won, undermined company favoritism, obliged firms to deal with the workers' elected delegates, and secured workers against arbitrary dismissal, thus strengthening their sense of collectivity and bolstering their courage in confronting management.

The response of the Roosevelt administration and Congress to this militancy involved both major concessions and a many-faceted effort to steer the organizing activities of workers into channels which would not threaten the economy's basic market and profit mechanisms. For all the hostility exhibited by most business leaders toward the unions which were trying to organize their workers, the idea of some formalized plan of employee representation within the firm had been a basic element of the American Plan of the twenties. Moreover, men as prominent as President Herbert Hoover and Gerard Swope of the General Electric Company had long argued that national unions (under the proper leadership, of course) could help industry reduce price competition and "eliminate waste." The economic crisis and the ensuing efforts of the Roosevelt administration to rescue the economy by stabilizing prices lent special force to this argument. While some New Deal advisers, like Donald Richberg, looked forward to national economic planning by industrial councils in which industry, labor, and consumers would all be represented, others, like Senator Robert F. Wagner's aide Leon Keyserling, argued that only strong unions could raise popular purchasing power sufficiently to get the economy growing again.

On the union side, John L. Lewis and Sidney Hillman were but the most prominent of the many leaders, who had been persuaded by their experiences in the 1916–22 epoch both that unions had to collaborate in making those employers who would recognize them more efficient, and that no unions could ever bring the large corporations of basic industry to terms without the help of the government. Among the leaders of the Democratic Party, of course, all but the most conservative hoped that a strong union movement would bolster their party's electoral strength, while they enacted measures to revitalize and rationalize the economy.

All these motives contributed to the decisive support that was mustered in Congress for the Wagner Act of 1935. That law established a National Labor Relations Board to protect workers, who were trying to form unions, against persecution by their employers, and to conduct elections through which workers might select their "bargaining agent," with which their employers were legally obliged to deal. For at least the first three years after the Supreme Court had upheld its existence (April 1937), the board pursued its assignment vigorously, and, aided by the LaFollette Civil Liberties Committee's exposures of repressive activities by corporate managers and municipal officials, helped unions become firmly established in those basic industries which had most successfully fought them off between 1919 and 1922.[38]

The point to bear in mind is that this governmental activity was simultaneously liberating and cooptive for the workers. Lifting the suffocating burden of absolute managerial control from the working lives of Americans (an oppression which the depression had made even worse because it intensified workers' fear of discharge at the very time that most companies abandoned their expensive welfare schemes) was one of the greatest chapters in the historic struggle for human liberties in this country. Both the action at the base and the deeds of the government contributed toward that result. On the other hand, the government's intervention also opened a new avenue through which the rank and file could in time be tamed and the newly powerful unions be subjected to tight legal and political control.

The mere existence of governmental agencies which could help them secure contracts strengthened the union officialdom relative to the membership and tempted them to discourage factory occupations and unofficial strikes, in order to win favor in Washington. Moreover, astute advisors of the business community argued that, if management had found the unionization of its workers unavoidable, the urgent task facing it was then to encourage the development of such union structures and policies as would be least inhibiting to management's aims. Ideally, as Sumner Slichter contended in a study for the Brookings Institution, unions dealing with mass-production industries should be industrial in form and undemocratic in administration. The industrial form he found preferable to craft organization, because the latter was more resistant to technological change and to future erosion of skills, on which the very existence of a craft union might rest. The advantages of bureaucratized leadership Slichter explained in this way:

Because the officers of unions are both more willing and better able than the rank and file to take account of the consequences of union policies [for the competitive position of their employers], and because they attach less importance than the rank and file to immediate effects and more importance to long-run results, unions are more successful in adjusting themselves to technological and market changes when the officers are permitted to make policies and negotiate agreements without ratification by the rank and file.[39]

Such an objective, of course, was not to be achieved overnight, but wartime regulations pushed unions rapidly down the path desired by Slichter. By pledging not to strike for the duration and by taking their grievances and contract negotiations before government agencies, union officials ceased to rely on the action of the rank and file for support. Checkoff of dues from workers' paychecks and government guarantees of union security prevented disgruntled members from withdrawing, at a time when unions could not even win wage increases. By 1944, however, the percentage of workers who took part in strikes matched that of the peak period of sit-down strikes in 1937, and union stewards and local officers were evidently leading many of those work stoppages.[40] Moreover, government guarantees of company profits, through the cost-plus pricing formula of war contracts, reduced the employers' incentive to discipline their workers, and tales abounded of workers flouting long-standing rules against smoking, gambling, reading, sleeping, eating, and cooking on the job.[41] At the war's end, the confluence of workers' determination to catch up with inflation through large wage increases and management's determination to tighten up its control over the shop floor (through retiming jobs, punishing obstreperous stewards, reimposing shop rules or unilaterally inventing new ones, and so on) provoked the largest strike wave in the country's history; 4.6 million people walked off their jobs in 1946.[42]

At this point legal restraints on union activity were severely tightened. The 1947 amendments to the Wagner Act, which were known as the Taft-Hartley Act, banned sympathetic strikes, secondary boycotts, and mass picketing. They required elected union officers to sign affidavits that they were not members of the Communist Party, and they outlawed political contributions by unions. Perhaps most important of all, they authorized the president to seek injunctions ordering strikers to return to their jobs, and they made unions legally liable for damages if their members struck in violation of written contracts. In effect, the only union activity which remained legal under Taft-Hartley was that involved in direct bargaining between a certified "bargaining agent" and the employers of the workers it represented. Both actions of class solidarity and rank-and-file activity outside of the contractual framework were placed beyond the pale of the law.

Since 1947 successive court rulings (especially those of the 1970s) have progressively tightened the legal noose around those historic forms of working-class struggle which do not fit within the certified contractual framework. Injunctions against wildcat strikes are now routine, and local officers, stewards, or others whom the company suspects of leading them may expect its disciplinary reprisals. National unions seldom support such activists, and where they do, they may anticipate injunctions and damage suits. Not only has the Supreme Court upheld suits against work stoppages in violation of no-strike clauses in contracts, it has also said that the law will imply such a clause even if it does not exist, when the contract contains a provision for arbitration of disputes (as most do). The Third Circuit Court of Appeals, which hears cases from the industrial belt of Pennsylvania and Ohio, has gone so far as to hold a union liable for damages suffered by an employer unless it does everything in its power to end an unauthorized strike – including expelling its errant members and replacing them with union scabs.[43]

The case of legal protections for collective bargaining resembles that of government stimulation of economic growth. In both instances a New Deal reform which initially offered substantial (if limited) benefits to the struggle for workers' control has evolved into a restrictive quagmire, from which working people are now striving to escape. The long coal miners' strike of 1977–8 dramatized the severity of the prohibitions under which workers must now operate, as well as the miners' readiness to defy them. After three years of continuous conflict over working conditions, safety, and work assignments in the coal fields, the mine owners were determined to obtain the United Mine Workers' consent to a contract which would guarantee punishment of miners who struck while it was in force. Knowing that almost half of the country's bituminous coal came from non-union mines, that ownership of the industry was highly concentrated in conglomerates, which could readily shift their resources between coal and other forms of energy, and that the companies had openly and se-riously threatened to destroy the miners' welfare fund and clinics if the union did not yield, the leadership of the UMWA surrendered to the major demands of the operators in December. But the miners rejected that agreement, and a second one, which emerged from national nego-tiations two months later, in spite of a Taft-Hartley injunction, which among other things prevented them from receiving any funds from their union. All over the Middle West other workers held support rallies, raised money and supplies for the miners, and denounced the injunction. A million dollars was donated by the International Association of Machinists and two million by the United Auto Workers, to help feed the strikers' families.

The determined unity of the miners made many of them declare that, despite the incompetence of their national officers, their union at the base was the strongest they had ever known it. Nevertheless, the coal companies, bolstered by the government's "legal protections" of collective bargaining, ultimately prevailed. The miners reluctantly accepted a third agreement, which was scarcely superior to the overwhelmingly rejected second offer. One miner from Pennsylvania's District 5 explained why the great majority in his region had defiantly voted against both of the last two agreements, by referring to their covers: "This one's green. The other was blue. That's about the main difference between them."[44]

The coal strike clearly revealed the relationship between the economic and political aspects of the New Deal formula in crisis. "Giveback" bargaining has become a dominant theme in management's relationship with unions. Specifically, employers are complaining that "they are paying good money and not getting the production."[45] The complaint goes back at least to the beginning of the seventies, when Chairman James Roche of General Motors protested that "management and the public" had "lately been shortchanged" by workers who "reject responsibility" and "fail to respect essential disciplines and authority." The management of U.S. Steel's South Works in Chicago took 34 hundred disciplinary actions against its employees in a single year.[46]

Three years later the Goodyear Tire and Rubber Company, by threatening to move its operations out of Akron, Ohio, forced the United Rubber Workers to surrender both established work practices and the 6-hour day, which it had won in the 1930s – and this in spite of unprecedented international solidarity shown by European rubber workers on behalf of the Americans. Then in 1976, when the union balked at wage reductions into the bargain, Goodyear closed out its production of passenger tires in Akron and moved to Governor Wallace's Alabama.[47] "Unions are going to have to give up those parts of the contract that reflect managing of the work force," predicted economist Audrey Freeman of the Conference Board, a business research institution. A recent report in the New York Times added that university-trained negotiators with a "gamesmanship" philosophy, gunning for "win situations" and encouraged by their ready access to injunction judges, are out to prove the point.[48]

Washington and the workplace

The end of the consistent, tangible improvement in living standards, which workers had enjoyed between 1940 and 1965, the increasingly aggressive posture of corporate management in its dealings with unions, and the tightening noose of legal restrictions around strikes all underscore the importance of the third element of the New Deal formula, the alignment of the labor movement with the Democratic Party. This alliance was originally secured between 1934 and 1938, when state and national party leaders threw their support behind massive relief projects for the unemployed, the Wagner Act, social security legislation, and minimum wage laws. At the same time, local Democrats from working-class neighborhoods of eastern European, southern European, and Afro-American ethnicity were swept into office (alongside of representatives from traditionally Democratic constituencies), and independent labor parties, like those in Minnesota, Wisconsin, and New York, gradually became virtually indistinguishable from New Deal Democrats, before passing off the stage.

This process will not be analyzed here, in part because its top level manifestations are so well known, and in part because so little research has been done into its meaning at the neighborhood and plant levels.[49] Nevertheless, three points should be kept in mind. First, although the alliance was formed while the Democratic Party was moving toward the Left, it held firm after 1938, when the Roosevelt administration stopped crusading for social reform. In the crisis of the New Deal following the economic slump of 1937, the labor movement, for all its new-found strength and militancy, offered no political alternative to the moribund capitalist system and its two parties.[50]

Second, attachment to the Democratic Party meant support of its foreign policy, both during the Grand Alliance against the fascist Axis and during the cold war which followed. In fact, loyalty to the government's foreign ventures became a test of loyalty to the Democratic Party, and even of fidelity to the AFL and the CIO. The result was a draconic purge of alleged Communist sympathizers, especially from the CIO between 1946 and 1949, which plunged the movement into internecine warfare.

In a more general sense, the combined impact of the unions' loyalty to the Democrats' cold war policies, widespread dismissals and police harassment of leftwing workers, and the purge within the union movement served to suffocate political and ideological debate in working-class America. The movement's intellectual vitality reached its nadir between 1969 and 1972, when building trades unions and employers jointly mobilized "hard hat" demonstrations against the peace movement, and George Meany threw the whole weight of the AFL-CIO against opponents of the Vietnam war and other liberal reformers, who had rallied around the candidacy of George McGovern.

As the cold war gave way to Washington's search for detente with the Soviet Union, and as the government's economic policies became increasingly attuned to the global needs of multinational corporations, the AFL-CIO drew ever closer to the most nationalistic and protectionist wing of the Democratic Party, represented by Senator Henry Jackson. During the first year of the Carter administration a serious rupture developed between the AFL-CIO and the president over the question of tariffs. The union leaders called for barriers against imports in order to revive the steel industry and to keep the shoe and clothing industries from virtual extinction. In April 1977, the needle trades unions called a national one-day strike to underscore their point. The close alliance of Carter with the multinationals, as exemplified by the participation of virtually every leading figure of his incoming administration on the Trilateral Commission, prevented the president from offering any concessions on this score. His only recourse to mollify the unions was to endorse important parts of their legislative program then before Congress, especially the Labor Law Reform bill, which would improve the position of unions in NLRB elections. The Congress, however, despite its Democratic majorities in both houses, voted down virtually every measure labor wanted, and the Labor Law Reform measure was defeated by a Senate filibuster. Years of loyalty to the Democrats are now yielding the most paltry rewards for the labor movement.

Simultaneously, an increasingly concerted movement from the "New Right," pounding away against the "perils" of women's equality, homosexuality, pernicious textbooks, and "forced bussing," greatly strengthened openly anti-union forces. One or another of its many "morality" crusades often picked up support from many workers, despite abundant evidence of their big business sponsorship and financing. No single issue served more to alienate workers from New Deal liberalism, however, than the ever-increasing burden of taxation which it placed upon them.[51]

George Meany's response to these threats was to convert the AFL-CIO bit by bit into a great snapping turtle, plodding along when it moves at all, hiding within its shell to shield the working class from contamination by the ideological currents which have swept around it, and from time to time snapping out at "new polititics freaks" or "hippies," who ventured too close (especially within the caucuses of the Democratic Party).

Third, these developments completed a long historic process of reducing the American labor movement to a trade union movement – or rather to an immobile and isolated aggregation of legally certified bargaining agents. The labor movement of the late nineteenth century, after all, had encompassed much more than unions. It had also included labor parties, both reformist and revolutionary, cooperatives, a proliferation of fraternal and reform associations (like the Turnvereins and the 8-Hour Leagues), and that vast all-embracing institution, the Knights of Labor, whose fifteen thousand local assemblies had touched every corner of the land in the 1880s. Elsewhere in the world the term "labor movement" still implies diverse forms of organization and activity. It is a stunning tribute to the power and pervasiveness of American capitalism, as well as to the dogged determination of American workers to organize in their own defense at the workplace, that in this country the union has become the one surviving agency of working-class action, and its character is determined, at least formally, by law.

American workers today, therefore, face the central question of how to break out of this isolation chamber. They seem to be rising to the occasion on two fronts: by producing a new socialist grouping of trade union activists and by generating new types of struggle at the base. Both of these developments threaten the fundamental roots of corporate power (private ownership, the profit and market mechanisms, the interlocking educational and business systems, and governmental confinement of union activity), and consequently both of them would rupture the New Deal formula.

Given the historic reduction of the labor movement to certified trade unionism, it is understandable that many of the best daughters and sons of the working class either hold union offices or aspire to them, despite all the restrictions to which such office holders are subject. Moreover, the ubiquitous workplace struggles and membership revolts of the last decade have stimulated a proliferation of individual candidates and of organized reform movements within virtually all unions, promising to "get tough" with the bosses.[52] Few have captured as much national attention as Edward Sadlowski and the Steelworkers' Fight Back movement. A young crane operator from the Burns Harbor plant of Bethlehem Steel explained his support for Sadlowski's successful 1973 campaign for the presidency of the union's District 31 this way:

The big reason why it looks like our mill is going for Sadlowski is that we're tired of hassling with the union staff and the management about discipline problems. We're making good money and all that, but we always have people being sent home for smoking dope and coming in late and things like that. We've been waiting for someone a little younger to come along and talk about getting some basic change the way the union is run. I don't think there is any real feeling that the discipline is going to change much with the new leadership, but the guys don't feel the [incumbent] Germano people really know anything about us or our grievances . . . When we had our mass meeting the people went big for Sadlowski . . . [because he was] gutsy and he showed he knows where our heads are at.[53]

Like most of the new crop of reform candidates, Sadlowski linked this posture of "toughness" toward the company (a readiness to be the workers' advocate, rather than to "see all sides" as an expert negotiator) with a determination that the labor movment take the initiative in the great issues of social change now facing the country. Many of the young leaders have recently joined with reinvigorated older progressives, who are still numerous despite the purges of the 1940s and 1950s, and even with a few presidents of national unions (particularly Albert Fitzgerald of the UE, Douglas Fraser of the UAW, Jerry Wurf of AFSCME, and William Winpisinger of the IAM) in staging national conferences independently of the AFL-CIO leadership for the promotion of mass campaigns for a shorter work week and full employment legislation. A most notable departure from the snapping turtle doctrine was the participation at the full employment conference in November 1977 of delegates from feminist organizations, environmentalist groups, tenants' movements, and Black and Hispanic associations.[54] Similar labor sponsorships in the struggle against the energy trust gave birth to the Citizen Labor Energy Coalition.[55]

These endeavors have thrust William ("Wimpy") Winpisinger into the limelight as the most highly placed champion of what might be called the respectable Left within the AFL-CIO. Under his leadership the International Association of Machinists has vigorously supported the Democratic Socialist Organizing Committee (as if the union had rediscovered its political orientation of 1911), and Winpisinger has confronted George Meany with the first consistent and principled opposition from within the executive council since the formation of the AFL-CIO. Although Winpisinger shies away from both the Old Left and the New, and has dissociated himself from Sadlowski's workplace confrontation with the bosses, and although he campaigns only for issues which are already to be found in the official program of the AFL-CIO, his prominence is important for two reasons. First, he calls incessantly for popular mobilizations, which both activate the labor movement and unite it with other social forces. "We need to set aside our knee-jerk reaction to other groups," he explains.[56] Second, he bases his campaign to "fire Meany" explicitly on the premise that labor must repudiate "the economic ground rules of big business," and on the frequent declaration that he is a socialist.[57]

But the Wimpy phenomenon exists only because of the rebellion at the base, and that insurgency has also produced its indigenous forms of struggle, which are very different from national conferences or Washington lobbying. On many occasions wildcat strikes have produced organizations of local activists, which cover many companies and at times hundreds of miles of territory, but which remain totally independent of the unions. A 1973 strike of drivers and warehousemen of United Parcel Service in a dozen Pennsylvania and Ohio communities, was well coordinated by a council of delegates from the struck shipping centers, in open defiance of the threats and sanctions of the International Brotherhood of Teamsters. The strikers even forced the IBT to pay them strike benefits, by petitioning the NLRB for a decertification election – a petition which was withdrawn when the union paid. Three years later, an unofficial strike of coal miners, which began in West Virginia, not only took out half the membership of the United Mine Workers, but also forced a judge to quash all fines and contempt charges for the massive violation of his injunction, as the only condition on which the strikers would return to their jobs.[58]

Workers engaged in such struggles are sorely tempted to shut the door to all outsiders, because they know they are vulnerable to manipulation. More often than not, however, it is the union officialdom which tries to seal them off from potential allies, while the wildcatters themselves are hungry for support, ready to test strangers by their deeds, and eager to learn those things about the world which their schools, the media, and their certified leaders kept hidden from them. For instance visitors to the picket lines established by the young employees of the huge Westinghouse works of East Pittsburgh in September, 1976, when they had closed the plant and padlocked their IUE union hall into the bargain, found the pickets initially suspicious of strangers. As soon as they had walked out, they had been visited by members of the so-called U.S. Labor Party, who advised them that their strike was foolish, because only a debt moratorium and revitalized economic growth could solve their problems. As the pickets became familiar with other people, who appeared to offer support, however, they became very friendly. Before long they were asking visiting rebel truck drivers about their techniques of organization, friendly lawyers about the intricacies and uses of labor law, and sympathetic historians about "the real story" of their union. In other words, they totally repudiated the snapping turtle mentality.

When workers have turned their attention from organizing strikes to organizing production, they have been obliged to establish alliances with other groups, at the same time that they have demonstrated in practice that they can operate complex modern industries collectively. For example, in September 1977 the management of the *Capitol Times* of Madison, Wisconsin, broke off relations with all its workers' unions at one blow. In recent years several major American newspapers have recreated the open shop in this manner. What was new in Madison was the response of the workers – they established their own newspaper. At the end of six months the *Madison Press Connection* was a flourishing daily, owned and controlled by the strikers – from reporting to financial direction and from layout to printing. Its pleasant and orderly workrooms were a tribute to what experienced women and men can do when they design their own work arrangements. The most important testimony of all was the quality of the newspaper, its columns free of editorial censorship and its composition governed by considerations of quality, instead of profit.

To bolster their circulation representatives of the *Press Connection* regularly consulted with Wisconsin's local unions and neighborhood groups, seeking advertisements and subscriptions, but also learning what their members wanted to see in the newspaper. Their own conclusion from the experience was summarized by one of their writers, who attended a conference of academic and union people on "job enrichment" and "workers' participation in management." He remarked: "We have learned that we don't need management's participation."[59]

Forming coalitions from the bottom up has been evident wherever workers have tried to take control of their own enterprises. When the Youngstown Sheet and Tube Company announced its intention to close the Campbell Works and dismiss five thousand employees forever, the workers organized a citizen's committee to campaign for community purchase of the mill and for federal aid to put the publicly owned enterprise back into operation. Not only did these steelworkers mobilize the townspeople to save themselves (instead of saving the corporation, as is usually attempted in such crisis), they also openly broke with their union's official doctrine that foreign imports are the primary cause of American steelworkers' problems. Instead of demanding import restrictions, these workers engaged the talents of some radical economists to help them propose specific governmental programs for mass transit, railroad improvements, solar energy, and pollution control, which could utilize the output of the Campbell Works. In the process, these steel-workers have illustrated the sane, sorely needed uses to which the nation's productive capacity might be put, if it were programmed around social needs rather than around maximizing corporate profit.[60]

Both the consolidation of an articulate socialist leadership within the labor movement and the proliferation of broadly-based grass roots struggles represent important alternatives to George Meany's "snapping turtle." The large number of workers, who have engaged in one or the other form of activity (or in both), have cut away at the very roots of their employers' power over them. Just as American workers have never in the past fit into the mold which the captains of industry have cast for them, so it now seems probable that they will not much longer be confined within its New Deal variant.

Perhaps the day will even come when workers will "regain mastery over collective and socialized production," as Harry Braverman put it, "by assuming the scientific, design, and operational prerogatives of modern engineering."[61] Their struggles have always implied an aspiration for such powers, which this century's industrial evolution has seemingly placed beyond their reach. When the cost of expert mismanagement and treadmill productivity has become too great to bear, will they reclaim them?

Notes

* This essay had its origin in a lecture which I gave at the University of Turin, May 30, 1977. I am very grateful to the participants in that seminar for their stimulating discussion and to Betti Benenati-Marconi for the notes which she took on that occasion.

1 George E. McNeill, *The Labor Movement: the Problem of To-Day* (New York, 1887), 455.

2 Marinette General Hospital, 67 LA 785. I am indebted to Staughton Lynd for bringing this case to my attention.

3 Studs Terkel, *Working* (New York, 1974), 59, 57–8.

4 See Lloyd Zimpel, ed., *Man against Work* (Grand Rapids, Mich., 1974); Barbara Garson, *All the Livelong Day: The Meaning and Demeaning of Routine Work* (Garden City, N.Y., 1975); Jeremy Brecher and Tim Costello, *Common Sense for Hard Times* (New York, 1976); John Zernan, "Organized Labor versus 'The Revolt Against Work:' The Critical Contest," *Telos*, 21 (Fall 1974), 194–206; David Meakin, *Man & Work: Literature and Culture in Industrial Society* (New York, 1976); Alasdair Clayre, *Work and Play: Ideas and Experiences of Work and Leisure* (New York, 1974); Dan Georgakas and Marvin Surkin, *Detroit: I Do Mind Dying* (New York, 1975); Daniel Mothé, *Autogestion et conditions de travail* (Paris, 1976); Solomon Barkin, ed., *Worker Militancy and Its Consequences, 1965–75. New Directions in Western Industrial Relations* (New York and London, 1975); Harry Braverman, *Labor and Monopoly Capital: The*

Degradation of Work in the Twentieth Century (New York and London, 1974).

5 See section on "control strikes" in Ch. 4.

6 F. J. Roethlisberger and W. J. Dickson, *Management and the Worker: Technical vs. Social Organization in an Industrial Plant* (Cambridge: Harvard University Business Research Studies, No. 9, 1934), 16–17.

7 Cornelia Straton Parker, *Working with the Working Woman* (New York and London, 1922), 32.

8 Stanley B. Mathewson, *Restriction of Output among Unorganized Workers* (New York, 1931).

9 F. F. Corcoran to M. K. Hovey, Chevrolet Motor Company memo, 1935, Henry Kraus Papers, Box 9, Wayne State University Archives of Labor History and Urban Affairs, Detroit, Mich. I am indebted to Steven Sapolsky for bringing this document to my attention.

10 Steve Packard, *Steelmill Blues* (San Pedro, Calif., 1978), 13–14. For a revealing analysis of the various abilities of different groups of steelworkers to affect their conditions in this way, see William Kornblum, *Blue Collar Community* (Chicago and London, 1974), 45–65.

11 See section on Worker Response to Rationalized Industry in Ch. 4.

12 Although the interpretation is my own, this description of dock work is based on Reg Theriault, *Longshoring on the San Francisco Waterfront* (San Pedro, Calif., 1978).

13 Cf., Zernan; Stanley Aronowitz, *False Promises: The Shaping of American Working Class Consciousness* (New York, 1973); Jeremy Brecher, *Strike!* (San Francisco, 1972). In an extreme case of this self-indulgent folly, Stanley Aronowitz wrote of the striking miners, "You can't kill a culture like you can kill a union," (*In These Times*, March 15–21, 1978) as though a culture floats on air, or the miners had done just as well without a union in the 1920s.

14 Sumner H. Slichter, *Union Policies and Industrial Management* (Washington, D.C., 1941), 345–69; Daniel Creamer and Charles W. Coulter, *Labor and the Shut-Down of the Amoskeag Mills* (WPA National Research Project, Report No. L–5, Philadelphia, Pa., 1939).

15 Argus Research Corp., *Steel: An Industry in Flux* (New York, 1977).

16 Quoted in Braverman, 447.

17 Samuel Bowles and Herbert Gintis, *Schooling in Capitalist America: Educational Reform and the Contradictions of Economic Life* (New York, 1976).

18 David F. Noble,. *America by Design: Science, Technology, and the Rise of Corporate Capitalism* (New York, 1977).

19 Ibid., 34, 175.

20 Ibid., 243–56. The quotations are on pp. 248, 254.

21 "Programs to Teach Free Enterprise Sprout on College Campuses," *Wall Street Journal*, May 10, 1978. I am indebted to Neil Basen for bringing this item to my attention.

22 Sidney L. Harring, "Class Conflict and the Suppression of Tramps in Buffalo, 1892–1894," *Law & Society Review*, 11 (Summer 1977), 879, 886.

23 Alexander Keyssar, "Men out of Work: A Social History of Unemployment in Massachusetts, 1870–1916," (unpublished Ph.D. dissertation, Harvard University, 1977). On the migrations of nineteenth-century workers, see Stephan Thernstrom, *The Other Bostonians: Poverty and Progress in the American Metropolis, 1880–1970* (Cambridge, Mass., 1973), 9–44.

24 U.S. Department of Commerce, Bureau of the Census, *Historical Statistics of the United States, Colonial Times to 1970*, 2 vols. (Washington, D.C., 1975),

114; William Preston, Jr., *Aliens and Dissenters: Federal Suppression of Radicals, 1903–1933* (New York, 1966), 332.

25 Preston, 236.

26 Samuel Yellen, *American Labor Struggles* (New York, 1936); Philip S. Foner, *History of the Labor Movement in the United States*, 4 vols. (New York, 1947–65); Alan Dawley, *Class and Community. The Industrial Revolution in Lynn* (Cambridge, Mass., 1976); Jerry M. Cooper, "The Army as Strikebreaker – The Railroad Strikes of 1877 and 1894," *Labor History*, 18 (Spring 1977), 179–96; Gerald G. Eggert, *Railroad Labor Disputes: The Beginnings of a Federal Strike Policy* (Ann Arbor, Mich., 1967); Graham Adams, Jr., *Age of Industrial Violence, 1910–15* (New York and London, 1966); Irving Bernstein, *The Turbulent Years: A History of the American Worker, 1933–1941* (Boston, 1969).

27 Preston, 245. Fine reporting of the strikes of 1921–22 may be found in the magazine *Labor Age* from that period.

28 Herbert G. Gutman, "Class, Status, and Community Power in Nineteenth Century American Industrial Cities – Paterson, New Jersey: A Case Study," in Frederic C. Jaher, ed., *The Age of Industrialism in America: Essays in Social Structure and Cultural Values* (Glencoe, N.Y., 1968); Dawley, *Class and Community*; Edward Levinson, *I Break Strikes: The Technique of Pearl L. Bergoff* (New York, 1935); Sidney L. Harring, "The Buffalo Police – 1872–1915: Industrialization, Social Unrest, and the Development of the Police Institution," (unpublished Ph.D. dissertation, University of Wisconsin, 1976).

29 Edwin E. Witte, *The Government in Labor Disputes* (New York and London, 1932).

30 For a very different interpretation of this period, one which finds a pro-union bias among leaders of business and government, see Ronald Radosh, "The Corporate Ideology of American Labor Leaders from Gompers to Hillman," *Studies on the Left*, 6 (November–December 1966), 66–88; James Weinstein, *The Corporate Ideal in the Liberal State, 1900–1918* (Boston, 1968).

31 Irving Bernstein, *The Lean Years: A History of the American Worker, 1920–1933* (Boston, 1960), 144–89; Ronald W. Schatz, "American Electrical Workers: Their Work, Struggles, and Aspirations, 1930–1950," (unpublished Ph.D. dissertation, University of Pittsburgh, 1977), 44–75; Paul Taylor, *Mexican Labor in the United States: Chicago and the Calumet Region* (Berkeley, 1932); Francis M. Vreeland and Edward J. Fitzgerald, *Farm-City Migration and Industry's Labor Reserve* (WPA National Research Project, Report No. L–7, Philadelphia, 1939); Peter Gottlieb, "Making Their Own Way: Southern Blacks' Migration to Pittsburgh, 1916–30," (unpublished Ph.D. dissertation, University of Pittsburgh, 1977).

32 Quoted in H. Dubreuil, *Robots or Men? A French Workman's Experience in American Industry* (New York and London, 1930), 187. On Kimball see Noble, 83, 278. On the Hawthorne experiment, see Roethlisberger and Dickson; Elton Mayo, *The Human Problems of an Industrial Civilization* (Cambridge, Mass., 1933).

33 On New Deal economic policy, see Gabriel Kolko, *Main Currents in Modern American History* (New York, 1976), 100–56. On Harding's conference on unemployment, see Kolko, 109; Paul H. Douglas, C. N. Hitchcock, and W. E. Atkins, *The Worker in Modern Economic Society* (Chicago, 1923), 500–6.

34 Kolko, 100–56, 310–47. The figures on output and unemployment in 1938 and 1929 are from U.S. Bureau of the Census, *Historical Statistics*, 126, 224. See also Charles Levinson, *Capital, Inflation, and the Multinationals* (New York,

1976); Barry Commoner, *The Poverty of Power: Energy and the Economic Crisis* (New York, 1976); David M. Gordon, "Recession is Capitalism as Usual," *New York Times Magazine*, April 27, 1975, 49–63; Fred Gaboury, "Wage Controls One Step Closer," *Labor Today* (May 1978), 7.

35 See Bernstein, *Turbulent Years*, 37–125; Charles R. Walker, *American City: A Rank-and-File History* (New York, 1937); George Powers, *Cradle of Steel Unionism: Monongahela Valley, Pa.* (East Chicago, Ind., 1972). On changes in treatment of aliens under the New Deal, see Louis Adamic, *My America, 1928–1938* (New York, 1938), 195–209. The intensely antiradical attitude of the Federal Mediation and Conciliation Service in 1933–4 can only be appreciated by examining its field reports in the National Archives.

36 The Goodyear Tire and Rubber Co., "What is Happening in Akron," May 29, 1936, Adolph Germer Papers, Box 23, State Historical Society of Wisconsin, Madison. See also Alice and Staughton Lynd, eds., *Rank and File: Personal Histories by Working Class Organizers* (Boston, 1973); Sidney Fine, *Sit-Down: The General Motors Strike of 1936–1937* (Ann Arbor, Mich. 1970); Peter Friedlander, *The Emergence of a UAW Local, 1936–39, A Study in Class and Culture* (Pittsburgh, 1975), 75–9.

37 Schatz, 116–226; Lynd, *Rank and File*, 105–10.

38 Radosh, "Corporate Ideology"; Barton J. Bernstein, "The New Deal: The Conservative Achievements of Liberal Reform," in *Towards a New Past: Dissenting Essays in American History*, Bernstein, ed. (New York, 1967), 263–88; Mathew Josephson, *Sidney Hillman, Statesman of American Labor* (New York, 1952); Melvyn Dubofsky and Warren Van Tine, *John L. Lewis: A Biography* (New York, 1977); Harry A. Millis and Emily C. Brown, *From the Wagner Act to Taft-Hartley* (Chicago, 1950); Jerold S. Auerbach, *Labor and Liberty: The LaFollette Committee and the New Deal* (Indianapolis, 1966).

39 Slichter, 378 and passim. See also C. Wright Mills, *The New Men of Power: America's Labor Leaders* (New York, 1948); Jesse T. Carpenter, *Competition and Collective Bargaining in the Needle Trades, 1910–1967* (Ithaca, N.Y., 1972).

40 Nelson Lichtenstein, "Ambiguous Legacy: The Union Security Problem during World War II," *Labor History*, 18 (Spring 1977), 234. See also Joel Seidman, *American Labor from Defense to Reconversion* (Chicago, 1953); Martin Glaberman, "The Struggle against the No-Strike Pledge in the UAW during the World War II," (unpublished MS, 1975).

41 James Boggs, *The American Revolution: Pages from a Negro Worker's Notebook* (New York, 1963), ch. 1.

42 Schatz, 174–315; Neil Chamberlain, *The Union Challenge to Management Control* (New York, 1948); James J. Matles and James Higgins, *Them and Us: Struggles of a Rank-and-File Union* (Englewood Cliffs, N.J., 1974); Art Preis, *Labor's Giant Step: Twenty Years of the CIO* (New York, 1972), 257–83.

43 Staughton Lynd, *Labor Law for the Rank & Filer* (San Pedro, Calif., 1978); Lynd, "Issues Raised by the Coal Strike," *In These Times*, April 5–11, 1978.

44 Mike Healey, "Two Mine Unionists Hurl Gripes of Wrath as UB Crowd Cheers," *Buffalo Courier-Express*, March 25, 1978. See also Linda and Paul Nyden, *Showdown in Coal: The Struggle for Rank-and-File Unionism* (Pittsburgh, 1978).

45 Arnold Weber, quoted in "Bigger Concessions from Unions Sought," *New York Times*, March 26, 1978.

46 Zimpel, 63, 44.

47 "Goodyear's Decision, Akron's Loss," *New York Times*, section 3, February 26, 1978.

48 "Bigger Concessions from Unions Sought," *New York Times*, March 26, 1978. For earlier phases of the battle for "management's prerogatives," see Neil Chamberlain, *The Union Challenge to Management Control* (New York, 1948).

49 For political developments on the national level, see, Bernstein, *Turbulent Years*; Preis, *Labor's Giant Step*; Bernstein, "The New Deal"; James Weinstein, *Ambiguous Legacy: The Left in American Politics* (New York, 1975); Samuel Lubell, *The Future of American Politics* (New York, 1965); Len De Caux, *Labor Radical: From the Wobblies to the CIO* (Boston, 1970). For suggestive beginnings of research into New Deal politics at the local level, see St. Clair Drake and Horace Cayton, *Black Metropolis: A Study of Negro Life in a Northern City*, 2 vols. (New York and Evanston, 1962), 342–77; Friedlander, *Emergence of a UAW Local*; Kornblum, *Blue Collar Community*; Lynd, *Rank and File*; Thomas Bell, *Out of This Furnace* (Pittsburgh, 1977); Adamic, *My America*; John Bodnar, *Immigration and Industrialization: Ethnicity in an America Mill Town, 1870–1940* (Pittsburgh, 1977), 127–58.

50 There has been little serious historical analysis of the political possibilities and Left strategies of 1937–40, but see Al Richmond, *A Long View from the Left: Memoirs of an American Revolutionary* (New York, 1972), 220–49; Weinstein, *Ambiguous Legacy*, 57–86.

51 On the cold war purge of the unions, see Bert Cochran, *Labor and Communism: The Conflict that Shaped American Unions* (Princeton, 1977); James R. Prickett, "Communists and the Communist Issue in the American Labor Movement, 1920–1950," (unpublished Ph.D dissertation, University of California, Los Angeles, 1975); Schatz, 227–310. For literary treatments of the purge's impact on the intellectual and political lives of workers, see K. B. Gilden, *Between the Hills and the Sea* (Garden City, N.Y., 1971); Clancey Sigal, *Going Away: A Report, A Memoir* (Boston, 1962); Emanuel Fried, *Drop Hammer* (Cambridge, Mass., 1977). See also the incisive comparison of labor education in the 1930s and 1970s in Frank Marquart, *An Auto Worker's Journal: The UAW from Crusade to One-Party Union* (University Park, Pa., 1975). On the New Right, see "Who's Who in the Right Wing," *The Machinist*, October 1977; "The New Right," *Steel Labor*, February 1978. On corporate sponsorship of New Right activities, see Kornblum, 150.

52 For a revealing account of the relationship between workplace struggles outside of the union framework and reform candidates for union office, see Dodee Fennell, "Beneath the Surface: The Life of a Factory," *Radical America*, 10 (September–October 1976), 21–41.

53 Kornblum, 224.

54 *In These Times*, November 23–9, 1977; April 19–25, 1978.

55 Ibid., May 17–23, 1978.

56 "Wimpy calls 'em like he sees 'em," *Labor Today*, March 1978.

57 "IAM's Winpisinger blasts Carter at E. V. Debs dinner," *In These Times*, May 17–23, 1978. McGovern's campaign for the presidency in 1972 split the Socialist Party into two parts. One of them, the Democratic Socialist Organizing Committee has become a rallying point for the emerging socialist bloc in the unions. The other, the Social Democrats-USA, has provided the brain trust for Meany's snapping turtle policy.

58 On the mine strike, see Nyden, 6, and the excellent coverage in the New York *Times* during August and September 1976. The account of the United Parcel Service strike is based on personal conversations with participants.

59 *Madison Press Connection*, passim; interview with Ronald McCrea, *Press Connection* offices, March 30, 1978.

60 Gar Alperovitz and Jeff Faux, "Youngstown Lessons," New York *Times*, November 3, 1977. Since 1973 the Jamestown Metal Products Co. of Jamestown, N.Y., and the specialty steel plant in Dunkirk, N.Y., formerly owned by Allegheny-Ludlum have all been kept open by joint employee-community groups, which acquired ownership of them, and the South Bend Lathe Co. has been taken over completely by its workers. *Congressional Record*, Wednesday, March 1, 1978, 1. I am deeply indebted to Staughton Lynd for documents on this movement.
61 Braverman, 444–5.

Bibliographical essay

As the notes to these essays suggest, information concerning workers' control struggles, or even simply work customs and workers' responses to employers' reforms, is to be found scattered in small morsels through innumerable, different types of historical records. There are few sources or studies which provide large amounts of data in a single convenient location. In fact, the most useful finding aid consists of a lot of friends, who know one's concern and offer to share interesting bits of information, which they have stumbled across in the course of their own research into totally different subjects.

What this bibliography does, therefore, is to identify sources which provided a significant amount of information or valuable insights, which were used in these essays, and to list some of the better books and articles which are in some way related to the theme of workers' control. They are arranged under the following eight general headings:

> work customs and culture
> managerial reform
> trade union practice and strikes
> the National Civic Federation and the socialist movement
> workers' control movements of the World War I epoch
> the American Plan and the triumph of scientific management
> the New Deal Formula and its present crisis
> historical perspectives on the problem of work

Work customs and culture

A few archival sources offer enough information on both daily work practices and managerial efforts to change them, to be worth careful scrutiny. Among them are the Frederick Winslow Taylor papers at Stevens Institute of Technology, the David J. Saposs papers and the Adolph Germer papers at the State Historical Society of Wisconsin, the William Martin papers in the Darlington Room of the University of Pittsburgh, and the voluminous papers of John Mitchell, Terence V. Powderly, and John W. Hayes, all at Catholic University of America, Washington, D.C. In the National Archives the records of the Federal Mediation and Conciliation Service and the National War Labor Board both provide abundant information on the workplace issues involved in strikes.

Among the many useful published documents of the United States government two reports of the U.S. Commissioner of Labor are indispensable: the Thirteenth Annual Report, *Hand and Machine Labor*, 2 vols. (Washington, D.C., 1899), and the Eleventh Special Report, *Regulation and Restriction of Output* (Washington, D.C., 1904). Revealing testimony may be found in the following reports: *Report of the Committee of the Senate upon the Relations between Labor and Capital*, 3 vols. (Washington, D.C., 1885); *Report of the U.S. Industrial Commission*, 19 vols.

(Washington, D.C., 1901); *Report on the Strike at the Bethlehem Steel Works* (Senate Document 521, 61st Congress 2d session, Washington, D.C., 1910); *Final Report and Testimony Submitted to Congress by the Commission on Industrial Relations*, 11 vols. (Washington, D.C., 1916); and especially *Hearings before the Special Committee of the House of Representatives to Investigate the Taylor and other Systems of Shop Management*, 2 vols (Washington, D.C., 1912). Rich material on railway workers may be found in United States Circuit Court, District of Nebraska, *Oliver Ames, Second, Et Al vs. Union Pacific Railway Company, Et Al, Record* (Omaha, Neb., 1894). For aggregate data on occupational groups, see United States Bureau of the Census, *Sixteenth Census of the United States: 1940. Population. Comparative Occupational Statistics for the United States, 1870–1940* (Washington, D.C., 1943).

Transactions of the American Society of Mechanical Engineers and the *Bulletin of the (Taylor) Society to Promote the Science of Management* are two serials of special importance, though four other management journals are also very useful: *American Machinist, Engineering Magazine, The Iron Age*, and *Factory*. By the 1920s every major industry had one or more periodicals, which often devoted considerable space to innovations in managerial practice, and *The Survey* was always concerned with corporate welfare work. Few journals from the labor movement are as useful, though precious items can be found in all of them, especially among the letters to the editors. *John Swinton's Paper* from the 1880s and the *Machinists' Monthly Journal* (called the *Monthly Journal of the International Association of Machinists* from 1888 through 1901) have been heavily used for these essays.

Reminiscences of workers and managers are often disappointing, because they devote far more attention to labor organizations or the company office than to the shop floor. Some of them, however, are quite rewarding: Abraham Bisno, *Abraham Bisno, Union Pioneer* (Madison, Wis.: University of Wisconsin Press, 1967); James J. Davis, *The Iron Puddler: My Life in the Rolling Mills and What Came of It* (Indianapolis: Bobbs-Merrill Co., 1922); Marie Hall Ets, *Rosa, the Life of an Italian Immigrant* (Minneapolis: University of Minnesota Press, 1970); Holden A. Evans, *One Man's Fight for a Better Navy* (New York: Dodd, Mead & Co., 1940); Clarence J. Hicks, *My Life in Industrial Relations: Fifty Years in the Growth of a Profession* (New York and London: Harper & Row, 1941).

There were some fine descriptions of work and working-class customs written during the late nineteenth and early twentieth centuries. Worthy of note are Elizabeth Beardsley Butler, *Women and the Trades: Pittsburgh, 1907–1908* (New York: The Russell Sage Foundation, 1911); Carlos C. Closson, Jr., "The Unemployed in American Cities," *Quarterly Journal of Economics*, 8 (January 1894), 168–217, 257–8; H. Dubreuil, *Robots or Men? A French Workman's Experience in American Industry* (New York: Harper & Row, 1930); Carter Goodrich, *The Miner's Freedom: A Study of Working Life in a Changing Industry* (Boston: Marshall Jones Co., 1925); Alfred Kolb, *Als Arbeiter in Amerika. Unter deutschen-amerikanischen Grossstadt Proletariern* (Berlin: Karl Siegismund, 1904); E. Levasseur, *The American Workman* (Baltimore: Johns Hopkins University Press, 1900); George E. McNeill, *The Labor Movement: The Problem of To-Day* (New York: The M. W. Hazen Co., 1887); Fred J. Miller, "The Machinist," *Scribner's Magazine*, 14 (October–December 1893), 314–34; Virginia Penny, *How Women Can Make Money, Married or Single* (Springfield, Mass.: D. E. Fisk and Co., 1870); Mary K. Simkhovitch, *The City Worker's World in America* (New York: Macmillan, 1917); Octave Thanet, "The Working-Man: Sketches of American Types," *Scribner's Magazine*, 16 (October–December 1894), 100–7; Leon Stein and Philip Taft, eds., *Workers Speak: Self Portraits* (New York: Arno Press and the New York

Times, 1971); Charles R. Walker, *Steel: The Diary of a Furnace Worker* (Boston: Atlantic Monthly Press, 1922); Whiting Williams, *What's on the Worker's Mind, by One Who Put on Overalls to Find Out* (New York: Charles Scribner's Sons, 1921).

Finally, some historians discussing the turn-of-the-century decades have displayed a keen sensitivity to work practices and work relations. See, John W. Bennett, "The Iron Workers of Woods Run and Johnstown: The Union Era" (unpublished Ph.D. dissertation, University of Pittsburgh, 1977); Alan Dawley, *Class and Community: The Industrial Revolution in Lynn* (Cambridge, Mass.: Harvard University Press, 1976); Herbert G. Gutman, *Work, Culture, and Society in Industrializing America: Essays in Working-Class and Social History* (New York: Alfred A. Knopf, 1976); William Haber, *Industrial Relations in the Building Industry* (Cambridge, Mass.: Harvard University Press, 1930); Katherine A. Harvey, *The Best-Dressed Miners: Life and Labor in the Maryland Coal Region, 1835–1910* (Ithaca, N.Y.: Cornell University Press, 1969); Bruce Laurie, Theodore Herschberg and George Alter, "Immigrants and Social History: The Philadelphia Experience, 1850–1880," *Journal of Social History*, 9 (Winter 1976), 219–67; Gerd Korman, *Industrialization, Immigrants and Americanizers: The View from Milwaukee, 1886–1921* (Madison: State Historical Society of Wisconsin, 1967); Louis Lorwin, *The Women's Garment Workers. A History of the International Ladies' Garment Workers' Union* (New York: B. W. Huebsch, Inc., 1924); Robert Ozanne, *A Century of Labor-Management Relations at McCormick and International Harvester* (Madison: University of Wisconsin Press, 1967); Benson Soffer, "A Theory of Trade Union Development: The Role of the 'Autonomous' Workman," *Labor History*, 1 (Spring 1960), 141–63; Katherine Stone, "The Origins of Job Structures in the Steel Industry," *Review of Radical Political Economy*, 6 (1974), 115–80; Daniel Walkowitz, "Working-Class Women in the Gilded Age: Factory, Community and Family Life among Cohoes, New York, Cotton Workers," *Journal of Social History*, 5 (Summer, 1972), 464–90.

Managerial reform

The literature dealing with the reform of management practices in the twentieth century is abundant and increasing steadily. The authors of most such works disclaim at the start any intention to deal with "the workers' response" to the innovations being analyzed. Nevertheless, there are some books on the coming of modern management of special relevance to the study of the working class, a few which treat the reactions of the trade unions, and a number of writings by the apostles of scientific management themselves, which offer important insights into the customs and initiatives of workers.

Within the last category may be found, Horace L. Arnold and Fay L. Faurote, *Ford Methods and Ford Shops* (New York: The Engineering Magazine, 1915); John Calder, "The Overvaluation of Management Science," *Iron Age*, 91 (March 6, 1913), 605–6; Frank P. Copley, *Frederick W. Taylor. Father of Scientific Management*, 2 vols. (New York: Harper & Row, 1923); Federated American Engineering Societies, Committee on Elimination of Waste in Industry, *Waste in Industry* (New York: McGraw-Hill, 1921); Henry L. Gantt, *Work, Wages, and Profits*, 2nd. ed. rev. (New York: The Engineering Magazine, 1919); Frank B. Gilbreth, *Primer of Scientific Management* (New York: D. Van Nostrand Co., 1914); William B. Leiserson, *Adjusting Immigrant and Industry* (New York: Harper & Row, 1924); Henry J. Rehn, *Scientific Management and the Cotton Textile Industry* (Chicago:

private edition, 1934); Frederick Winslow Taylor, *Principles of Scientific Management* (New York: Harper & Row, 1911); F. W. Taylor, "Shop Management," *Transactions of the American Society of Mechanical Engineers*, 24 (1903), 1337–456; William H. Tolman, *Social Engineering. A Record of Things Done by American Industrialists Employing Upwards of One and One-Half Million of People* (New York: McGraw-Hill, 1909).

Useful historical studies include the following: Hugh G. J. Aitken, *Taylorism at Watertown Arsenal: Scientific Management in Action, 1908–1915* (Cambridge, Mass.: Harvard University Press, 1960); Harry Braverman, *Labor and Monopoly Capital: The Degradation of Work in the Twentieth Century* (New York: Monthly Review Press, 1974); Monte A. Calvert, *The Mechanical Engineer in America, 1830–1910: Professional Cultures in Conflict* (Baltimore: Johns Hopkins University Press, 1967); Alfred D. Chandler, *The Visible Hand: The Managerial Revolution in American Business* (Cambridge, Mass.: Harvard University Press, 1977); Paul H. Douglas, *American Apprenticeship and Industrial Education* (New York: Columbia University Press, 1921); Michael Maccoby, *The Gamesmen: The New Corporate Leaders* (New York: Simon and Schuster, 1976); Daniel Nelson, *Managers and Workers: Origins of the New Factory System in the United States, 1880–1920* (Madison: University of Wisconsin Press, 1975); and David F. Noble, *America by Design: Science, Technology, and the Rise of Corporate Capitalism* (New York: Alfred A. Knopf, 1977).

The response of union leaders to scientific management has been chronicled in Samuel Haber, *Efficiency and Uplift: Scientific Management in the Progressive Era, 1890–1920* (Chicago: University of Chicago Press, 1964); Robert F. Hoxie, *Scientific Management and Labor* (New York: Appleton-Century-Crofts, 1915); Jean Trepp McKelvey, *AFL Attitudes toward Production, 1900–1932* (Ithaca, N.Y.: Cornell University Press, 1952); and Milton J. Nadworny, *Scientific Management and the Unions, 1900–1932* (Cambridge, Mass.: Harvard University Press, 1955).

The interest of management experts in workers focused increasingly on turnover and alienation after 1910. Revealing studies of this type may be found in Magnus W. Alexander, "Waste in Hiring and Discharging Men," *Iron Age*, 94 (October 29, 1914); Daniel Bloomfield, ed., *Selected Articles on Employment Management* (New York: H. W. Wilson Co., 1922); Alma Herbst, *The Negro in the Slaughtering and Meat-Packing Industry in Chicago* (Boston: Houghton Mifflin Co., 1932); Stanley B. Mathewson, *Restriction of Output among Unorganized Workers* (New York: The Viking Press, 1931); Elton Mayo, *The Human Problems of an Industrial Civilization* (Cambridge, Mass.: Harvard University Press, 1933); Carlton H. Parker, *The Casual Laborer and Other Essays* (New York: Harcourt Brace Jovanovich, 1920); F. J. Roethlisberger and W. J. Dickson, *Management and the Worker: Technical Vs. Social Organization in an Industrial Plant* (Cambridge, Mass.: Harvard University Press, 1934); Ordway Tead, *Instincts in Industry: A Study of Working-Class Psychology* (Boston: Houghton Mifflin Co., 1918).

Trade union practice and strikes

Within the vast corpus of historical, sociological, and economic literature dealing with American unions, the most important to the student of workers' control have been the richly empirical institutional monographs, which were modeled after Sidney and Beatrice Webb, *Industrial Democracy* (London: Longmans, Green, 1897). Examples of such books are: John B. Ashworth, *The Helper and American Trade Unions* (Baltimore: Johns Hopkins University Press, 1915); George E. Barnett, *Chapters on Machinery and Labor* (Cambridge, Mass.: Harvard University

Press, 1926); John R. Commons, ed., *Trade Unionism and Labor Problems* (Boston: Ginn & Co., 1905); Commons, ed., *Trade Unionism and Labor Problems. Second Series* (Boston: Ginn & Co., 1921); John A. Fitch, *The Steel Workers* (New York: Russell Sage Foundation, 1911); Augusta E. Galster, *The Labor Movement in the Shoe Industry, With Special Reference to Philadelphia* (New York: Ronald Press Co., 1924); Jacob H. Hollander and George E. Barnett, *Studies in American Trade Unionism* (New York: Holt Rinehart & Winston, 1912); Robert F. Hoxie, *Trade Unionism in the United States* (New York: Appleton-Century-Crofts, 1917); David A. McCabe, *The Standard Rate in American Trade Unions* (Baltimore: Johns Hopkins University Press, 1912); Gladys L. Palmer, *Union Tactics and Economic Change: A Case Study of Three Philadelphia Textile Unions* (Philadelphia: University of Pennsylvania Press, 1932); Mark Perlman, *The Machinists: A New Study in American Trade Unionism* (Cambridge, Mass.: Harvard University Press, 1961); and Vertrees J. Wyckoff, *The Wage Policies of Labor Organizations in a Period of Industrial Depression* (Baltimore: Johns Hopkins University Press, 1926).

Historical studies of a far broader scope, which provide important insights into the connection between workplace practice and union leadership include the following: David Brody, *Steelworkers in America: The Nonunion Era* (Cambridge: Harvard University Press, 1960); David Montgomery, *Beyond Equality: Labor and the Radical Republicans, 1862–1872* (New York: Alfred A. Knopf, 1967); Selig Perlman, *A Theory of the Labor Movement* (New York: Macmillan, 1928); Philip T. Silvia, Jr., "The Spindle City: Labor, Politics, and Religion in Fall River, Massachusetts, 1870–1905" (unpublished Ph.D. dissertation, Fordham University, 1973); and Warren R. Van Tine, *The Making of a Labor Bureaucrat: Union Leadership in the United States, 1870–1920* (Amherst, University of Massachusetts Press, 1973). Two books from the 1920s offer especially valuable views of the changes in unionism during that decade: J. B. S. Hardman, ed., *American Labor Dynamics in the Light of Post-War Developments* (New York: Harcourt Brace Jovanovich, 1928), and William English Walling, *American Labor and American Democracy* (New York: Harper & Row, 1926).

Studies of strikes in the United States have far more often been episodic than analytical. A few which have fit into the latter type, however, have proven very useful in the study of workers' control struggles: Jon Amsden and Stephen Brier, "Coal Miners on Strike: The Transformation of Strike Demands and the Formation of a National Union," *Journal of Interdisciplinary History*, 7 (Spring 1977), 583–616; Alexander M. Bing, *War-Time Strikes and Their Adjustment* (New York: E. P. Dutton, 1921); John H. Griffin, *Strikes. A Study in Quantitative Economics* (New York: Columbia University Press, 1939); Fred. S. Hall, *Sympathetic Strikes and Sympathetic Lockouts* (New York: Columbia University Press, 1898); Ernest T. Hiller, *The Strike: A Study in Collective Action* (Chicago: University of Chicago Press, 1928).

The National Civic Federation and the socialist movement

Here the literature is abundant, though attention to the workplace and community significance of the movements is still rare. Two documents published by the National Civic Federation are well worth close examination: "Joint Trades Agreement Conference of the National Civic Federation, Held at the Fifth Avenue Hotel, New York City, Saturday, May 7th, 1904, at 10 A.M.," typescript in John Mitchell Papers, box A3-10, Catholic University of America, Washington, D.C., and *The National Civic Federation, Its Methods and Its Aims* (New York: The

National Civic Federation, 1905). On the history and role of the NCF, see Marguerite Green, *The National Civic Federation and the American Labor Movement, 1900–1925* (Washington, D.C.: Catholic University of America Press, 1956); Bruno Ramirez, *When Workers Fight: The Politics of Industrial Relations in the Progressive Era, 1898–1916* (Westport, Conn.: Greenwood Press, 1978); James Weinstein, *The Corporate Ideal in the Liberal State, 1900–1918* (Boston: Beacon Press, 1968); and Robert H. Wiebe, *Businessmen and Reform: A Study of the Progressive Movement* (Cambridge, Mass.: Harvard University Press, 1962).

Among the many studies of the Socialist Party, IWW, and syndicalist movement, some are especially important in the study of workers' control. Frederick A. Barkey, "The Socialist Party in West Virginia from 1898 to 1920: A Study in Working Class Radicalism" (unpublished Ph.D. dissertation, University of Pittsburgh, 1971); Henry F. Bedford, *Socialism and the Workers in Massachusetts, 1886–1912* (Amherst: University of Massachusetts Press, 1966); Joseph R. Conlin, *Bread and Roses Too: Studies of the Wobblies* (Westport, Conn.: Greenwood Press, 1969); William M. Dick, *Labor and Socialism in America: The Gompers Era* (Port Washington, N.Y.: Kennikat Press, 1972); Melvyn Dubofsky, *We Shall Be All: A History of the Industrial Workers of the World* (Chicago: Quadrangle Books, 1969); Philip S. Foner, *History of the Labor Movement in the United States*, vols. 3 and 4 (New York: International Publishers, 1964, 1965); William Z. Foster and Earl C. Ford, *Syndicalism* (Chicago: William Z. Foster, n.d.); Robert Hunter, *Labor in Politics* (Chicago: The Socialist Party, 1915); Marc Karson, *American Labor Unions and Politics, 1900–1918* (Boston: Beacon Press, 1965); Ira Kipnis, *The American Socialist Movement, 1897–1912* (New York: Monthly Review Press, 1952); John H. M. Laslett, *Labor and the Left: A Study of Socialist and Radical Influences in the American Labor Movement, 1881–1924* (New York: Basic Books, 1970); Patrick M. Lynch, "Pennsylvania Anthracite: A Forgotten IWW Venture, 1906–1916" (unpublished M.A. thesis, Bloomsburg State College, 1974); Sally M. Miller, *Victor Berger and the Promise of Constructive Socialism, 1910–1920* (Westport, Conn.: Greenwood Press, 1973); Carl E. Person, *The Lizard's Trail: A Story of the Illinois Central and Harriman Lines Strike of 1911 to 1915 Inclusive* (Chicago: Lake Publishing Co., 1918); Bruce M. Stave, ed., *Socialism and the Cities* (Port Washington, N.Y.: Kennikat Press, 1975); William English Walling, *Socialism as it Is: A Survey of the World-Wide Revolutionary Movement* (New York: Macmillan, 1912); James Weinstein, *The Decline of Socialism in America, 1912–1925* (New York: Monthly Review Press, 1967).

Workers' control movements of the World War I epoch

After World War I overt and explicit workers' control struggles assumed a variety of shapes, ranging from strike demands through union programs to the activities of the Communist Party and the Trade Union Educational League. The following books, articles, and documents shed light on that period: Earl R. Beckner, "The Trade Union Educational League and the American Labor Movement," *Journal of Political Economy*, 33 (August 1925), 410–31; James P. Cannon, *The First Ten Years of American Communism* (New York: Pathfinder Press, 1962); Evans Clark, "The Industry Is Ours," *Socialist Review*, 9 (July 1920), 59–62; William Z. Foster, *The Great Steel Strike and Its Lessons* (New York: B. W. Huebsch, 1920); W. Z. Foster, *Trade Unionism: The Road to Freedom* (Chicago: International Trade Union Education League, 1921); Louis C. Fraina, *Revolutionary Socialism: A Study in Socialist Reconstruction* (New York: The Communist Press, 1918); History Committee of the General Strike Committee, *The Seattle General Strike* (Seattle, 1919, reprinted as Root & Branch Pamphlet 5, Charlestown, Mass., 1972); Sylvia Kopald, *Rebellion in Labor Unions* (New York: Liveright Publishing Co., 1924); James O. Morris, *Conflict within the AFL: A Study of Craft Versus Industrial Unions, 1901–1938* (Ithaca, N.Y.: Cornell University Press, 1958); Nat Hentoff, ed., *The Essays of A. J. Muste* (Indianapolis: Bobbs-Merrill Co., 1967); Nationalization Research Committee of United Mine Workers of America, *How to Run Coal: Suggestions for a Plan of Public Ownership, Public Control, and Democratic Management in the Coal Industry* (Clearfield, Pa.: UMWA, 1922); Glenn E. Plumb and William G. Roylance, *Industrial Democracy: A Plan for Its Achievement* (New York: B. W. Huebsch, 1923); C. E. Ruthenberg, *Are We Growing Toward Socialism?* (Cleveland: Local Cleveland, Socialist Party, 1917); David M. Schneider, *The Workers' (Communist) Party and American Trade Unions* (Baltimore: Johns Hopkins University Press, 1928).

Five studies of European workers' struggles during these years provide an important international and comparative perspective on developments in the United States: G. D. H. Cole, *Workshop Organization* (Oxford: At the Clarendon Press, 1923); Patrick Fridenson, ed., *1914–1918, l'autre front* (Paris: Editions Ouvrières, 1977); Carter L. Goodrich, *The Frontier of Control: A Study of British Workshop Politics* (New York: Harcourt Brace Jovanovich, 1921; reissued by Pluto Press, London, 1975); James Hinton, *The First Shop Stewards' Movement* (London: George Allen & Unwin, 1973); Ernest Mandel, *Contrôle ouvrier, conseils ouvriers, autogestion. Anthologie* (Paris: François Maspero, 1970).

The American Plan and the triumph of scientific management

Management journals and studies of workers' discontent by industrial psychologists provide much of the best material for the 1920s. The thinking of leading management figures is revealed in the *Report of the Special Conference Committee. Revising and Supplementing the Progress Report Published July 24, 1919, and Including Annual Reports dated December 15, 1922, and December 6, 1923* (New York: Special Conference Committee, 1924). Useful published surveys of the period include: Ray S. Baker, *The New Industrial Unrest: Reasons and Remedies* (Garden City, N.Y.: Doubleday & Co., 1920); Clarence E. Bonnett, *Employers' Associations in the United States: A Study of Typical Associations* (New York: Macmillan, 1922); Robert W. Bruére, "West Lynn," *Survey*, 56 (April 1, 1926), 21–7, 49; John R. Commons et al., *Industrial Government* (New York: Macmillan, 1921); Harry W. Laidler and Norman Thomas, eds., *New Tactics in Social Conflict* (New York: Vanguard Press, 1926); and Sam A. Lewisohn, *The New Leadership in Industry* (New York: E. P. Dutton, 1926).

The New Deal Formula and its present crisis

Only a highly selective description of the voluminous literature on the New Deal can be offered here. The writings which follow offer perceptive analyses of the role of the state during the Great Depression and its impact on the local activities of workers. Louis Adamic, *My America, 1928–1938* (New York: Harper & Row, 1938); Horace S. Cayton and George S. Mitchell, *Black Workers and the New Unions* (Chapel Hill: University of North Carolina Press, 1939); Len DeCaux, *Labor Radical: From the Wobblies to the CIO, a Personal History* (Boston: Beacon Press, 1970); Sidney Fine, *Sit-Down: The General Motors Strike of 1936–1937* (Ann

Arbor: University of Michigan Press, 1969); Peter Friedlander, *The Emergence of a UAW Local, 1936–39, A Study in Class and Culture* (Pittsburgh: University of Pittsburgh Press, 1975); John A. Garraty, *Unemployment in History: Economic Thought and Public Policy* (New York: Harper & Row, 1978); Martin Glaberman, "Wartime Strikes: The Struggle against the No-Strike Pledge in the UAW during World War II" (unpublished manuscript in possession of author); Matthew Josephson, *Sidney Hillman: Statesman of Labor* (New York: Doubleday, 1952); Gabriel Kolko, *Main Currents in Modern American History* (New York: Harper & Row, 1976); Nelson Lichtenstein, "Ambiguous Legacy: The Union Security Problem during World War II," *Labor History*, 18 (Spring 1977), 214–38; Alice and Staughton Lynd, *Rank and File: Personal Histories by Working Class Organizers* (Boston: Beacon Press, 1973); Harry A. Millis, *How Collective Bargaining Works: A Survey of Experience in Leading American Industries* (New York: Twentieth Century Fund, 1942); Ronald Radosh, "The Corporate Ideology of American Labor," *Studies on the Left*, 6 (November–December 1966), 66–92; Al Richmond, *A Long View from the Left: Memoirs of an American Revolutionary* (New York: Houghton Mifflin Co., 1972); Ronald W. Schatz, "American Electrical Workers: Their Work, Struggles, and Aspirations, 1930–1950" (unpublished Ph.D. dissertation, University of Pittsburgh, 1977); Sumner H. Slichter, et al., "The Changing Position of Foreman in American Industry," *Advanced Management*, 10 (December 1945), 155–61; S. H. Slichter, *Union Policies and Industrial Management* (Washington: The Brookings Institution, 1941); James Weinstein, *Ambiguous Legacy: The Left in American Politics* (New York: New Viewpoints, 1975).

The crisis of the New Deal formula has too many facets to allow a comprehensive coverage here. The books and articles which follow devote special attention to the role of workplace struggles in that crisis. Stanley Aronowitz, *False Promises: The Shaping of American Working Class Consciousness* (New York: McGraw-Hill Book Co., 1973); James Boggs, *The American Revolution: Pages from a Negro Worker's Notebook* (New York: Monthly Review Press, 1963); Neil W. Chamberlain, *The Union Challenge to Management Control* (New York: Harper & Row, 1948); Ely Chinoy, *Automobile Workers and the American Dream* (Garden City, N.Y.: Doubleday, 1955); Dodee Fennell, "Beneath the Surface: The Life of a Factory," *Radical America*, 10 (September–October 1976); Philip S. Foner, *Organized Labor and the Black Worker, 1619–1973* (New York: Praeger Publishers, 1974); Barbara Garson, *All the Livelong Day: The Meaning and Demeaning of Routine Work* (Garden City, N.Y.: Doubleday, 1975); Dan Georgakas and Marvin Surkin, *Detroit: I Do Mind Dying: A Study in Urban Revolution* (New York: St. Martin's Press, 1975); David M. Gordon, "Recession is Capitalism as Usual," *New York Times Magazine* (April 27, 1975), 18, 49–63; Michael Harrington, *Full Employment: The Issue and the Movement* (New York: Institute for Democratic Socialism, 1977); William Kornblum, *Blue Collar Community* (Chicago: University of Chicago Press, 1974); Harvey Swados, *On the Line* (Washington, D.C.: U.S. Government Printing Office, 1966); Studs Terkel, *Working* (New York: Pantheon Books, 1972); U.S. Department of Health, Education and Welfare, *Work in America* (Cambridge, Mass.: MIT Press, 1973); John Zernan, "Organized Labor versus 'The Revolt Against Work': The Critical Contest," *Telos*, 21 (Fall 1974), 194–206.

Historical perspectives on the problem of work

The struggle for workers' control has reached far beyond the boundaries of the United States, appearing wherever capitalism has emerged, and it has persisted in those countries where formal capitalist relationships have been abolished. Moreover the connection between that struggle and philosophical discussion of the problem of human alienation has generated profound intellectual controversies. Karl Marx, *Capital: A Critique of Political Economy*, 3 vols. (Chicago: Charles H. Kerr, 1906) is, of course, the centerpiece of the debate. Two little known socialist writings deserve careful attention: Paul Lafargue, *The Right to Be Lazy* (Chicago: Charles H. Kerr, 1907); and William Morris, *Factory Work as It Is and Might Be* (New York: New York Labor News Co., 1922).

Historical discussions of the problem of alienation have proliferated in recent years. Among them are Daniel Bell, *The Cultural Contradictions of Capitalism* (New York: Basic Books, 1976); D. Bell, *The End of Ideology: On the Exhaustion of Political Ideas in the Fifties* (New York: The Free Press, 1961); Alisdair Clayre, *Work and Play: Ideas and Experience of Work and Leisure* (New York: Harper & Row, 1974); Siegfried Giedion, *Mechanization Takes Command: A Contribution to Anonymous History* (New York: W. W. Norton & Co., 1969); James B. Gilbert, *Work without Salvation: America's Intellectuals and Industrial Alienation, 1880–1910* (Baltimore: Johns Hopkins University Press, 1977); Melvin Kranzberg and Joseph Geis, *By the Sweat of Thy Brow: Work in the Western World* (New York: G. P. Putnam's Sons, 1975); Henri de Man, *Joy in Work* (London: George Allen and Unwin, 1929); David Meakin, *Man & Work: Literature and Culture in Industrial Society* (New York: Holmes and Meier Publishers, 1976); Daniel T. Rodgers, *The Work Ethic in Industrial America, 1850–1920* (Chicago: University of Chicago Press, 1978); Peter N. Stearns, *Lives of Labor: Work in a Maturing Industrial Society* (New York: Holmes and Meier Publishers, 1975); Keith Thomas, "Work and Leisure in Pre-Industrial Society," *Past and Present*, 29 (December 1964), 50–62; E. P. Thompson, "Time, Work-Discipline, and Industrial Capitalism," *Past and Present*, 38 (December 1967), 56–97.